THE SMALL BUSINESS SURVIVAL GUIDE

By Jason Reid

Course Technology PTR

A part of Cengage Learning

COURSE TECHNOLOGY
CENGAGE Learning™

Australia, Brazil, Japan, Korea, Mexico, Singapore, Spain, United Kingdom, United States

COURSE TECHNOLOGY
CENGAGE Learning™

The Small Business Survival Guide

Jason Reid

Publisher and General Manager, Course Technology PTR:
Stacy L. Hiquet

Associate Director of Marketing:
Sarah Panella

Manager of Editorial Services:
Heather Talbot

Marketing Manager:
Mark Hughes

Acquisitions Editor:
Mitzi Koontz

Interior Layout Tech:
Bill Hartman

Cover Designer:
Luke Fletcher

Indexer:
Kelly Talbot Editing Services

Proofreader:
Sandi Wilson

For product information and technology assistance, contact us at **Cengage Learning Customer & Sales Support, 1-800-354-9706.**

For permission to use material from this text or product, submit all requests online at **cengage.com/permissions**. Further permissions questions can be e-mailed to **permissionrequest@cengage.com.**

All images © Jason Reid unless otherwise noted.

All other trademarks are the property of their respective owners.

Library of Congress Control Number: 2010928009

ISBN-13: 978-1-4354-5780-5

ISBN-10: 1-4354-5780-3

Course Technology, a part of Cengage Learning
20 Channel Center Street
Boston, MA 02210
USA

Cengage Learning is a leading provider of customized learning solutions with office locations around the globe, including Singapore, the United Kingdom, Australia, Mexico, Brazil, and Japan. Locate your local office at:
international.cengage.com/region.

Cengage Learning products are represented in Canada by Nelson Education, Ltd.

For your lifelong learning solutions, visit **courseptr.com.**

Visit our corporate Web site at **cengage.com.**

Printed in the United States of America
1 2 3 4 5 6 7 12 11 10

To my wife Kim, and kids Derek,
Ashlyn, Kyle, and Ryan.
Thanks for dealing with my crazy
schedule and hobbies

— and —

To 20 years of experience that
no amount of money can buy

About the Author

Jason Reid is the co-founder of National Services Group, a $40 million services company. Jason is the veteran of 10 startups in multiple industries, from contracting to mortgage finance. Over the past 17 years, Jason has been involved in TEC, Vistage, YPO, and YEO, essentially serving on the board of advisors for scores of companies in multiple industries. Jason and his partners have been twice finalists for the Ernst and Young Entrepreneur of the Year awards.

Contents

Introduction: Doing Business Today

Unless you live in a cave in the middle of nowhere, you are all too aware that the world we live in is different today than the world we lived in just last year.

Every day there are new headlines about more foreclosures, the stock market reaching new lows, companies, big and small, laying off more workers, the impact of the recession, and of course the idea that recovery will be slow at best. It is enough to make people grab the kids, any cash they have, and move to a place where they can hunt their own food and grow their own vegetables.

The recessionary paralysis that many business owners fall into spreads across almost every industry. Everywhere you look, people seem to be cautious and scared. Many business owners are cutting back to make sure they can "weather the storm" and everyone seems to be hunkering down for a long winter's night or years of intrepid weather.

Not me. I relish these types of economic environments. During the boom times anyone could make a dollar, most of the time just by showing up. Customers buy what you have during these times whether you are good at what you do or just the first one to show up to the party.

The competition is different during boom times. Everyone is starting a new business and everyone is an expert. New businesses pop up everywhere almost every day. When the unemployment rate is below six percent, employees are in the driver's seat. Raises that are ridiculous in size and proportion become the norm as owners try desperately to hold on to anyone who is willing to work. Employee quality and pride of workmanship drop, as employees know they can always go down the street for a dollar more an hour if they don't like working for you.

When times get tight, though, the fly-by-night operators all but disappear. The companies that survive are the ones that focus on quality, customer service, and value.

Work ethic trumps luck. Money from successful companies can be poured into training. These employees appreciate it more and are less likely to jump ship, because opportunities in a down economy are few and far between! These are the times to capitalize on the fact that the bar is set very low in most industries and most of your competitors are closing their doors or shrinking down to one- and two-man shops. There really is no better time to be in business!

Most of the population is not all that affected by a recession. They may have less equity in their homes, but they still own them. They still have jobs that need to be done and things will still need to be repaired, maintained, and upgraded in that great big investment we all call home sweet home. They still need to put clothes on their kids, and they still want the newest gadget.

You don't need the entire population to run a successful business—you can do just fine with ones who are still around.

The great thing about hard economic times is that your competition has all but disappeared. If you run a legitimate, well-organized, and professional company there is even more work out there for you to acquire!

This book will help you make sure you are doing all the things that you need to do to run a first-class organization and grow during the good times and the bad. Keep this book with you at all times and refer to it daily. If you follow all the steps that are outlined here, you will have a successful business that will be the envy of all your competitors!

Why Small Businesses Stay Small

I have spent the last 20 years learning how to be a successful businessperson. In those 20 years, my partners and I have built National Services Group. We started from nothing and today we are one of the largest residential repaint contractors in the country with thousands of employees spread across the USA doing approximately $40 million in business per year.

Among the many things that I have seen and learned over the last 20 or more years is that the world is full of tens of thousands of extremely hard-working business owners who are stuck in a rut. They are in a constant struggle to make payroll and pay the bills, all the while trying to figure out how to bring in new customers and keep the lights on.

The small business owners who I have met over the years share many of the same characteristics. They are all very hard-working and driven individuals who are very passionate about their chosen industries. They care greatly about the finished product that they provide to their customers and they dream of getting their businesses to the next level.

I have spent my career watching small business owners and have spent hour upon hour talking with them. I have watched the mistakes they make (I made most of them myself at one point or another). I have witnessed their solutions and strategies they try to implement and have seen the results of those efforts. I have also asked myself why it seems to be so hard for many to build a business they have dreamt about most of their adult lives. Over the years I believe I have figured out not just the reason for this difficulty, but the solution as well.

They Love Their Product or Service More Than They Love Business

Most small business owners started their businesses by going down very similar paths. They ended up making a profession out of a passion. They became good at that passion and eventually good enough that they thought they could run the business better than the guy who they worked for.

Most also had the unfortunate misconception that the people who they were working for made money hand over fist. They quickly discover, though, as they start out on their own, how erroneous that thinking is.

This Book Is for You Regardless of Your Company's Size

When the time comes that you decide to run a business, you need to make some decisions. Do you want to run a business that is a good-paying job where you have yourself and an employee or two? Do you want to run 1, 2, 3, 10, or 20 projects at a time? Do you want to have 1, 2, 3, 4, or more locations? Are you ready to start taking the steps to learn about what it takes to succeed in business?

Regardless of how you answer these questions, this book is valuable to you. The principles of running a solid first-class business are still the same whether the business employs two people or 2,000. So if you decide that you want to be extremely hands-on during all of your projects or you eventually would rather manage the business by looking at reports generated from the systems you develop, the basic building blocks are all still here in this book.

How You Ended Up Here

Passion for a Hobby

You are in the business you are in simply because you were passionate about an idea or a hobby. That passion has benefits with regards to running your business. The most important benefit is that you truly understand everything that is important about the job you are doing. Your passion means that quality is high and your customers (assuming you follow the customer service rules) are satisfied with you and refer new work to you.

You Fell Into It

I never had a love of painting. I started painting in the summer when I was 16 at a pharmaceutical plant in Quebec where my father worked. I was the only English-speaking person at an all-French-speaking unionized plant. This meant that I was given every job that no one else wanted to do. Hence, I spent most of my summers painting.

I have great stories from those days, but basically they put me in the basement, on the roof, and on ladders painting pipes and anything else that needed to be painted that no one else wanted to do. That was my job. When I did it too fast, I got in trouble for making everyone else look bad. When I took a nap because I was done too fast, I'd get criticized for that, as well. You get the picture.

I moved away to go to college and got a job painting houses for the summer. Why? Because I needed money to pay for college and I knew how to paint. I stayed in the painting business not because of a love of the trade, but because it was what I knew how to do and I had a love of business.

When I was younger, I remember hearing people say that, after all, Procter & Gamble just sells toothpaste and Coca-Cola just sells sugar-flavored water. Business is business. And a service business will always be needed. I decided that painting was a service that almost everyone needed.

Wanting to Be Your Own Boss

At some point in time, some of you decided that you really wanted to be your own boss. Running a business is a great way to do that. In fact, a very high percentage of business owners end up in their businesses primarily because they were tired of working for someone else and felt that they could do a better job.

How Low Is the Bar in Your Industry?

This is where I will offend many of you. What I love about the business I am in, and the contracting business in general, is that the bar has been set so low. In many cases all you have to do is call back your clients on time and show up on time and the job is yours.

Consumers have been conditioned over the years to expect the lowest levels of customer service from most contractors. If you are just slightly better than terrible, you're going to win the contract. These customers follow the line of thinking that comes from the saying, "If you give a starving man a cracker, that cracker will be the best darn cracker he ever ate!"

This low bar syndrome exists in almost every industry where small businesses rule. The great thing about almost every business in every industry is that you are almost always guaranteed to come across competition that is less than stellar. By following the basic concepts in this book, you will be miles ahead of your rather incompetent competition.

You: CEO and Owner

It is lonely at the top. Regardless of why you chose to do what you are doing, you can't escape the fact that you are where you are.

You have ultimate responsibility for the success or failure of your business.

You are the one who goes without a paycheck in order to make sure your people get paid.

You are the one who cares the most about each customer. You are the one who will be here for the long run.

You are the one who lies in bed at night and cannot sleep as everything from new ideas to stressful thoughts race through your head.

You are the one.

Working on Your Business, Instead of in It

As CEO you have a responsibility to everyone who works in your organization. You need to understand what your job actually is.

At times you are the "chief cook and bottle washer."

At times it may seem like you are the only one who gets it.

At times it may seem like you are the one who needs to do all the work.

The most important job you have, though, is to take the time to step back and work on the business.

Working on the business means that you are not working on the day-to-day operations of the business, but are using your mind to think and plan where your business is headed.

Working on the business means spending time to work on new ideas such as marketing strategies, sales trainings, two-year projections, and so on, not always just about getting today's job done.

It means finding time to think, read, learn, talk to mentors and advisors, and to figure out just how others built their companies.

Your Dream

You started your company because you had a dream of building a great business.

It may have been to build a better company than all of your competitors.

It may have been to make a bunch of money or to be partners with your kids some day.

Whatever the reason, chances are, as time goes by, things have not exactly ended up as you planned.

Maybe your company has exceeded your expectations. But, more than likely, you've been frustrated because you are not quite where you had always planned on being.

Not meeting your expectations tends to be the natural course of business.

A wise man once said that entrepreneurs tend to overestimate what they can do in five years and underestimate what they can do in 15.

Staying in the game, and working every day to make progress, is what running a business is all about.

I hope this book helps you on your journey to success—however you define success.

What This Book Is and Is Not

This book is short and to the point.

This book is heavily weighted toward finding business and growing your company.

This book is fast paced.

This book will give you great ideas you can use *now*.

This book will help grow your business as you implement its ideas.

This book is not a magic feather. You still need to do the hard work.

This book is not an encyclopedia of everything about each topic.

This book is not all there is to learn about running a small business.

This book will not do the hard work for you.

That is up to you.

Chapter 1

Branding

Branding, marketing, and lead generation. So they are all the same, right? No, no, no! One of the most important lessons in generating business is to understand that branding, marketing, and lead generation are all uniquely different and play different, albeit important, roles in building your business. Throughout the next three chapters you'll learn the basics that you need to understand each of these unique concepts in order to help you build your business.

Branding is all about who you are and what you stand for as a company. How do you want to be known? How do you want your customers to remember you and what do you want your reputation to be? Some examples of branding are:

- **Empire Community Painting: The Company That's Easy To Do Business With**
  It is Empire's goal to make the painting experience easy for its customers. Empire wants to communicate to potential customers that it takes all of the typical headaches that are generally associated with painting jobs out of the customer experience.

- **Mike Diamond Plumbing in Los Angeles: "I guarantee my plumbers will smell nice."**
  Mike Diamond Plumbing wants to make the point that its plumbers are not like other plumbers and that its customers have a much more enjoyable and professional experience.

Although these examples are really "taglines," they are designed to convey what the company stands for and how, in this one simple sentence, the potential customer can identify with the company.

The following exercise can help you decide what your company stands for and ultimately what your brand and tagline will be.

After you have interviewed your customers, take a look at the 25 points that your customers listed as the most important aspects they look for in choosing a business in your trade. Chances are you will see some common themes. You will probably be able to narrow these 25 items down to five common themes.

Compare what you listed as most important with the customers' themes. If you are in tune with your customers, the lists will match.

Next you need to look at the first two lists. In a perfect world, the ways you want your company to be known match what your customers told you they want. If this is the case, you are off to the races and ready to pick a tagline. If you and your customers are not aligned, it is time to go back and retool your company.

BRANDING EXERCISE

List three areas in which your company excels and why.

1. _____
2. _____
3. _____

List three ways you want your company to be known.

1. _____
2. _____
3. _____

List the five benefits of your company's services you believe are most important to your customers.

1. _____
2. _____
3. _____
4. _____
5. _____

Now comes the hard part. Go out and talk to five of your customers and ask them what they think are the most important aspects of working with someone in your trade.

1. _____
2. _____
3. _____
4. _____
5. _____

One of the many keys to building a successful small business is to offer a product or service in a manner that your potential customers want. The key to building any business is to effectively communicate to your customers that you deliver exactly what they seek.

If what your company is best at and what you want your company to be known for are not matching up with what your customers want, you really do need to do some soul searching. Are you out of touch with your customers? Are you marketing to the right customers? Is it time to rethink how you run your business?

For example, if you think your company is great at solving very challenging problems that no one else can solve, but your customers are more interested in great customer service, your business is out of alignment with your customer's expectations.

Or, if you think one of your greatest strengths is that you provide expertise on a specific type of material, but your customers believe that a solid mix of quality and price is most important, your business is out of alignment with your customer's needs.

In general, the company that has the best branding is the company that truly understands what is important to its potential customers.

Identifying Your Brand

Your brand should convey what your company stands for and match the top five qualities that are important to your customers. Your brand will sometimes be defined in an entire paragraph on your website or in your marketing materials, but should also be boiled down to one sentence that states the most important quality of your company. This is your company's *tagline*.

Creating a Tagline

At this point you have taken the time to really understand what your customers want and you have taken the steps to make sure that your customers' wants match the goods or services you provide.

Here comes the creative moment. The tagline is the one sentence that you want your company to be known for. It should be simple, but needs to remind your customers that you know what is important to them.

Some simple taglines that you might recognize are as follows:

- *When you got it, flaunt it*—Braniff Airlines
- *All the news that's fit to print*—The New York Times
- *It takes a licking and keeps on ticking*—Timex
- *Have it your way*—Burger King
- *M'm! M'm! Good!*—Campbell Soup
- *When it absolutely, positively has to be there overnight*—Federal Express
- *The quicker picker upper*—Bounty
- *Capitalist tool*—Forbes

Write down five simple phrases that could be your tagline:

1. _____

2. _____

3. _____

4. _____

5. _____

Not as easy as it sounds? Then get some help. You will be amazed at how creative the people are around you. Your employees, family, customers, and friends can help. Show them the list of five qualities that you want to be known for and have a contest. Offer $100 to the one who comes up with the best tagline for your company. You will be amazed at what they contribute.

The choice is yours. Once you have a list of five or more options from yourself, friends, employees, and family, choose the one that best fits your own style. It's your decision. After all, this is your company!

Creating a Logo

Logos convey the look of your company name. Logos are meant to be recognizable and memorable. The important point to remember here is that logos can mean an awful lot if you are, or want to be, a recognizable national brand. We all recognize the golden arches of McDonalds, the Disney logo, and so on. The reality is that, for the most part, few of us are creating national brands that need the perfect logo.

There are companies that specialize in logo creation, many of which have free tools to get you started. Simply Google "free logo creation." These companies will give you inexpensive logo options that include your company name and tagline. The purpose of the logo is to help you communicate who you are and make your company look professional and reliable.

Your Elevator Pitch

The *elevator pitch* refers to a short persuasive speech given to someone during an elevator ride and was overused during the Dot Com days, whereby you pitch your company successfully to a venture capitalist by the time the elevator hits the 30th floor. Even if you'll never be riding an elevator with a venture capitalist, you (and all of your employees) need to be able to sum up your company's mission and goals in three or four succinct sentences.

You are essentially taking your brand identity and vocalizing it. This will not necessarily feel very comfortable in the beginning for you or your employees. Practice makes perfect.

Successful Branding

The key to successful branding is to make sure that everything that leaves your office with your company information on it has the exact same look and feel. Your logo, tagline, and who you are should never change. Even in a small market, you want your customers to recognize you easily and not be confused by a mess of different marketing materials, logos, or taglines. All of your marketing materials, signage, websites, invoices, and so on, should have the same look and feel. Make a commitment to this new image of yours and stick to it.

Branding: The Summary

You have now defined who your company is and what it stands for. You should have at this point:

- **A defined brand**
  You should have three to five points that summarize your company mission. These are created by matching what you are best at with what is important to your customers.

- **A tagline**
  This is a single sentence or phrase that summarizes who you are.

- **A logo**
  Your company name presented in a clean and professional graphic that incorporates your tagline.

- **A consistent message**
  Keep your branding the same all of the time. People will eventually start to remember your company's look and tagline.

Chapter 2

Marketing

The challenge in defining what marketing is has nothing to do with its definition.

Marketing is defined by the American Marketing Association as *the activity, set of institutions, and processes for creating, communicating, delivering, and exchanging offerings that have value for customers, clients, partners, and society at large.*

You knew that already, right?

The confusion comes from what most marketing "gurus" and companies say you need to do in order to get new business.

Many marketing gurus will tell you that a consumer needs to see your company's name in front of them something like 29 times before they are comfortable enough to use you. This may very well be true if your goal is to build a national brand—or even a local or regional brand where you are trying to make your company name synonymous with the sector you are in.

This strategy may be great for Coca-Cola, Pepsi, Taco Bell, Johnson & Johnson, and such, but it is a sure way to bankrupt a small business owner.

Marketing for the rest of us can be described as simply getting your name out to potential customers and communicating to them what it is that you offer and how you can help them. Following the "KISS" theory (Keep It Simple, Stupid), this chapter covers the marketing basics that will help move your company to the next level.

Businesses fall into three camps:

- Those who believe they have a "word of mouth" business and do nothing at all.
- Those who spend money on marketing and are constantly disappointed with the results.
- Those who have read this book.

Strategy #1: Doing Nothing and Loving It

It is possible to keep yourself busy by doing high-quality work and relying on the kindness of others to refer you to their friends and neighbors. This strategy may keep you busy during times of economic prosperity, but won't likely grow your business.

Using this "word of mouth" helped small businesses grow 40 years ago when people actually spoke to their neighbors. Today, people are becoming more and more insulated and family focused. It is not uncommon for neighbors to live in a suburban neighborhood for five or 10 years and never really know their neighbors. They may share an occasional wave as they pass each other going in and out of the driveway as they quickly slide in the garage, but rarely spend any time together.

Consequently, you may have just provided someone with an amazing customer experience, but if that customer doesn't talk to his or her neighbors, the hoped-for endorsement is a best-kept secret.

There is unfortunately an exception to that rule. Nothing brings a neighborhood together like a horror story of a bad customer experience. Neighbors who have not spoken two words to each other in six years suddenly are best friends bonded around the story of how their time was wasted or they felt cheated by your business. (More about that later.)

Word-of-mouth businesses are also the first to suffer during a downturn in the economy. It only makes sense. If fewer people are spending, there are fewer people to talk about you.

Strategy #2: Spending Your Way to the Poor House

Just because you spent money on a "marketing program" does not mean that it was worth the money you spent on it. The graveyard of small business owners is littered with the corpses of those who spent a ton of money and did not get the returns they had hoped for.

Before you dive deeply into the pool of marketing mistakes in this section, there are a few terms you need to understand:

- **Cost per Lead**
  Cost per lead is the actual dollar amount it ends up costing you to get a single lead from a marketing effort. For example, if you spend $2,000 for a particular marketing effort and it generated 40 leads, your cost per lead is $50.

- **Marketing Cost per Job**
  If you close 1 out of 10 of those leads, your marketing cost per job is $500. This would be terrific if your average job netted $6000, but would be upside down if your average job size is $300.

Caution, Will Robinson: Strategies That Don't Usually Work
Merged Mailers

Merged mailers are marketing ploys that gang a bunch of advertisements into a single mass-mailed envelope.

The merged mailer pitch sounds great. "Get your flyers into the hands of many qualified homeowners for a very low price."

Merged mailers, though, are the most ignored form of junk mail. And we all know how often typical junk mail goes directly into the trash. Merged mail packets are worse. Think about your own home. How much junk mail do you receive every day?

Your advertisement is not just a single stand-alone piece of junk; it is in an envelope (that has to be opened up) hidden with 25 more pieces of junk.

Remember the *cost per lead*. Merged mailers have a terrible cost per lead and are not worth your advertising dollars even if the salesperson is incredibly slick. These salespeople are also notorious for telling you that you need to buy their program for multiple months (getting your name out there the infamous 29 times) in order to see results.

With all of that said, if you have a very large average sale price and have a big part of each job's profits set aside for marketing expenses, perhaps this form of marketing will work for you.

Yellow Pages

Yellow page advertising is another perennial favorite of small business owners.

For years, having a yellow page ad seemed to be a "must-have" for small businesses. It was a perceived sign to others that you were a significant player in your market by showing that you, too, could afford a sacred yellow page ad.

But, in today's world, who uses traditional printed yellow pages?

Prior to the advent of the Internet, many people used yellow pages as a vehicle to find all types of businesses. Today, though, most people go to Google or another search engine to find a business. This gives them a list of all the Internet-savvy businesses in the area as well as actual reviews about these businesses.

Customers can then jump on the website and make well-informed decisions as to who to call. This search method is free, quick, easy, and thorough.

Let me illustrate. Today, I drove by the mailboxes in my neighborhood where people of neighboring households go to get their mail. You know the type. A group of about 16 mailboxes clustered together on a single pedestal. Stacked underneath the cluster are several yellow page books. They have been there for about a month. Obviously, many of my neighbors don't see the value in bending over to pick up their copy of the local yellow page book.

Let's discuss for a minute how yellow page advertisements are priced.

Also, in today's day and age, who would ever commit to an up-front astronomical monthly fee in order to hope to get a lead or two at a price point that no one can commit to? Don't do it. This tip alone will save you many times the cost of this book!

I speak from painful experience. Years ago, we spent tens of thousands of dollars on paint contractor yellow page ads. We received a call here and there, but once we started evaluating the cost per lead, we dropped out of the large-scale yellow page-advertising program.

There are some small businesses that still may see some value in yellow page advertising. These types of businesses would be the "crisis" type businesses. A crisis type business is a business that you need to call immediately when an urgent problem occurs. Examples include roofers and plumbers.

You may also benefit from the yellow pages if you live in an area with a very large elderly population that has a small local version of a yellow page book. Be careful, though. The elderly are becoming computer savvy, too.

SPENDING WITH CAUTION
Before you spend, remember these important points:
- Be very leery of marketing salespeople who want to take your money, but cannot guarantee you a cost per lead or, ultimately, a cost per job that makes sense to you.
- Test everything you do in very small dollar amounts. Make sure it works before you commit to spend your mortgage payment.
- Understand your marketing cost per lead and cost per job.
- Most importantly, understand your average job size and use that number to determine a sensible cost for finding new customers.

Strategy #3: Creating a Marketing Program that Works

Here is the section you have been waiting for. The section that gives you a leg up on your competition and saves you money!

Make an Inventory List

Make a list of everything that you use to promote your company. This should include everything from business cards and envelopes to flyers and advertisements.

1. _____
2. _____
3. _____
4. _____
5. _____
6. _____
7. _____

Everything you use to promote your business must have the same look. Here's a list of the items you'll typically need:

- Logo and tagline
- Phone number
- Website
- Email address

Marketing Materials: What You Really Need

This section covers the marketing materials that you really need to get some business on a fairly regular basis. It doesn't have to be incredibly expensive to arm yourself with the appropriate materials.

Business Cards

The simple business card is a great and inexpensive marketing tool. The most important point to remember about business cards is that their purpose is not as a tool for writing quotes on the reverse side! They are to be freely handed out to anyone and everyone who will take one. Better yet, they are to be given 10 at time so people can hand them to their friends. If you are not going through 500 business cards a month, you are not actively marketing your business!

A Basic Flyer

A basic flyer is the workhorse of your operation. It should be half of an $8^1/_2 \times 11$ sheet of paper (so you can get two out of each piece of paper). It should have all of your branding information that you came up with in the previous chapter, as well as any logos (with permission of course) from any trade groups (including the BBB) to which you belong.

Refrigerator Magnets and Other "Swag"

Swag has its place and can be helpful. If you happen to be in a service that a customer needs regularly, then something that the customer might save and use, such as a refrigerator magnet or a calendar has value.

However, if you are a roofer and you just put on a 20-year roof, why would you give anyone a one-year calendar with your name on it?

Pens that are cheap will only associate your company with something that does not work and needs to be thrown out. Squeeze balls get lost or given to the kids.

Pads of paper get used up eventually.

The best and least expensive item is a simple business card or two. Politely suggest they pin one up on their corkboard that most people seem to have to keep their important information.

The corkboard at my house has business cards of our plumber, handyman, hair salon, mechanic, pizza place, dry cleaner and pool service. When I need those businesses, I know exactly where to find them. All the other goodies well-meaning businesses give me tend to go to the kids, the dogs, or in the trash.

Ads in Local Papers

I am generally not a fan of print advertising, but there are times when it can have an impact and not be very expensive.

Small local newspapers tend to be read cover to cover by people who want to know what is going on in their community.

These papers generally have a very small distribution, but do have a classifieds section or a services section that many homeowners turn to in order to find a local business. These local papers will drive customers to your business.

Just like with anything else, test first and watch your cost per lead and cost per job.

Free Publicity

Nothing is more effective than free local publicity. An article written about you and your company in your local newspaper can bring you a flood of leads that will turn into jobs. And, best of all, it's free! Picture this…

LOCAL CONTRACTOR HELPS NEEDY DURING TOUGH TIMES

Harold Plumber, owner of Harold's Plumbing in Colorado Springs, doesn't just talk about helping out his neighbors during these challenging times, he actually does something about it. Harold and his employees took a Saturday afternoon and helped out the Smith family here in Colorado Springs. John Smith and his wife Abigale are both retired and living on their monthly Social Security check. What savings they did have was all but washed away in the stock market. Their home of 40 years had some significant plumbing issues and the Smiths needed help. Mr. Plumber came to their rescue after hearing about their plight on a local TV news report. After four hours of hard work by Harold's crew, the Smith's dire situation was resolved. When asked why he did it, Mr. Plumber was very frank. "In today's challenging times neighbors have to pull together and help each other out. The Smiths are great folk who just needed some help." This reporter wishes the world had more Harold Plumbers.

Some might think an article like this may result in people calling for more free work. Yes, some people may call you for free work, but no more than who already call you expecting to get a job for half your rate! This kind of publicity will also generate plenty of calls from people who read the story and want to support your business.

First find a needy family in your area and block off a day or so to help somebody. Make the arrangements and go to work! Make sure the family writes you a reference letter and take plenty of pictures. Enjoy the day. You and your employees are doing something worthwhile.

Before you go over to do the work, contact your local newspaper. Talk to someone in the features department. Small community newspapers are always looking for a "feel good" story of someone doing something to help somebody in need. With all the hardship going on in our communities, it is great to read a story about a local merchant volunteering to help put some "hope" back in somebody's life. When you call, make sure to let the reporter know that the purpose of your service is to show the community that people are still helping each other out.

If you do this properly you'll see two results. One will be that you will receive calls for some new business. Secondly, you will feel really good about helping people who need it.

A Reference Book

Some of the best marketing comes from showing potential customers samples of your work and what you're all about. This type of book works great for just about any business. Imagine how impressed a customer who just walked into your store will be after picking up a book that has picture after picture of satisfied customers with their new purchases and a handwritten note from each of them about how happy they were with your services.

Keep a simple three-ring binder up to date with the following:

1. One page about your company, including when it was founded and what you stand for (your branding message).

2. A quick note about you and your family, complete with your picture. Remember, customers want to feel safe about the person they are hiring.

3. Copies of your workers compensation and insurance policies, and any trade associations you belong to.

4. A few pages with pictures of smiling people working. Maybe add a bit about their personal family lives and comments from customers about them individually. Customers need to feel comfortable around your employees as well.

5. Testimonials that include a note about the service or product they bought, pictures of happy customers, and reference letters from the customers.

6. Product information that is relevant.

If you don't already have a reference book put together, this should be the first thing you work on when you finish reading this book. This tool alone will make you money right out of the gate.

Using Referrals to Get Repeat Business

Every satisfied customer should result in more business!

If you have done a good job and made sure your customer is happy, each and every satisfied client can lead to obtaining another customer. This does not happen by accident, though. To be successful at having each customer refer you to her friends and neighbors, you need to work the system!

Customer Service Survey with Referral Piece

Every time you complete a transaction with a customer you should hand him a customer service survey. This survey is to be filled out on the spot, not mailed back (very few people follow through on getting such a survey completed and in the mail). Design the survey to remind the customer of all the things you did well on the job. Additionally, the survey calls for the customer to write down the names and phone numbers of four friends who may be interested in receiving an estimate or product information.

The following are some sample questions for your customer service survey:

1. Did our product or service exceed your expectations?
2. Were our employees polite and courteous?
3. Did our employees take their shoes off or wear booties in your home?
4. Was our proposal clear, concise, and professional?
5. Did our employees arrive when they were scheduled?
6. Were our employees polite and courteous?
7. Did our employees treat your home with the respect it deserves?
8. Were all of your concerns addressed?
9. Are you 100% happy with our service or product?
10. Would you refer us to your friends and family?

If your customers answer no to any of these questions, you have the opportunity to resolve their concerns, either by actually fixing the problem or by apologizing for anything that was not up to their expectations.

The purpose of this survey is to simply reinforce, in a very positive way, how great your company is, what a superb job you just did, and, most importantly, to set them up to give referrals. Your competitors are not doing this! This survey alone makes you stand out from the rest.

Referral: Call to Action

Your customers are very busy people and, in most cases, even if they loved your product or service, they will not think about referring you to their friends or take the time to do so. You need to entice them to help you out.

One great way is to offer your customers a reward for introducing you to your next customer. This can be as simple as a $20 Starbucks gift card. You will be surprised how hard someone will work for you so they can get $20 worth of coffee.

Referrals 2.0: Using Facebook to Market Your Business

Facebook is an overlooked marketing tool. Have your happiest customers put a quick recommendation of you on their "wall" on Facebook. Facebook fans are addicted to the site.

Facebookers do three main things:

- Collect new friends.
- Update their wall to tell their friends what they are doing.
- Get constant updates from their friends about new things in their lives.

Facebook friends trust each other. Don't think that teenagers are the only ones who use Facebook—there are countless adults who use Facebook as a primary tool to communicate with friends near and far. Asking each of your satisfied customers to just post a quick referral to friends can lead to referral after referral.

Consider these statistics directly from Facebook:

- More than 400 million active users
- 50% of Facebook's active users log on to Facebook in any given day
- More than 35 million users update their status each day
- More than 60 million status updates posted each day
- More than 3 billion photos uploaded to the site each month
- More than 5 billion pieces of content (web links, news stories, blog posts, notes, photo albums, and so on) shared each week
- More than 3.5 million events created each month
- More than 3 million active Pages on Facebook
- More than 1.5 million local businesses have active pages on Facebook
- More than 20 million people become fans of pages each day
- Pages have created more than 5.3 billion fans
- Average user has 130 friends on the site
- Average user sends eight friend requests per month
- Average user spends more than 55 minutes per day on Facebook
- Average user clicks the Like button on nine pieces of content each month
- Average user writes 25 comments on Facebook content each month
- Average user becomes a fan of four pages each month
- Average user is invited to three events per month
- Average user is a member of 13 groups

The power of Facebook is truly amazing for small businesses. No other advertising vehicle even comes close to delivering the eyeballs that Facebook does every day. Facebook friends read each other's posts daily and trust what is posted as being factual. They trust their close network of friends.

Just imagine someone who has a great experience at your restaurant, or who found the perfect dress at your shop, and was completely blown away by the customer service. If this was only a few short years ago, that customer may tell their story to one or two friends in passing. If their experience with you was exceptional, they may tell four or five people. The chances of additional business actually being generated from these discussions are probably very small.

Today that same customer can go home and tell all 130 of their closest friends what an amazing experience they had with your business. Not only can they write something about that experience but since Facebookers generally read each other's posts daily, then that post will be read by not one or two people but closer to 80% of their 130 friends. What kind of advertising medium can possibly deliver that number of eyeballs?

Creating a Facebook Fan Page

In order to truly harness the power of Facebook you need to create a Fan Page. The instructions for doing so are simple and can be found on Facebook itself. A Fan Page is essentially a page about your company. Some of the top Facebook Fan Pages are Starbucks, which has 5,300,000 fans, Coca-Cola with 4,100,000 fans, YouTube with 3,800,000 fans, and Skittles with 3,500,000 fans. (I did some rounding on these numbers, but they're probably even higher by now.) These companies are great examples of businesses that are using Facebook to market directly to their customers. Just like a regular Facebook page, when a status is updated on a Fan Page, it is sent to all fans. This means that every time you post a satisfied customer status on your page it will also get posted on the pages of all your fans.

Here are some tips to keep your Fan Page interesting:

- Don't overpost; once a week is plenty
- Keep your posts interesting and fun
- Do not use your Fan Page as your personal blog
- Pictures of happy customers work great
- Special offers for your Facebook fans are always a winner

You can also buy targeted ads on Facebook that will reach out to the exact demographic in a geographic area. These ads show up on the right side of the page. Check out Facebook advertising on the site for more info.

Facebook is a huge game changer for the way small businesses reach out to their customers. It is the single best way to advertise and you can't beat the price—it's free!

Using LinkedIn to Market Your Business

If you live in the business-to-business world, LinkedIn is an amazing tool for your business.

Wikipedia describes LinkedIn best, as indicated in the following sidebar.

MEMBERSHIP

LinkedIn has more than 60 million users worldwide, of which approximately half are in the United States.

The purpose of the site is to allow registered users to maintain a list of contact details of people they know and trust in business. The people in the list are called *Connections*. Users can invite anyone (whether a site user or not) to become a connection.

This list of connections can then be used in a number of ways:

- A contact network is built up consisting of their direct connections, the connections of each of their connections (termed *second-degree connections*) and also the connections of second-degree connections (termed *third-degree connections*). This can be used to gain an introduction to someone a person wishes to know through a mutual, trusted contact.
- It can then be used to find jobs, people, and business opportunities recommended by someone in one's contact network.
- Employers can list jobs and search for potential candidates.
- Job seekers can review the profile of hiring managers and discover which of their existing contacts can introduce them.
- Users can post their own photos and view photos of others to aid in identification.

The "gated-access approach" (where contact with any professional requires either a preexisting relationship, or the intervention of a contact of theirs) is intended to build trust among the service's users. LinkedIn participates in EU's International Safe Harbor Privacy Principles.

LinkedIn also allows users to research companies with which they may be interested in working. When typing the name of a given company in the search box, statistics about the company are provided. These may include the ratio of female to male employees, the percentage of the most common titles/positions held within the company, the location of the company's headquarters and offices, or a list of present, past, and former employees.

The feature LinkedIn Answers, similar to Yahoo! Answers, allows users to ask questions for the community to answer. This feature is free and the main difference from the latter is that questions are potentially more business-oriented, and the identity of the people asking and answering questions is known.

The searchable LinkedIn Groups feature allows users to establish new business relationships by joining alumni, industry, or professional and other relevant groups. LinkedIn groups can be created in any subjects and by any member of LinkedIn. Some groups are specialized groups dealing with a narrow domain or industry whereas others are very broad and generic in nature.

The newest LinkedIn feature is LinkedIn Polls, still in alpha.

A mobile version of the site was launched in February 2008, which gives access to a reduced feature set over a mobile phone. The mobile service is available in six languages: Chinese, English, French, German, Japanese, and Spanish.

In mid-2008, LinkedIn launched LinkedIn DirectAds as a form of sponsored advertising.

In October 2008, LinkedIn revealed plans of opening its social network of 30 million professionals globally as a potential sample for business-to-business research. And, in doing so it's testing a potential social-network revenue model-research that to some appears more promising than advertising.

In October 2008, LinkedIn enabled an "applications platform" that allows other online services to be embedded within a member's profile page. For example, among the initial applications were an Amazon Reading List that allows LinkedIn members to display books they are reading, a connection to Tripit, and a Six Apart, WordPress, and TypePad application that allows members to display their latest blog postings within their LinkedIn profile.

In summary, LinkedIn allows you to stay in touch with and build new business contacts over the web.

Back to Basics: Using Handwritten Notes

Actual old-fashioned handwriting has its purpose!

There was a time when people routinely took the time to handwrite a note or a letter to offer thanks. Back 25 years ago, people handwrote them because not everybody owned typewriters and very few owned a personal computer. Email was definitely not mainstream and definitely not a common practice.

Over the last 25 years, the art of the handwritten note has slowly disappeared. When was the last time anyone sent you a handwritten note or letter? Check out last year's group of holiday cards and note how many included handwriting.

If you really want to have a huge impact on your customers, send them handwritten notes thanking them for their business or the time they took with you on the estimate. (Many will stare at the card reading it over and over again wondering where you downloaded the interesting font!)

The handwritten note will have impact. You will be remembered as one of the few that took the time to go the extra mile.

And, with the note, don't forget to include a few business cards in the envelope.

Use handwritten cards to:

- Thank someone for his or her interest in your business.
- Apologize for a problem on the job.
- Thank someone for the business.

For those of you who want to go out on a limb, send them a $20 Starbucks gift card in advance of their first referral, letting them know that you are confident that they will more than earn the gift card (of course, only where this is legal). You will be surprised how many people will feel the need to make sure you get a referral because you already paid them for it!

Sending Out Cards: Almost as Good

For those of you who have tried and tried to get on the program of sending out handwritten cards and have continually failed, shame on you (okay, and on me, too).

I can honestly say that a handwritten card to thank a customer or an employee is the best way to make a substantial impression on your customers.

There is an easier alternative, though.

Sendoutcards.com is an online service that simplifies the process. You input all of your customers' and employees' information into it. You pick the appropriate card and type a note on it. Another site, senditout.com, will print the card, put it in an envelope, and mail it out for you—all with the click of a button. The site also includes a handwriting feature that will copy your handwriting or printing so that the card actually looks like it came from you. What will they think of next?

Email Not for a Thank You, But...

Email simply does not have the same personal touch as cards and notes. Most working people today will receive 20 to 200+ legitimate emails a day.

The majority of business people view email as a necessary evil. They see it as more of a challenge to their daily life than as a savior.

Your message of "Hey, thanks for your time" will be forgotten almost immediately.

There is, however, a useful purpose to email.

Email to Respond to Customer Questions

Always respond immediately to a customer email. (Yes, as if you were sitting around the computer just waiting for his or her message.)

Even if your answer is "I will call you in 30 minutes" or "I will have to get back to you later today," you need to always respond immediately.

Email Information

It is always a great idea to email to potential customers pictures of similar jobs and scanned copies of the reference letters that go along with them.

Taking the time to email your customers information about your suppliers, products, and your website link will really make an impression on those that are data-driven and want to know more about you and your operation.

All You Never Wanted to Know About the Internet!

Yes, you need a website. How elaborate your website needs to be depends on many things, including how much of your business is conducted over the web. Generally speaking, if you are not actually selling products via the web and are using your site only to promote your product or service, it does not need to be expensive. It can be done by any teenager in your neighborhood and it can include just one page. The content really depends on how ambitious you are. There are a couple of points to remember when setting up your website.

The Why of the Website

A website is not going to suddenly drive new business to your door. Truth be told, when you put up a website no one may ever find you unless they are specifically looking for your company. Try typing in Italian restaurants, Mechanics, or Landscape Contractors into Google and you'll see pages of listings. The chances of your website finding its way to the front page of such a generic search are almost as good as winning the lottery.

Your website's main purpose is to act as an online brochure about your company. Your website is a visible and effective place for you to post photos of your happy customers, your location, and other basic information. Customers can anonymously go to your site and get a better feeling of the company.

Your URL (Otherwise Known as Your Web Address)

Ideally, your URL is *yourcompanyname.com*. Depending on the unique nature of your business name, this may be very difficult to obtain. The best way to find a URL is to use Godaddy.com where a feature exists that allows you to search for various versions of your name until you find something simple that works (and hopefully uses the .com suffix instead of .net, .biz, or the other less common extensions).

The chance that your first pick is available is probably next to zero (unless the name of your business is incredibly unique). If you have not already secured yourname.com years ago, someone else has probably taken it. Take a cue from the movie industry. Have you ever noticed that every movie has a website, but is always *moviename*movie.com? The movie industry realized that it would be next to impossible to always get the URL that it wanted. It understands the value of the .com extension, so it generally uses *moviename*movie.com to ensure nobody else has it.

If you can't find your companyname.com, try adding your trade to the end. For instance, AlltheMechanic.com or HelentheFlorist.com or SmiththeLandscapers.com

Once you have your URL, you will need to purchase the .net, .biz, and .org extensions. It is better to be safe than sorry. After all, after you implement the strategies in this book you are going to be on your way to developing a large business—you might as well be prepared for the future. Also these extensions will only cost you about $10 each per year. Ten bucks isn't much of an investment to make sure a competitor doesn't grab a similar URL.

Don't forget to renew your URL yearly or to buy the three-year package. Most URL providers allow you to "auto renew" so that you don't run the risk of losing the URL. Letting your URL expire is disastrous and needs to be avoided at all costs. Someone else can purchase your expired URL. Confused previous customers trying to find you fail and tons of printed marketing material is wasted!

Less Is More

A picture is worth a thousand words. This old saying holds true on the Internet as well. In fact, if your front page has no pictures and just a thousand words, no one will stop to read it or even look at it. They will go somewhere else. In the website game, less is more. Stick with these guidelines:

- Fewer long paragraphs (that people won't read) and more bullet points that jump off the page.
- Fewer colors and more white background and whitespace.

- Fewer words in general and more pictures.
- More pictures of you, your family, and your workers are great! Remember people come to your site to get comfortable with your company. They want to feel good about you and your employees. The more your site can make them feel comfortable, the better.

References

A references section is a must for your site. Continually update the section with pictures and letters from your customers. There is nothing better than a site that shows your recent, happy customers. Customers tend to be suspicious of a company whose site shows references from five years ago.

Important Website Tips

Your website should be simple and uncluttered. Remember, less is more, but some things must be included.

Include Contact Information

This should jump off the page at your customers. Don't make them hunt for it. When they click on the contact info button it should take them to a nice clean page that has all of your contact information, as well as a form to fill out if they would rather email you than call you.

Your contact information should be big and bold at the bottom of every page, as well.

Include a Buy Now Button

If you are selling products online, the link that takes your customer to the catalog page should be obvious and easy to see. No one wants to hunt on a cluttered website to find the products they are looking for. Make everything easy for your customers.

Provide Your Branding Message

Your branding message (the one you came up with in the last chapter) needs to be front and center on your site. This is who you are and what your customers have told you is most important about you. This message, communicated in bullet points, is a key part of getting someone to choose you!

Remember that you only have 60 seconds to get a browser's attention. You all know how this works. You go to a website and in the first 60 seconds you decide if you are going to spend more time there or just go somewhere else. Your website needs to grab your potential customers' attention and speak directly to what they are looking for. If it doesn't, they'll move on to a competitor's website.

In most situations, your website is your customer's first impression of you and your company. If your website is crowded, dated, or just plain boring, your customer will naturally assume that is the kind of work you do.

Using a Blog To Market Your Business

Think about creating your own blog. Go to blogger.com and follow the easy instructions to create a blog. Blogs are a great way to keep your potential customers updated on jobs in progress and references in general. You can post reference pictures and letters from past customers and have general updates on company happenings.

Keep in mind that your company blog is not the place to share your personal, political, or religious views, or your thoughts about Paris Hilton. This is a space dedicated to just how cool your company is.

Just because you may have never read a blog and have absolutely no intention of ever reading one does not mean that your customers don't read blogs. Many of your customers obtain a great deal of their daily information not from newspapers or television, but from their Facebook account and from miscellaneous blogs on the Internet. And this trend is on the rise.

Your blog should have a direct link from your site and also be listed on all your marketing materials.

Once you start your blog make sure you are committed to updating it at least weekly. People expect to see recent information on a blog. That is a blog's purpose.

Website Optimizing and Other Expensive Hobbies

In recent years, website optimization has become a new up and coming business. The minute you launch your site you will be pitched from multiple companies that will claim to be able to make you show up on the front page of a Google search. These salespeople will tell you that they have a service that, for a fee of thousands of your dollars (and many months of patience), they can get your site to show up on the search engines. They are right about one thing. It is very expensive and it does take months. But, there still is no guarantee that your site will show up any where close to the front page.

SEO (Search Engine Optimization) is all about getting Google and Yahoo to recognize your site as being relevant to the search that someone performs. This is done primarily by using keywords that Google recognizes on your site. Google uses these keywords (and other information it gathers on your site) in order to evaluate whether your site has more relevance than another site.

The main issue with being found by Google is that Google does not recognize images as being relevant, so the more text you have on your home page with more relevant "keywords" and terms, the better your website will rank. You may rank high on the search results, but if you agree with the "60 Second Rule," people may actually click on your site, but will disappear just as quickly as they got there because of a lack of interest in a home page flooded with text and no pictures.

No One Really Knows Besides Google

Beware of any SEO company that claims it can guarantee you top rankings on Google. The algorithms that Google uses to rank its search results rival the secrecy of the Coca-Cola formula and Kentucky Fried Chicken secret recipe. No one really knows what items on your website will guarantee ranking success. And as soon as an SEO company starts getting some success, Google changes the parameters. It's an ever-changing game.

The real question you need to ask yourself is do you need to show up on the first page of a Google search? The majority of small businesses operate on a local level. If your business is in San Diego, is it valuable to you that a person who searches for "Car Detailing" in Boston finds your site among the search results? Let the big national players spend the money and worry about what happens when somebody types "Landscaper" or "Florist" into a search box.

Searches That Do Matter

People have become much more skilled at how to find the information they are searching for on Google, Yahoo, MSN, Bing, and all the other search sites. Most people now will type in "Handyman in Sacramento" or "Toyota Mechanic in Boise". By putting in their local city, the search engine will deliver local results only.

Own Your Local Searches

Owning the local searches is where you want to focus all of your Internet energy. Whenever someone types in your trade and the cities in which you operate, you want to make sure that your company comes up front and center. This is how you drive leads to your business. Keep in mind, though, that this is an expensive project if you plan on using SEO.

Much easier, less expensive, and guaranteed solutions exist.

Using Google: The One Stop Shop for All Your Web Marketing Needs

There are many search engines out on the Internet. Some people have their personal favorites, but Google owns 67% of the Internet search market, followed by Yahoo at 20%, and the rest make up the remaining 13%. If all you do is make sure that you are set up properly on Google, you will reach 67% of the people looking for your trade in your area. Trying to figure out how all the other search engines work becomes a project with diminishing returns at a certain point. Focus on Google local search and capture two-thirds of the market looking for you. Let the other third go—there are just not enough hours in the day to try and make all that work worth your while.

Google Maps

Utilizing Google Maps is an important part of your strategy. Make sure you are working with a company that understands how to use this technology to improve your local search results.

Google Ad Words

A great way to show up on the first page of a local search is to "buy" the spot on the Google home page. For what can range from pennies to dollars per click, your business can show up every time someone searches for your trade in your area.

Pay per click means that you only pay when someone clicks on your ad. This is the only way in which you should do Internet advertising. This is a strictly pay for performance model. If no one clicks on your ad, you don't pay.

Don't get carried away with your ad words. You don't need to be paying top dollar for the first spot on Google. That game is for people who did not read this book. Let them waste their money. There is usually a premium for being the one in the first spot of the search results. It is amazing how much the price drops when you are number three or four on the pay per click ads. People who are searching for any business will look at the first three to five ads. They click on the links and go to the respective sites. At this point, they will decide from whom they want to get an estimate. (Go back to how to build an amazing site!) You can end up paying 1/20 the price as your competitor paid who bought the number one spot—and the potential customer ended up viewing both of your sites.

The easiest way to make sure you show up when someone searches for "your business" and "your city" is to buy the key words that will guarantee your business will show up each time that search is performed.

With a little extra reading, you can figure this out for yourself. If this is how you like to spend your spare time, check out www.perrymarshall.com. You can learn everything you ever wanted to know about ad words at his site.

Using a Web Marketing Company

For those of you who have no interest in learning an entirely new business, hire a web marketing company to do it for you.

Finding a search company that understands your need to drive local traffic is the most important thing you can do with your online marketing money. Interview them thoroughly and make sure that you call at least three or four references. These references are vital in determining if their customers have been successful winning the local search battle.

One of the most important things to find out is how much of your money will go to the marketing company versus for your actual ad words.

This business sector is full of new companies that just started their businesses yesterday, so do your research!

When setting up your ad word account, start with a $100 limit or so and test, test, test. Monitor how many people are clicking on your site and if this is indeed turning into contacts and estimates.

Yes, There Is More You Can Do on the Web

Try Craigslist

Craigslist can be a tremendous source of leads for service-based companies. Unless you have been living in a cave, you have heard of Craigslist! It is a relatively new phenomenon and is the "go to" place for almost any type of service:

- **Posting is easy.** Go to craigslist.com and click on "post to classifieds." Then click on "services offered" and finally on "skilled trades." At that point just follow the directions. Make sure you are careful to use your "tag line" and put your company in the best light. Put a phone number that someone will answer and will not go to voicemail. Don't forget your email address as well as your company website.

- **Post in every city you have coverage.** Craigslist covers very specific geographic areas so be sure to post your ad in each city in which you do work.

- **Re-post every three days.** Craigslist is just that, a list. The key with any list is to keep yourself on top of the list. The only real way to do this is to keep posting your ad every three days so that you stay on top. This process only takes four or five minutes. There should be no excuse for not doing it.

- **Don't give up.** Over time you will get leads from Craigslist. The key to success is to keep updating your entry in Craigslist as part of your weekly routine. Write it in your calendar and follow through!

Try Backpage.com

Backpage.com is a competitor to Craigslist. Take the time to post your listing with them as well. The process is the same.

Try eBay

This section would not be complete without a mention of the Grand Daddy of the Internet: eBay. Again thanks to Wikipedia, here is the history of eBay.

EBAY

The online auction website was founded as AuctionWeb in San Jose, California, on September 3, 1995, by French-born Iranian computer programmer Pierre Omidyar as part of a larger personal site that included, among other things, Omidyar's own tongue-in-cheek tribute to the Ebola virus. The very first item sold on eBay was a broken laser pointer for $14.83. Astonished, Omidyar contacted the winning bidder to ask if he understood that the laser pointer was broken. In his responding email, the buyer explained: "I'm a collector of broken laser pointers." The frequently repeated story that eBay was founded to help Omidyar's fiancée trade Pez candy dispensers was fabricated by a public relations manager in 1997 to interest the media. This was revealed in Adam Cohen's 2002 book, *The Perfect Store*, and confirmed by eBay.

Chris Agarpao was hired as eBay's first employee and Jeffrey Skoll was hired as the first president of the company in early 1996. In November 1996, eBay entered into its first third-party licensing deal, with a company called Electronic Travel Auction to use SmartMarket Technology to sell plane tickets and other travel products. Growth was phenomenal; in January 1997 the site hosted 2,000,000 auctions, compared with 250,000 during the whole of 1996. The company officially changed the name of its service from AuctionWeb to eBay in September 1997. Originally, the site belonged to Echo

Bay Technology Group, Omidyar's consulting firm. Omidyar had tried to register the domain name echobay.com, but found it already taken by the Echo Bay Mines, a gold mining company, so he shortened it to his second choice, *eBay.com*. (Echobay.com is now owned by Echobay Partners, Ltd., a private equity firm based in Nevis.)

In 1997, the company received approximately $5 million in funding from the venture capital firm Benchmark Capital.

Meg Whitman was hired as eBay President and CEO in March 1998. At the time, the company had 30 employees half a million users and revenues of $4.7 million in the United States. eBay went public on September 21, 1998, and both Omidyar and Skoll became instant billionaires. eBay's target share price of $18 was all but ignored as the price went to $53.50 on the first day of trading.

As the company expanded product categories beyond collectibles into almost any saleable item, business grew quickly. In February 2002, the company purchased iBazar, a similar European auction website founded in 1995 and then bought PayPal on October 14, 2002.

In early 2008, the company had expanded worldwide, counted hundreds of millions of registered users, 15,000+ employees and revenues of almost $7.7 billion. After nearly 10 years at eBay, Whitman made the decision to enter politics. On January 23, 2008, the company announced that Whitman would step down on March 31, 2008, and John Donahoe was selected to become President and CEO. Whitman remained on the Board of Directors and continued to advise Donahoe through 2008. In late 2009, eBay completed the sale of Skype for $2.75 billion, but will still own 30% equity in the company.

If you have a retail location of any type, you should also have an eBay storefront. You have probably driven by small specialty shops in your neighborhood and wondered, "how do these people stay in business, no one is ever in there…" The answer is that the small specialty jewelry shop is actually a large global business selling to customers in 20 countries and that its jewelry that you would never be caught dead wearing is actually a top seller in Japan.

eBay makes it easy to set up your own storefront. Simply go to eBay and follow the simple steps to build your store. You will be selling globally in no time!

Chapter 3

When Things Go Very Bad

In the old days, small businesses could survive even though they provided a poor quality product and left a wake of destruction and angry customers behind them.

Ten years ago it was literally possible to just do enough to get by. "The customer is always right" was a phrase that people would say, but only half-heartedly believed.

Truth be told, 10 years ago a home small business could actually grow over time despite not taking care of its customers. There wasn't much concern at the time because the dissatisfied customers didn't have a way to get their irate voices heard.

It is now simple for customers who are not happy with your product or service to get the word out. Not only will they tell a couple of friends and neighbors about how dissatisfied they are with you, but they'll tell the whole world.

And damage isn't done with just the completely unhappy customers, but with customer comments that the job was only "satisfactory," not "outstanding." In today's world of customer-driven review websites, "satisfactory" is about the same as "Oh, and they killed my cat as well."

"Satisfactory" Will Kill Your Business!

What is wrong with doing a satisfactory job? You'd think there would be nothing wrong with a satisfactory job, but it simply isn't enough in today's electronic age. "Satisfactory" today means you are not planning to grow your business or maybe not even planning to stay in business.

Beware: Customers will research you on the web!

Things have changed in the last 10 years. Wake up! Check out your local competitors. Consumers now have a wealth of information available to them on the web. Consumers will spend hours and hours researching and reading the reviews on different sites before they take the plunge to buy a $200 digital camera. Customer review websites are available for just about every product or service imaginable.

Chances are they will spend hours doing their homework on the Internet before making a final decision.

Their research has been made easier by a new group of entrepreneurs whose websites are driven not just to make money, but by social responsibility. One of their main purposes is to make sure that businesses are held to a higher standard than they have been held to in the past. These service review sites do what consumer groups across the country have been trying to do for years.

Their aim is to scare you straight. And it's working!

Service Review Sites

Here are some popular service review sites and their *modus operandi*.

Pissedoffconsumer.com

Pissedoffconsumer.com is an online consumer product review and complaint site. If a consumer has received terrible service, been scammed, cheated, or something similar, he or she can post a complaint and share feedback with site members about products or services.

Angieslist.com

Angie's List is a word-of-mouth network for consumers with thousands of first-hand reports from members in your area. It is a respected source for recommendations for contractors or other home improvement service providers.

Ripoffreport.com

Ripoff Report is a consumer reporting website and publication, by consumers and for consumers, to file and document complaints about companies or individuals.

Unlike the Better Business Bureau, Ripoff Report does not hide reports of "satisfied" complaints. All complaints remain public and unedited in order to create a working history on the company or individual in question.

Ripoff Reports covers over 1,000 topics and categories. Users can browse the latest reports, search the reports, or submit a report now for free, by clicking on File Report.

HomeStars.com

HomeStars enables homeowners to connect with neighbors online to read and write reviews with no membership fees.

Checkbook.org

Consumers' Checkbook is the independent, non-profit consumer authority. Consumers' Checkbook rates the local service firms that consumers use in everyday life.

Kudzu.com

This is another great site for customers to tell the world about their favorite—or least favorite—businesses. Consumers rate businesses from one to five stars and then write a short review about the businesses. These ratings and reviews are then posted for others to read.

Google.com

Google also has the ability for users to do a review on their local searches. Then, when other potential customers look up the business online, they'll see the good, the bad, and the ugly that has been written about the business.

Yelp.com

Yelp.com was founded in 2004 to help people find great local businesses. Yelpers have written over 10 million local reviews, over 85% of them rating businesses three stars of higher. Yelp also features local events, special offers, lists, and a community discussion forum.

Dine.com

Dine.com recommends groups of restaurants that the user may like according to preferences based on ambiance, price ranges, and other restaurants the user likes. If a member of Dine.com likes many of the restaurants that the user likes as well as some that the user has not yet visited, it's pretty likely that the others may be of interest to the user. By playing an active role in Dine.com (for example, posting reviews and listing their own favorite restaurants), users are simultaneously improving the quality of the site for everyone.

Retail Sites

If you are in retail and think you are off the hook, you had better be aware of these sites.

RateItAll.com

RateItAll.com offers a fun and social way to find and share reviews about anything from local bars and restaurants, products, people, places, and music to movies, celebrities, pets, poems, art, games, and travel.

On this site, users can build "Top Ten" style lists about anything, take compatibility quizzes in areas such as music and movies and meet people who share similar tastes, promote a product, site, brand, self, and so on

There are nearly 3 million things to rate on the site. In 2009, nearly 15,000,000 people used RateItAll.

The site also offers DoubleDutch, a location-based game for the iPhone and mobile web that was created by the RateItAll team. DoubleDutch incorporates elements of social gaming, location, and reviews to provide a fun, social, and useful tool for keeping track of where people are and discovering new hangouts in a particular town.

Mechanic-Review.com

The goal of Mechanic-Review.com is to make sure "A good mechanic is easy to find."

Dentists and Doctors Beware!

At this point some of you are saying, "Well, of course, there are sites for *those* kinds of businesses, but I am a professional and we don't play by the same rules."

Just to prove you wrong, here's what is going on out there about you and your colleagues.

Doctoroogle.com

DR.Oogle (doctoroogle.com) is a website designed to review dentists. It has 120,810 patient reviews and recommendations of dentists and dental specialists to help users when selecting a new dentist. Users can also post dental questions and receive dental advice from interested dentists in a particular location. DR.Oogle is a nationwide dentist directory and is a registered dental referral service in the State of California.

RateMDs.com

RateMDs.com allows users to rate a doctor or dentist, view state medical board records, and find doctors or dentists and read their ratings.

PhysicianReports.com

This site not only allows you to review your doctors, but also to get a complete background check them.

Lawyers: Avvo.com

Yes, even lawyers get reviewed. Avvo rates and profiles attorneys, so that people can choose the right one. Lawyer profiles contain helpful information including a lawyer's experience, areas of practice, disciplinary history, and ratings from clients. Profile data comes from many sources, including state courts and bar associations, lawyer websites, and information provided by lawyers.

Ratingz.net

The Ratingz Network features a variety of topic-specific sites where users can read and post anonymous and independent ratings and reviews of places and services in your community and across the US. Check out its sites:

- AccountantRatingz.com: Audit your accountant!

- CampRatingz.com: Real experiences from real camp families

- ChildCareRatingz.com: Who's watching your kids?

- ClubRatingz.com: Find the right nightclub for you!

- CollegeDormRatingz.com: Where do you want to live?

- DrugRatingz.com: Share your experiences with prescription drugs and pharmaceuticals

- LawyerRatingz.com: You be the judge!

- MechanicRatingz.com: Tell us what's "under the hood" at your local garage!

- RadioRatingz.com: Where the listeners talk back!

- RealEstateRatingz.com: Buyers and sellers rate real estate agents

- RestaurantRatingz.com: What's on the menu tonight? Find the best places to eat throughout the United States and Canada!

- SalonRatingz.com: Where do you go for style?

- SkiRatingz.com: Where do you go for snow?

- TherapistRatingz.com: Patients rate therapists

- TVratingz.com: Where the viewers are the critics!

- VetRatingz.com: Who's caring for your pets?

- WeddingRatingz.com: All the people who make your wedding a success!

Scared Yet?

After reading the missions of these various sites, if you're not just a little intimidated, you're not yet getting the point. The world has changed and you can no longer hide your faults or mistakes. These sites are real and customers are using them more and more every day to help them make decisions as to who to hire and who not to hire.

The Customer Is Not Always Right

You know I really do agree that customers are sometimes wrong.

I'm convinced that 98% of the time, customer problems are caused by something the business did, but in 2% of the cases, the customer is the one at fault and possibly is trying to take advantage of the situation.

Up until about five years ago, we all knew exactly what to do with those 2%. Every business owner has his or her favorite stories of those 2%.

The challenge today is that even when consumers are dead wrong, you can't afford not to make them happy.

That customer who did not pay you because of some bogus claim can still make your life hell. His access to all of these websites will cost you much more business than just biting your tongue and giving in.

Unfair? Of course. But, trust me, even if you feel like you have won the battle by standing firm on your not bending ways, you will definitely lose the war.

Make the customer happy and move on.

All it takes is one or two upset customers to post something negative about your company on any of these websites and your future business will start flying out the window.

How many customers will decide to call your competitor because you had a poor or average review and your competitor had a positive review?

What do you do when you see negative reports about somebody you are considering doing business with? If you were researching companies on the web and one business had negative or satisfactory reviews and the other one had great reviews, whom would you choose?

The answer is simple.

The Review Is Incorrect!

"The site is wrong. They had better take down the negative posting about my business! They can't do this! I will sue them!"

You're not going to be successful in either getting the various sites to delete the negative review or in suing the website owner. The best way to summarize why you will not win is to show you exactly what is on RipoffReport.com's site.

RIPOFFREPORT.COM

From time to time, the Ripoff Report receives notices from companies and individuals who claim that false or inaccurate information about them has been posted on this site. Sometimes we receive letters from lawyers with similar allegations. These people sometimes threaten to sue Ripoff Report for defamation and other claims unless the statements they do not like are removed.

If you are considering sending us a notice or demand (or if you have already done so), this page is intended to provide you with information that may help you to better understand the situation and your rights, as well as the rights of the people who post reports here. You need to understand that threats against Ripoff Report are not effective, nor will they result in the removal of any reports. Here's why.

As is our policy, we never remove reports even when they are claimed to contain defamatory statements, and even if the original author requests it.

The reasons for this policy are simple.

First, this site is only effective when all complaints are maintained and preserved so that over time patterns of truly bad business practices are exposed. If we removed complaints this would give companies an incentive to pressure authors (or us) to remove true and accurate reports in exchange for money or simply to avoid a costly lawsuit. For that reason, we will never agree to remove reports, even if someone can show that a report is probably inaccurate. Under this policy, no reports are ever removed, so there is no benefit to companies who threaten or pressure a customer hoping to get them to retract a valid complaint. Even if this means that one or more questionable reports are left up, we think that removal of any reports would ultimately make this site less credible and thus less effective as a tool for educating consumers. That's why we have made this strict policy decision.

If this seems unfair or unreasonable, consider this—if someone sues you in court and makes outlandish claims that are completely false, you can fight the case and win, and at the end of the case a judgment will be entered in your favor proving that you were right and your accuser was wrong. However, the court clerk will not destroy the file or seal the records of the case simply because you won. Even when a lawsuit is shown to be 100%

baseless, the documents remain part of a public record that is maintained for years or perhaps forever (trust us, we know about this from first-hand experience). In this situation, the remedy you are entitled to is a court order or judgment proving that you did nothing wrong, not destruction of the public records about the case.

Some Anti-Ripoff Report sites (who will remain nameless) have tried to spread "truthy" stories that Ripoff Report has been sued and has lost, having to pay millions of dollars in damages in some cases. Just so you know the real truth, here it is.

Because we will not remove reports, Ripoff Report has been sued on many occasions based on the content that our users have created and posted. If you are considering suing Ripoff Report because of a report that you claim is defamatory, you should be aware that to date, Ripoff Report has never lost such a case. This is because of a federal law called the Communications Decency Act or "CDA", 47 U.S.C. § 230.

So, why should you care about the CDA? Well, it's simple—if someone posts false information about you on the Ripoff Report, the CDA prohibits you from holding us liable for the statements that others have written.

So there you have it. If a negative review goes up on Ripoff Report's site, it stays up on the site forever. Even if it is a total lie.

The new rule in customer service is the same as the old rule: The customer is always right.

You need to take that mantra seriously. If you don't, you will eventually be out of business!

You Have a Problem: Now What?

So, somehow you managed to get yourself a bad review on one of these sites…now what are you supposed to do? The first thing to do is to take a deep breath and realize that this does not need to be the end of your business as you know it. There are things you can do to actually help fix the problem.

First, call the customer and resolve his or her concerns. This may be the last thing you may want to do at this point—especially if they are part of the 2%—but you just have to do it.

Call or visit and offer to fix the problem. Give the customer all his/her money back if you have to. Do *anything* you can to get the customer to post another comment saying that you did indeed take care of the problem.

No one really knows how much business a bad review will actually cost you! You have no idea how many people were impacted by it. Ignoring the bad review will only make bad things worse.

Be Proactive

It is imperative to stay ahead of any bad press you get.

The best way to do this is to make sure that you are offering the highest level of customer satisfaction possible. Above all, when something gets screwed up (and it will), apologize right a way, fix the problem, and apologize again.

Once you have resolved the issue, send the customer an apology note and a Starbucks gift card, and then re-read the customer satisfaction part of this book. You simply cannot afford to have any bad press on the web.

Bad Review Half-Life

So, what is the half-life of a bad review on the web?

WHAT IS A HALF-LIFE?

According to Wikipedia, the half-life of a quantity whose value decreases with time is the interval required for the quantity to decay to half of its initial value. The concept originated in describing how long it takes atoms to undergo radioactive decay but also applies in a wide variety of other situations.

Unfortunately, the life of a bad review on the web is about the same as a plastic bottle in a landfill. It almost never goes away.

A bad review on the web will be around as long as the website is around and just like a fine wine—it gets better and stronger with age!

A bad review on the web grows stronger and stronger the more often people look at it. It will move up the list when searched in Google, and so on. The more clicks it gets, the more relevant Google will deem it to be and the higher it will rank on Google's search results list.

That 2% of people who used to just go away can now haunt you forever with one simple posting.

They may forget about you, but you (and all those who find that bad review online 10 years from now) will never forget about them.

The moral to this section is that if you slash and burn your customers, they will slash and burn you. They just carry a bigger sword and will do much more damage to you in the long run.

But This Customer Is Dead Wrong!

We have all had a customer who tries to take advantage of the system. If you think we as small business owners have it bad, spend a little time with employees from Home Depot or Macy's and listen to their stories about customers trying to push the boundaries of right and wrong.

The problem with drawing a line in the sand and taking a stand is that you really can't win anymore. This may sound like you should always just give up and not fight back, but the truth is that in today's Internet age, it is much better to retreat so that you can live to fight another day. Fighting a fight based on principle, even when you are absolutely right, just isn't worth it.

The World Is Generally Good

I tend to believe that most people are inherently good and are not out to take advantage of their fellow man. I also believe that most of your customer challenges can be traced back to something that you did as a business and therefore you're the actual source of the problem, however small. As for the little group who is truly evil and spends its time plotting against unsuspecting business owners, they'll get theirs. Karma is a wonderful thing.

What You Can and Should Do Now

Constantly Google Yourself

Spend the time to go online and Google your company so that you see what comes up. Don't forget to search your company under all of the customer websites so that you know what people are saying about you.

Encourage the Positive

Take advantage of your positive customer relationships and ask customers who really like you to go onto each of the sites and post a rave review of your company. Maybe even have an inexpensive business card printed with all of the sites' web addresses on it.

Why can't you have 10 or more positive reviews on each site? All it takes is for you to take the time to ask people to help you out.

Chapter 4

Leads

There is no such thing as a bad lead.

The car business has a saying, "They don't walk onto the lot if they are not looking to buy." Essentially, this means that every customer who walks onto a car lot has an interest in buying a new car.

For what other reason would people go to a car lot? They could argue that they are "just looking," but, deep down, they have an interest in that new car they're looking at.

If the right deal could be made, they would buy. That "right deal" might be $0 down and zero payments forever (or more likely something slightly higher than that), but there is a deal out there that would make them buy.

Heck, if that car is the car of their dreams and the stars align just right, they may even be persuaded to pay full price and buy on the spot. Anything is possible. Those sales take place everyday.

Automobile salespeople are confident they "have you" the moment you walk onto the lot, because they know you were motivated enough to make the trip to their dealership to take that first step. The interest is there, and they know it!

Ever walk into a fast food restaurant just to check out the prices?

People do things for a reason. We go into restaurants because we are hungry, we walk in to grocery stores to buy food, and we go to shoe stores to buy shoes.

Everyone Window Shops

Actually, no one really window shops…they always end up purchasing *something*.

When was the last time you ever saw a person spend a day window shopping and not buy anything?

If they are out wandering around the mall they will buy *something*. It may be small, but they'll buy something. If not, they would have gone to the park or stayed at home.

Have You Ever Been to Mexico?

If you want to see the best example of believing that the world is your customer and that everyone will buy from you, all you need to do is go south of the border for a day or so.

Just walk around any open-air market and you will be accosted by vendors beckoning you to come into their shops.

If you happen to be wearing any type of identifiable clothing, they will address you straight away. Your clothing logo becomes your name. "Hey, Nike! Come on over here. I have a great deal for you."

"Utah! Hey, Utah! Yes, you, Utah! Come in my shop. I have exactly what you are looking for. I'll make a great deal—real cheap—just for you, Utah."

You tell the aggressive vendor that you don't have time and that you're on the way to the beach. There is no obstacle large enough to keep him from making a sale. "No problem. I'll bring everything directly to you on the beach." He brings that and a whole lot more, including a bunch of stuff you never knew you wanted.

Only in Mexico will people sell you wool blankets on the beach in 95-degree heat! Why? Because, the gentlemen selling the blanket really believes that you came to his beach today looking to buy that blanket.

And guess what? In his world, he is right. If he works hard enough, talks to enough potential customers, smiles his best smile, and says the right thing to make you laugh, you'll end up looking at his blankets. If he gets you to respond to him, he knows that he has a 50/50 shot of making the sale. If he gets you to ask, "How much?", he's 80% there. All it takes to close the deal is the right price.

You came to Mexico and you walked onto *his* beach. You are his lead and you are his customer. He just needs to cut you the right deal for the blanket that you will ultimately take home, put in a closet, and only get it out when the kids have a sleep over.

How many of you would choose to sell wool blankets on the beach in 95-degree heat? How many of you would even have a chance to succeed at it?

The Leads Are Weak!

When you have some time, you need to rent one of the greatest sales movies ever made, *Glengarry Glen Ross*.

There is a fantastic line by Alec Baldwin in the movie when he says, "The *leads* are weak? *You* are weak!"

This movie is a fantastic example of how most of us are always looking for the perfect "lay down."

That lay down is something like the person who tells us, "Yes, of course, please charge my credit card for the full price of the job before you come over and see my house. I want to thank you in advance for taking the time to do the work for me. I will make sure my wife has lunch ready for you—what would you like to eat?"

Have You Ever?

Have you ever been absolutely sure that a customer was going to buy from you?

You know the customers I am talking about.

The potential customers who tell you on the phone how they saw your last job and how great the work was. They walk into your shop and are glowing with excitement. They were best friends with your last customer and "Wow, did you ever make them happy! And, by the way, they are really tough to make happy. You really must be something special."

They want to know what your schedule is and how soon you can get started, even before you have met them or they spend 45 minutes asking question after question.

When you meet the customer, she practically gives you a hug at the door. You finally get to the "close" and they tell you how great it looks and that they just need to check over a couple of things, but starting in two weeks sounds about right.

You leave the house with a smile on your face and then cancel your next customer meeting because they only wanted a couple hundred bucks worth of work done. Or you don't pay much attention to the next customer who walks in as you are confident that your dream customer will be right back. You may even decide to take the rest of the day off.

A week later, you can't get back in touch with these sure-fire customers and you're not sure what is going on. But…guess what? You never talk to them again.

Have you ever? I bet you have.

Have you ever met potential customers who rubbed you the wrong way and that the only reason you even talked with them was because you could not find a convenient excuse not to? You were convinced these customers were made of stone or some other type of indestructible matter?

Customers who believed that "stoic" is an emotion that is well suited for all occasions?

Customers who you notice even their own dogs don't like them?

Have you ever?

And then, have you ever been completely shocked when they look at you and say, "Looks great, where do I sign?" or "I'll take three." They grab the contract from your hand, sign it before you get a chance to go through it, and ask you when you are going to start?

I bet you have.

Have you ever met customers who don't want to spend a bunch of money?

Customers who start the conversation with, "I am thinking of doing this myself," "show me your most economical…", or "last night while I was changing my oil…"

Have you ever?

And then, have you ever seen that customer end up deciding to buy your most expensive option?

I bet you have.

Have you ever had customers promise you that they were *absolutely* going to buy from you, and then you never see them or hear from them again?

Have you ever had a simple estimate turn into a huge job you were not expecting?

Have you ever seen a customer with a brand new BMW or Mercedes in the garage ask for the cheapest materials possible?

I bet you have.

We all have experienced these types of situations.

So why do most businesses still feel the need to keep "grilling" prospective clients?

The Customer Qualification Game

Over-qualifying a potential customer is a mistake that most of us are guilty of making. I subscribe to the idea that if people give you their phone number, or if they walk into your place of business, they are looking to buy.

If they are looking to have some work done, they all have the same potential. It is your job to unlock that potential!

All the World Is a Stage...

Every customer is an actor. They act in the way they believe they need to in order to get the best deal possible.

Some believe that the more friendly and positive they are, the better deal they will get.

Others believe that if they are really tough and no nonsense, that *they* will get the best deal.

Some believe that if they act like they are willing to do it all themselves, you will be forced to bring down your price in fear of losing the job.

What they all have in common is that at one time they all walked onto a car lot, went window shopping, bought a blanket in 95-degree heat in Mexico, gave you their number, want some work done at their home, and they don't really want to do it themselves.

Some Undeniable Truths About Customers

Good Leads Die Young

Prospective customers want you to call them back now, not later.

The best time to call the customer back is not to have to call them back at all. The ideal situation is that when a customer calls you have someone in your organization who can take that call immediately.

Think about it. When potential customers decide they want to talk to someone about getting some work done, they are in a buying mode. They have sat down, blocked off the time, are mentally prepared to speak about their project and have dialed the phone.

They did not do all of that so that they can get a call back in four hours or four days. They're ready to talk now—on their schedule, not yours. They called so that they could talk to *you* about using *your company* for work on their home.

If you don't talk to them right away, what will they do? Will they wait for you to get back to them? Will they give up in frustration and decide not to get their project done?

No, what they will do is keep dialing the phone until they talk to someone. They will be at their best—most excited and most receptive—to the first person they talk to.

Their enthusiasm drops the more times they have to tell the story.

Old Customer Leads Are Not Bad Leads

Another common misconception is that a lead that is a week or a month old is no longer good.

Generally, business owners will call on a lead once or twice. If nothing happens, they throw it in the trash and mutter something about people wasting their time.

A lead is only dead when the customer says they don't want the work done or you are too late and someone who was more persistent got the job.

If They Don't Call Back, They Must Not Be Interested

Another great misconception about customers is the idea that if they don't call you back, they don't want to hire you.

The truth of the matter is that you are not as important to them as they are to you.

Customers are very busy. They are working more hours than ever before, balancing spouses and kids, as well as activities and whatever personal life they can fit in.

This does not mean that they are not still interested in having the work done. It only means that they don't have the time to talk to you at the moment you called and they didn't respond.

Last Man Standing

Persistence is the key to success when reaching customers. Call regularly and at different times.

Leave messages only once a day, but call more often. Mix up your messages. Make it lighthearted and fun.

If you have their cell phone, send a text message. Don't stop calling until they tell you to stop calling.

In 90% of the cases, they simply have not called you back because they have been too busy.

When you actually do end up writing quotes for customers who required 10 phone calls, in many cases they end up booking with you. The reason why they booked with you is because all of your competitors gave up calling them back. They feel obliged to go with you after all they put you through to get a call back. Yours, oftentimes, is their only estimate.

Every Lead Is Different, But the Same

Leads will come from a variety of sources. They will come as responses from referrals, vehicle signs, your staff on a job site, a flyer in the neighborhood, your website, a door you knocked, or from the Internet. Each lead is unique and the first phone call needs to be tailored a little differently depending on the characteristic of the lead.

CHARACTERISTICS OF LEADS

Referral

- Already has heard about you
- Most likely going to have something done
- Arguably the warmest of the lead family
- Most likely not a competitive bidding situation

Do:

- Answer the phone or call back right away
- Talk up the customer they know
- Get a letter of reference from the friend
- Get out there ASAP to book the job

Don't:

- Take your sweet time getting back to them
- Assume the job is yours at any price
- Get lazy with your presentation because you assume it is yours
- Overcharge because it is a referral

Flyer/Yard Sign/Truck Sign

- May or may not have seen your work
- Most likely going to have the work done
- Most likely knows very little about you
- May or may not be a competitive bid situation

Do:

- Take the call right away or call back in five minutes
- Find out where they heard about you so that you can see what marketing is the most effective
- Ask a ton of questions to understand what they are looking to do
- Educate them about you and your company so that they have confidence and are looking forward to meeting you in person

Don't:

- Wait two days to call them back
- Assume that they will or won't buy based on the phone call

- Be arrogant or standoffish on the phone
- Wait too long to set up the estimate—get out there right away

Your Website

- Most likely has read about you on your site
- They will do their research on you
- Most likely a competitive bidding situation

Do:

- When speaking to them, refer to your website often and even get them to go online while you are on the phone to walk them through the highlights of the site
- Recognize that they will do their research and will want lots of information
- Take your time and don't rush to get them off the phone
- Make sure they get all the information they need

Don't:

- Forget that your competitor's site is just a click away
- Ignore email and texts
- Assume the website will take your place in the sales process
- Assume that they are already sold

Cold Call

- Most likely has never heard of you
- May be just at the beginning phases of the project
- You may have put the idea in their head
- You may be the first and only bid or one of many

Do:

- Set the date and time of the estimate immediately
- Call back multiple times; people are busy
- Educate the customer about who you are
- Convince them to meet you

Don't:

- Be put off if they are not as excited as you would like
- Expect them to be excited to talk to you yet
- Stop calling until they say no

Store-Bought Leads

- Customer may or may not remember filling out an online form
- They are now receiving calls, not in the mode of making a call
- May or may not be ready to talk when you call back
- This will be a competitive situation with three to eight businesses

Do:

- Get the lead on a text on your phone
- Call as soon as the lead comes through
- Get to the customer's house for the estimate right away
- Educate the customer about your company

Don't:

- Assume the customer knows anything about your company
- Be put off by the fact that at this point you are just one of six people calling them
- Give up on a lead until they say no

Article in the Newspaper

- They already like you because of the article
- You have a smidgen of "celebrity status"
- May not be a competitive bidding situation

Do:

- Talk about the article and what a great experience the event was
- Bring a copy of the article with you to the estimate
- Take advantage of your celebrity status

Don't:

- Assume that you have the job because of your article
- Be overly cocky just because you got some free press
- Forget that fame is fleeting and this is your 15 minutes—use it wisely

Yellow Pages or Newspaper Ads

- They are actively looking for a business
- They know very little about you
- They want you to answer the phone or they will call someone else

Do:

- Realize these buyers, more than likely, are attracted to doing business with a local company
- Take the call right away or call back within five minutes
- Ask what about your ad made them call you

Don't:

- Assume that your ad has told them all they need to know about your company
- Think that they will remember calling you off of the ad if you call them back three hours later
- Think they called only you

The Essential Rules of Leads

The essential rules are about the same for almost every lead.

Make sure you take customer calls immediately.

Take the time to listen to what they want. Sell them on you, as an individual, as well as your company and team.

Continue to be responsive throughout the process.

If you follow these basic rules, you are already miles ahead of your competition.

Internet Lead Providers—A Few Important Thoughts

Over the past few years, Internet lead providers have popped up all over the web. These sites, such as *Service Magic* and *Reliable Remodeler*, spend hundreds of thousands of dollars advertising on the web for people who want to have home improvements done.

There are now a plethora of sites where you can now purchase leads. All you need to do is Google "your business leads" to see just how many are really out there.

If you Google "mortgage," "painter," "dentist," "landscaper," and so on, you will most likely see these lead providers show up on the first page of the search results. They will show up in the top 10 and probably on the side panel where the paid searches appear.

These sites are very powerful and gather thousands and thousands of leads for small businesses.

Why They Are So Popular

Customers love these sites because they are able to go to one location, fill out one form, and get "pre-screened businesses" to call them.

They view it as a time-saving and quality-control system.

With this service, they don't have to take the time to find quality businesses. The work has already been done for them.

The Customer Experience

The customer experience tends to be quick, easy, and mostly painless.

That is, of course, unless they filled out a form on multiple sites. They'll soon be inundated with as many as 12 companies calling them.

Customers tend to be pleased with the experience, though, because they end up getting a very competitive bid by a qualified business.

The Internet Is Not Going Away

Everyone has the crazy old uncle (or maybe *you* are the crazy old uncle) who swore that the Internet was just a fad. The old crone was convinced that, soon enough, just like the pet rock, the Internet, too, would pass.

Well, the crazy old uncles are wrong and the Internet is only getting stronger.

Websites like *Service Magic* and *Netquote* (for insurance agents), and *1800Dentist* are growing in popularity amongst consumers. If you don't take them seriously, you will be missing out on potential new business.

You will end up being the guy you heard stories about growing up.

You know the one. The one that believed that new-fangled television thing was just another fad.

If You Can't Beat Them, Join Them

So now that you are a believer, it is important to truly understand how this game is played. Each site is a little different, but here is the basic process.

INTERNET LEAD SETUP

1. Choose a site and click on the "business owners only" section.
2. Sign yourself up as a business.
3. Make sure you have a valid credit card to pay for your leads.
4. Provide whatever references and insurance documents are needed.
5. Define the geographic territory from which you are willing to take leads.
6. Define the type of leads you are willing to take.
7. Set your preferences to receive the leads via email or cell text.

If You Are Not First, You Are Last

In the immortal words of Ricky Bobby from *Talladega Nights*, "If you are not first, you are last."

The most important thing to remember about these types of leads is that this absolutely is a race!

Each lead is given out simultaneously to multiple business owners. They will all be attempting to contact the customer.

If the customer has made requests on multiple sites, he or she might have 12 or more companies calling.

You want to be the first to contact the customer. You want to set the bar high enough that the others who will follow you won't be able to measure up.

Set an appointment to meet the customer in person as soon as possible.

Enjoy the Pain

I won't mislead you. These leads are not as fun to call on as leads from people who are best friends with your last customer or who read an article about you in the local newspaper.

They don't know you. You are going to have to earn their trust and business the hard way.

These are real leads, though, and will turn into real jobs if you work them properly.

Bad Internet Leads

From time to time you will come across a lead that is not legitimate. Maybe someone put in their friend's name and number just as a joke.

These leads won't cost you anything, though. You can return them to the vendor and get credit for these bogus leads. Keep in mind, though, that 90+% of the leads you will get off of these sites are real homeowners who really want to have the work done.

If you feel you are getting higher than a 10% "junk lead" rate, then the problem is most likely you and not the lead.

The Secret

There are some business owners who do a substantial portion of their business through buying leads off of these sites.

The vast majority of businesses will sign up for leads, take five or six, take their time calling them back, and end up not booking a single job.

These businesses will then go back to sitting at home hoping that the phone is going to ring.

The secret is in being first, not last!

Invest

When you sign up, realize that you will probably mess up the first few leads while you get accustomed to dealing with these types of customers.

Commit to taking 20 leads and aggressively working them. If you follow the steps you read in this book, you will have success with these sites.

The other benefit you have is that your competitors have not read this book. They will end up taking five leads, and then will get mad and quit.

All the more leads for you.

Branding/Marketing/Lead Generation Summary

Branding

Figure out who you are and what is important to your customers. Make sure that you are aligned in this area and then create your commercial, tagline, and company brand. Your branding message will be the same on all your marketing materials.

Marketing

Getting your name out into the community does not need to be an expensive endeavor. It does, though, need to be a constant effort.

Lawn signs need to go up on all of your jobs. Flyers should be passed around the neighborhood you are working in. You need to always be passing out flyers and business cards. Seek press coverage of the great things you do. Make sure you obtain referrals from past customers. These activities all need to be part of your daily schedule.

Lead Generation

Be sure to track and review the cost per lead and marketing cost per job. Every new effort should be tested and tracked against other methods of gaining work.

There is no such thing as a bad lead—just slow and lazy business owners.

Chapter 5

Sales, Sales, Sales

S ales is my favorite part of the business. Most business owners will see immediate improvement in both their personal sales skills and their sales management skills by following the principles in this chapter.

The first part of focusing on sales is to dispel any misconceptions about sales in general. The job of the owner or CEO of any business is to be the company's chief cheerleader and chief salesperson.

If you are not excited to sell yourself and your company to your customers, you should quit now and go get a job working for someone who does. Understanding that constantly-improving sales skills is an A priority for your business is crucial to any owner.

Okay. Enough of that. I am now officially finished with the lecture.

Sales Is Not a Dirty Word

Many business owners are amazingly talented and passionate about their chosen profession and because of years of working for less-talented people, decided to start their own business.

They are, and should be, very proud of the service or product that they deliver.

The challenge in starting up a business, though, is that their past employment responsibilities may not have involved talking to customers and selling them on themselves and their company. They tend to not know how to be this chief cheerleader and salesperson.

Then this book you're holding comes along and opens your eyes.

When many of us think of sales, we automatically think of used car salesmen like Robin Williams in *Cadillac Man* or we think of the aluminum siding salesmen in *Tin Men* (which are both very funny movies and worth watching, by the way).

Even the thought of being personally involved in sales can bring up an almost allergic reaction to some business owners.

Sales, though, shouldn't be so scary. You're involved in sales every day, whether you notice it or not.

Sales is the simple art of communicating your ideas, thoughts, plans, and dreams to someone else.

Sales is about finding out what someone else really wants and trying to determine if what he or she wants is something that you can provide.

We are selling daily and being sold to daily. Some of us are better at it than others, but it is utterly vital for company survival. Not being capable of effectively sharing your ideas with others will have devastating consequences.

All around us are people who are easily persuaded. They never end up going to the movies or the restaurants they want because someone else in their group convinces everyone that their movie or restaurant is better.

People are wearing clothes and living in houses and in towns that they really don't like purely because of their inability to speak up and share their desires.

People get passed over daily for promotions and end up reporting to a boss they hate because, even though their ideas were better, they could not sell them to the people in charge.

Relationships fail all the time because people are unable to take the time to listen and find out what the other person wants.

All of this, too, is "sales."

If there is only one thing that you take from this book, it should be to acquire a thirst to learn more about sales and become the best communicator that you can possibly be. And, if you don't, you will be doomed to a life of misery and will never experience the joy of getting your own way. (But, boy, will you make everyone around you happy!)

Is it really that magical?

Well no, but there is some truth in the last paragraph. Selling is a part of your daily life and, as CEO and owner of your business, you need to be amazing at it!

The Basics

Call When You Say You Will

With cell phone plans being as inexpensive as they are, there is absolutely no excuse for not calling customers back when you say you will call.

I am sure you are extremely busy, but so are your customers and they are waiting for your call. They are judging you on whether you do exactly what you say you will do.

The good news for the many of us is that 20+% of small business owners do not call when they say they will call. They are just "too busy" and "could not break away." To them, the rest of us would like to say "thank you" for making it so easy for us to take business away from you!

Call to Confirm

Calling to confirm an appointment is an often-missed, but very important step. Always call the customer 15 minutes or so before your appointment just to let them know you are on your way and what time you will be arriving.

If you are going to be late, and it happens, all tends to be forgiven with this one phone call. If you show up late with no call, your chances of getting the job plummet. It will go to your competitor who makes such a call three out of four times.

Show Up

This sounds simple, but you will automatically beat 10-15% of your competition by just showing up!

Far too many businesses have a horrible reputation for not showing up at all for set appointments.

You've seen it. Hopefully, you haven't done it.

Those who have just simply not shown up undoubtedly have amazing tales and excuses as to why they didn't keep the appointment. No matter the tale, there is absolutely no excuse for blowing off a customer.

If you are going to completely miss appointments, do us all a favor and go do something else for a living.

You give the rest of us a bad name.

First Impressions

How you look when you show up at a client's home or when a customer shows up at your place of business plays a crucial role the decision-making process.

You need to make sure that regardless of how your day has gone, that you are in a clean company logo shirt and clean pants with combed hair and breath that doesn't smell like the back of a trash receptacle.

Sound like basic stuff? Many businesses have a reputation of not adhering to these simple and obvious sales principles.

You only get one chance at a first impression. Don't blow it!

Keep a clean shirt and pants on a hanger in your car or truck. Stash a bag of toiletries in the trunk. Make sure your showroom or shop is always spotless; keep the stacks of paper and Taco Bell cups hidden behind the counter.

Think of this initial meeting as a first date where you need to impress.

The Vehicle

Customers pay attention to the car you drive. Believe it or not, it matters what you drive to a customer's home.

Ideally, you arrive in a company vehicle with your company's logo on the side. (Sign companies can make a relatively inexpensive removable magnet of your logo for the side of any vehicle.)

The vehicle needs to be clean inside and out. Customers may glance inside your vehicle, see the pile of McDonald's wrappers, and make assumptions about you that cause them to run to your competition.

Don't come driving up in a sports car or convertible. Customers associate theses cars with people who are out to have fun and will assume that you will not take their job seriously.

Stay away, obviously, from the high-end vehicles, like Mercedes, Porsches, BMWs, and so on. Even though you are doing well enough to own one, don't drive it to a potential customer's house. If you do, you'll soon not be able to afford the payments.

Again, customers don't want to pay for your excessive lifestyle.

Your Showroom, Shop, or Restaurant

This may go without saying, but people form opinions about you and your business after only 30 seconds in your place of business. If they see a mess or if things just seem in disarray, they will most likely walk out and never return. You have all done it yourselves. You walk into a restaurant, take a quick look around, you see some tables where people have obviously left and there are still dirty plates on the table or just a few crumbs scattered about. The hostess walks over to welcome you (sometimes smiling, sometimes not) and has a nice little stain on her outfit. Now this example may be extreme, but it is amazing how many small restaurants miss the basics and lose customers. You walk out after politely asking for a menu (which is code for, "I need to get out of here quickly before I catch something"). The same type of thing happens with almost any place of business: dust on the cabinets or merchandise, dirt on the floor or rugs, and employees who look like they just walked in off the street. All of these things can cause your customers to quickly walk out of the door.

My personal favorite is the auto repair business owner. Some of these guys think it's okay to leave their front office as much of a mess as the work area in the garage. This always makes me want to shake my head. It's not okay to leave your customer waiting area a mess. On a regular basis you will have customers who need to wait for their automobile repairs to be finished. If they're waiting in squalor, their opinion of you matches what they see.

It's the Little Things

The little things make the difference. I'll always remember a particular cab ride I had in San Francisco. I had just gotten off an early morning plane trip and was standing in line for a taxi. The attendant there saw the cab driver, looked at me, and said, "You're in for a treat." I was on the phone at the time and I wasn't really paying attention. I just looked at him quizzically, finished my call, and got into the taxi. I immediately noticed that something was different about this taxi and its driver. As I sat down, I first noticed the scent—not the typical "taxi smell," but a pleasantly fresh scent unlike any cab I'd ever been in before. This one was spotless and appealing. I noticed next the softly playing classical music. The cab driver looked back at me and politely said, "Hello, sir. My name is Phillip. I will be your driver today. Before we begin our trip may I offer you a bottled water and perhaps a snack?" I looked at him as if he had two heads and said, "Sure, I'll take a water."

"A snack, sir?" My new friend Phillip held out a basket full of granola bars and small bags of chips (a much better selection than I had just had on my much more expensive flight). I decided to take a granola bar. "Sir, I have the most recent copies of *Newsweek*, *Business Week*, *Time*, and, of course, *Sports Illustrated*. Would you be interested in reading anything on our journey to the city? If you prefer, I have a small laptop here with an Internet card you are welcome you use to surf the web during our drive." At this point I was almost choking on my granola bar. I took a copy of *Business Week* and sat back in my seat. "One more thing before we get going, sir. Do you have a music preference?" At this point I had had enough. I leaned forward and said, "Okay Phillip, what's the deal? I have never had anyone treat me this way in a cab before. What's the deal?"

"Well, sir, being a taxi driver just works out with my schedule. I was raised by my parents that if I was going to do a job, I need to be the best at that job."

"Is this your own cab?"

"No, sir. I lease the cab from the cab company, but this is my own business. I pay them per day for the car and then keep whatever profit I have at the end of the day. By the way, is the temperature okay for you? Would you like me to cool things off a bit?"

"No, no, everything is fine. So does this work out for you? You know, as a business?"

"Actually, I do quite well, sir, thanks for asking."

I was still in a state of shock, but I was intrigued.

"I'm curious, Phillip. Most taxi drivers I talk to have a hard time making ends meet. How do you make this work financially?"

"Well, sir, I am very busy actually. I tend to have an awful lot of repeat business. I spend my time picking up airport fares on Mondays and Wednesdays. I obtain plenty of new business in those two days and because most people are in town for a few days, they tend to call me whenever they need a ride. Honestly, my tips seem to be double to triple that of the other drivers I talk to … not that I am asking you for an extra tip, of course."

I smiled as the cab pulled up in front of my hotel. Phillip looked back and asked if I needed a receipt. I replied in the affirmative and he proceeded to fill one out and then handed me the receipt as well as three business cards.

"I hope you enjoyed your ride and please give my card to people you may meet at the hotel who need a ride around town or to the airport. I am happy to take care of getting you to any locations you may need on your trip. Just call my cell, text, or email me on my Blackberry."

I shook Phillips hand and tipped him four times what I would normally tip for the same ride. For the remainder of my trip and every trip since then I have continued to use his service.

I know that seems like a bit of an unbelievable story, but why should it be so unusual? Is it that difficult for any taxi driver to do the simple things that Phillip did? Would you not be excited to tell people about his service or tip him at a much higher rate than you would for the service that we all put up with day in and day out from other cab drivers? I bet you would.

Another great story is about a dentist who I used for years. Like most people, I really hated going to the dentist, and have for years… that is until I met Dr. Beal. I was amazed at the thriving practice he had built.

From the minute patients walk into the building they feel more like they're in a high-end spa than a dentist's office. The typical appointment starts with an amazing "spa like" reception area, complete with complimentary water, teas, and coffee. As patients are brought back into the "dental work" areas their first stop is at the video library where they're asked if they would like to choose a DVD to watch during their stay. Once they have chosen a movie to watch they are given a warmed pillow to wrap around their neck as they sit down in the dental chair. They lean back and enjoy the feeling of the warm neck pillow and look up at the ceiling just as their video appears on the video screen mounted above the chair. Headphones are gently placed on their head.

If they have a fear of dentists and need something to relax a little bit, "laughing gas" is available to take the edge off. Just as the hygienist is about half way through the cleaning, in comes the masseuse who removes their shoes in order to give a 15-minute foot massage.

I am not exaggerating when I say it is an amazing experience. Before I started with Dr. Beal, I was constantly out of date with my regular dentist appointments. When I finally did make the overdue appointment, the visit would take five hours to complete all the work. Looking back on my last dental appointment with Dr. Beal, the experience was one of the most relaxing ones I had had in a very long time. A day of laughing gas, movies (that I never am able to remember… gas works great), and my feet being massaged was almost appealing enough to make me want to stop brushing so I'd have an excuse to return. Alas, Dr. Beal had some health issues and had to stop practicing. The folks who took over his clinic never quite understood how important Dr. Beal's patient experience really was to their patients. I am still looking for a new dentist. See how rare a find this kind of business owner is in the dental world?

Shoes Count

There are people who pay close attention to others' shoes.

Homeowners don't want to see your work boots in their house. Their home is not a work site!

Upon entering someone's home, always remove your shoes, or at a minimum, wear the little booties that go over shoes to protect the flooring. If you have a place of business, make sure you and your employees understand the importance of wearing clean and attractive shoes.

The customer is watching and making mental notes of the things that bother them. More than 40% of your competitors overlook this shoe advice. Your customers do not!

Tattoos, Earrings, and Other Miscellaneous Adornments

There are those who enjoy cool tattoos, earrings, and flashy chains. A place of business or a customer's home, though, is no place to show off your bling. (That is, unless your place of business is a tattoo shop or flashy jewelry store!)

Assume that any of this stuff that you or your employees think is a fashion statement is a turnoff for almost all of the mainstream 55-year-old Baby Boomers. When you wear it or show it off your chances of making a sale dwindle. Enjoy your weekends and personal time. Show off whatever you got. But, during the week, cover the tattoo and get rid of the bling.

Long Hair

Reread the last paragraph.

Don't like what you hear? Go ahead and take your chances. There is an exception to every rule and this one would likely be a guitar shop. I am sure you can think of a couple more as well.

Got Smokes?

Do not smell like smoke when you are at work.

People who don't smoke (and that number is growing) can be absolutely indignant about being around it.

If your business involves going into a customer's home, your potential customers will assume that you will smoke in their home while they are away (even though you try to convince them otherwise). Many customers will walk right out of your place of business if there is even a hint of a smoky smell. (Yes, I know… cigar shops are an exception.)

In general, these nonsmokers will automatically pass on you for someone who does not smoke.

There are multiple studies that prove the point. Disagree at your own risk.

Smile All the Time

No one wants to do business with a negative and unhappy person.

No one cares about your personal life or how economically tough your business is right now.

Why would a person want to do business with someone whose life is falling apart?

The simple answer is they don't. They will choose the businessperson who is not a mess and who has a positive outlook on life.

Got a Funny Story?

If you have a good, clean, funny story, use it to break the ice. Get the customer laughing and break down the barriers that automatically go up when you walk into a house.

If you don't have one, find one and practice it. Go ahead and use the same one all the time (just be careful not to tell the same one twice to the same customer).

Understand Personal Space

No one wants to be crowded in your place of business or in his or her home. Customers want to know that you are available and want to be able to get their questions asked when they are ready. Most do not want a hug or to be close enough to smell your breath.

Ask Questions and Learn Something New

When I first started in sales, I absolutely loved in-home estimates. I would look forward to every single one of them.

I loved them because I knew that every day I was going to be able to meet new people who knew things that I did not know.

I took full advantage of this opportunity to look around customer's homes and ask a bunch of questions. Asking what they did for a living would sometimes start an interesting conversation. Asking about a picture on the wall or the hobby being displayed out in the garage almost always would get a conversation going.

Every time I entered the home, I had something that would spark a conversation that I could then expand on by asking more questions.

I gauged my success at the end of the day by what I learned at each stop, not by the deals I sold. (And, yes, I always sold a ton of deals!)

Understand Your Customers

Customers are going to fall into a few main categories.

Hard Driving and Fast Talking

You know the type; not a lot of room for small talk here. They talk really fast and breaking down the wall that may be between the two of you can be very tough.

You need to move as fast as they do. They want to get quick and easy facts— so give them the information they want quickly and easily.

This type of customer does not want to waste time. If you try to take too much time talking to them about something other than the purpose of your visit, this customer will assume that you will drive them nuts when you are working on their house with your constant questions and chatting.

They don't want to work with a "Chatty Kathy."

Get right down to business. Focus on how you understand exactly what it is they want and that they will barely know you are there.

Convince them that you will be in stealth mode the entire time, just like a ninja, getting your work done and leaving without bothering anyone.

The Technician

Technicians are the accountants, engineers, doctors, and people like my brother-in-law, who actually enjoy curling up with a good owner's manual (no joke).

These guys want the details. They want all the details. They want to know the exact details of every product you have and why you have chosen to stock them.

They want to know about your crew and who will be working on the job. They are interested in your hiring procedures and the details about you and your company.

They are not necessarily on a time frame and could spend most of the day with you (even for a $30 sale).

They are offended if you try to rush them and they appreciate follow-up emails with more information like product spec sheets.

The most important point to remember with these types of people is to never make anything up. They will know the minute you are lying. They have an extra gene that allows them to determine who is telling the truth and who is not. Ignore this one and you'll get caught. This is not to say that it is ever okay to lie to any of your customers…

If you don't know the answer, simply write it down and tell them you will find out for them. Answer all of their questions truthfully and honestly to the best of your ability and you will earn their trust.

Friend of the World

These people are the best. They want to talk and tell stories, share their family secrets, and friend you on Facebook.

They will tell all of their neighbors and friends what a great job you did that will keep you awash in work for months… but only if you take the time to talk and laugh and smile and share stories.

If you rush them or appear not to care about what they are trying to share with you, then they will not trust you. If they don't like and trust you, then they will not do business with you.

Salespeople

Salespeople are so special that they deserve a category all of their own. I love selling to salespeople for one reason and one reason only. Salespeople love the game. They love to be sold to.

They are preconditioned after years of sales training to buy!

They just want to make sure you give them your best presentation and made sure they had fun while you do it.

One of my favorite stories has to do with a time I was out training a new salesperson and we were to the point of "closing the deal." The young salesperson I was training asked for the job once and the "customer salesman" said, "No, I'll have to think about it."

The rookie got up, said "thank you" and excused himself. The customer and I were still sitting at the table.

The customer turned to me and said, "Is he really going to give up that easily?"

I said, "He may be, but I'm not." After 45 minutes of going back and forth, the customer signed the deal, looked at me and said, "Thanks. That was a lot of fun."

He then turned to the rookie and said, "I hope you learned something today."

Salespeople all love the game and just want to be sold to.

Got Nothing

The most challenging type of person to deal with is the one who gives you absolutely nothing to work with.

They are a blank slate—emotionless and disinterested. (The only thing that could possibly be worse than trying to sell to one of these folks is to be in the same family with one!)

The only thing you can do with the small part of the population who is completely uninterested in human communications or relationships is to be as professional as possible, stick to your presentation, and hope for the best.

When you get the signals that they are not interested in talking about their families, jobs, or listening to your amazingly funny stories, back off immediately and stick to the facts.

At that point, tuck your head between your knees and hope for the best.

Two Ears and One Mouth: Use Them Proportionately

The magical key to selling just about anything is to do one basic thing: listen.

Most salespeople simply don't listen. Instead, they decide to talk a person's ears off about why they are superior to the competition.

Even worse is showing up and not talking or listening!

If you listen close enough and ask the right questions, customers will tell you exactly what is going to be important to them in their buying decisions.

Competency

Customers want to know that you are good at what you do.

They want to see pictures and reference letters. They want numbers to call (even if they don't intend to call them).

They need to know that you fully understand your trade and that you are a professional who has chosen to do this as your life's work.

If they believe this to be true, you are closer to booking the job.

Trust

If you lie, they will catch you.

If you try to make things up or look the least bit shady, they will pick up on it and not give you the job.

If you don't show up when you say you will, or forget to call when you said you would, they will not give you the job.

Safety

A large number of service business owners forget that they work in people's homes. Their home is their castle. It is something that they actually have control over and, more importantly, it is where their families live.

Everybody will do everything possible to make sure that their homes are safe for their families, including being very careful about who they actually allow into their sanctuaries.

Homeowners base a significant portion of their decision to hire someone on the degree to which they feel like the person they are hiring is safe to have in their home.

They are highly in tune with these protective feelings. If they fear even in the least for their safety, for some reason don't trust you, or if something in their gut is uneasy, they will toss you away like day-old donuts.

Take this warning seriously. If you are not someone that they would like to have over for lunch with the kids, they will find someone who is and that person will get the business.

The Process

All the best sales presentations have a process. A good sales presentation is just like a play. They are done the same way each time. Think of this process as a Broadway show. In the following example from the construction industry, our show is made up of acts 1 through 11.

Act 1: The First Phone Call

The first phone call is the very first impression you are going to be leaving your customer. They will either leave your phone call looking forward to meeting you or questioning why they called you instead of someone else.

GOALS OF THE FIRST PHONE CALL

Obtain or exchange the following information:

- The scope of the project
- Any experiences have they had in the past with your service or trade
- Any special concerns that they have
- The time frame
- The budget
- Your 60-second commercial

Phone tips:

- Smile on the phone; your customers can tell the difference
- Speak clearly
- Make sure you are in a place with no background noise
- Write everything down, including the names of their dogs and kids, and bring the notes to the estimate

Do your best to make sure everyone who has an interest in the project will be home when you come over to do the estimate.

Take the time to ask what the customer is looking to have done. Get as much detail as you can.

Act 2: The Front Door

This is when you go back and reread the section on first impressions. Success or failure is dependent on these first impressions.

Act 3: Time to Chat

Act 3 is the part of the show where you learn about the customer.

Have some time to chat casually and build some rapport. This part of the show should not be rushed, unless of course the customer wants to rush it.

In general, the longer you are able to continue building your relationship with the customer, the better chance you have of closing the job.

Act 4: The Work

This is when you find out what the customer is looking to have done.

This is why you are there. Listen carefully and ask a lot of questions. With the notes from the first call, specifically ask to see the areas that they told you about.

WHAT WORK IS TO BE DONE?
- What is the scope of the work?
- Why do they want to have it done?
- What areas are they concerned about?
- What are their expectations for time frame and quality of work?

Take lots of notes. It is impossible for you to remember all the details at a later date. These notes will come in handy as you prepare your estimate. Note-taking also demonstrates to the customer how detail-oriented you are.

Act 5: Your Time to Shine

Act 5 is where you get to show off your stuff. All those years of hard work and experience are about to shine through.

Act 5 is all about you as a professional business owner showing how you are going to solve your customer's challenges.

This is where you talk about the way in which you will tackle the job, the products that you will use, and the experience that you have with this type of project.

Act 5 is where you show the customer things that they may have not thought of yet. Talk about the specifics that they as a "layperson" may not be aware of.

The most important thing about Act 5 is to realize that it is Act 5 and not Act 1. You need to go through all the first acts in their entirety and not just rush to Act 5.

If you walk into a play right in the middle of it, you will not understand or appreciate it. You need to see it from the beginning and be able to see how each act builds upon the others.

Act 6: Your Reference Book

Now that you fully understand what the customer is looking to have done, you can walk back over to the kitchen table and show them your reference book.

Take the time to show them your contractor's license (if necessary) and your insurance information. Pictures of your family and crew are always a great touch.

Include trade associations that you are a member of and of course the pictures and reference letters from local customers.

The last thing from the book you should show your potential customer is a section on the products and materials that you use, focusing on the fact that you only use the highest quality materials.

Act 7: The Measure

This is when you leave the customers to review your references and talk amongst themselves, while you review the project, take measurements, and then go back to your car or truck to write up the bid.

Write up the bid?

Yes, you will never have a better opportunity to close this deal than right now.

If you have taken the time to go through all the first six acts and have not rushed the process, as you are taking your time to get your measurements done, your customers are already making their decisions.

They have already decided if they like and trust you. If they do like and trust you, it is simply a matter of how well they liked your professional presentation and whether your price is in the general ballpark of their budget.

TIPS FOR WRITING UP BIDS
- Print, don't write. If your handwriting/printing is poor, fix it. People might view a sloppy contract as an example of the work you will do.
- Use a proper three-copy contract with your logo and information on it.
- Make sure you have spaces for the customer's home phone, cell, and email.
- Write specific areas of concern the customer had on the contract.
- Be extremely specific about the work being competed.
- You only get one shot at this, so don't mess it up—literally.
- Don't forget to include a very clear and legible price with all options listed in detail.

Taking your measurements home and getting back in touch later is an absolute no-no. Only the huge jobs (such as full remodels) require a second visit.

Never, ever, mail, fax, or email a bid. You need to be in person when a decision is being made. If you are making a second visit, start again with Act 1. You can go through those first acts a little faster this time, but your customer may have forgotten why they like you. You need to remind them.

Act 8: The Big Finish: The Climax of the Show

This is it. This is why you actually came to the customer's house.

This is now your opportunity to close the deal, to walk away with a signed contract and a job for you and/or your crew to start.

This is the moment where your hands get a little sweaty and you start mentally questioning your numbers.

Are you too high? Too low?

Now is the time to trust your estimating procedures and ignore the price.

The price is the price is the price. It is only one small part of what makes a consumer decide who to let into their home.

Do you really think that to save a few dollars the customer will hire the ex-con who has been asking questions about the house alarm system?

They will hire the person who they trust the most.

Is that person you?

STEPS TO THE CLOSE

- Get the customers to join you at the kitchen table, making sure anyone who is going to have a say in the project is sitting down with you.
- Sit down and place the contract in front of them on the table.
- Have a pen in your hand for the signature (I always had my lucky pen; every salesperson is a little superstitious).
- Get the price out of the way. "After going through your project in detail I have come up with a cost of X."
- Now move on. "What I would like to do now is go through the estimate with you and make sure I did not miss anything and that I am providing you with everything you asked for."
- Go through the estimate, making sure to restate all of their areas of concern.
- Double-check that you have the correct phone numbers and email addresses (just in case they don't sign the job on the spot).

Ask these closing questions:

- Is this the job you were looking for?
- Is it okay to have a small space in your garage for the equipment?
- Is this the exact color that you were looking for?
- I am going to spend a little extra time on this area, because I know you were concerned about it. Is that okay with you?

Going for the Close

"I am confident that I will give you exactly the job you are looking for. Do you have any questions?"

Remember after you ask a question like this, you need to SHUT UP! Sales is all about knowing when to SHUT UP.

It is like a game of tennis.

Once you have served the ball and it has gone over the net, what do you do? You do nothing more than get into position and wait for the ball to come back to you.

You are done. You don't sit there and keep swinging the racket like a madman. You get into position and wait for your turn.

Once you have asked a question, you need to sit there quietly and wait for an answer.

It does not matter how long it takes (if your customer is a salesperson, she will mess with you by sitting there and not saying anything for as long as she can, just to see if you blow it!).

This is the art of the close!

Back to the Show

Once you have answered the customer's questions or found out that they have none, your next step is to move in for the kill.

"Well then, the only thing left is for me to get your signature down here at the bottom of the agreement."

Now put the pen down and SHUT UP!

You don't need to do anything else. The customer knows that it is now their turn. They completely understand that you are expecting an answer from them.

They understand that you want them to pick up the pen and sign the agreement. You don't need to jump in and save them from this sometimes-awkward moment.

Just like in a game of tennis, the ball has been hit into their side of the court at 70 miles an hour and is coming straight at them.

They will react!

Act 9: Objections

Objections are opportunities to educate your customer about issues that they may be misinformed about or just need to be reminded of.

What are the typical objections that you come across and how do you handle them?

TYPICAL OBJECTIONS
- Trust or confidence in your company.
- Trust or confidence in you.
- Price: Does your price fit their budget?
- Price: Are they realistic about what they want to have done?
- Decision process: They cannot make the decision on their own.
- Lacks education: Wants other bids.

Act 10: Keep Closing!

This is a long play. Get used to it! This whole show can be an hour and a half to two hours.

Close at least three times. (The reality is you are supposed to close five times, but let's start easy.)

After each objection that you have handled successfully you need to go back and once again ask the tough closing question. If you want the job, you are going to need to ask for it more than once.

"No"—in Sales—Doesn't Always Mean "No"

Most customers are pre-programmed to tell you that they are going to get three estimates and that they will not be making a decision today.

They will typically say "no" the first couple of times that you ask them for the job simply because that is what they believe they are supposed to do.

If they like you, they are simply waiting for you to finish getting them comfortable before they say "yes."

They want to say "yes." It is time consuming and a hassle to get other estimates. They already trust you and like you.

Keep asking for the job (just not the same way each time) and you'll get it.

Act 11: Command Performances

Yes, there are times when even the best of us are not able to convince our customers to sign up with us on the spot.

Even though you should be able to close over half of your proposals on the spot (assuming no plans need to be drawn), there will be times when you will need to take the time to enter the final act of this play.

It is shocking the number of contractors who never call the customer back after they perform an estimate.

They are either so hurt by the fact that the customer did not choose them right there on the spot or are under some misguided notion that the customer will of course call them back when they are ready to have the work done.

THE CLOSING PROCESS AFTER YOU'VE LEFT

Closing jobs after you leave the customer's home requires a very specific step-by-step process.

Step 1 is to find out why they are not ready to agree today.

- Is it the financing?
- Do they want more estimates?
- Did you fail to win them over with your amazing show?
- Ask as many questions (without being too pushy) in order to find out exactly why they feel the need to wait.

Step 2 is to set up a specific time to call them back in the next 72 hours when they will be able to make a decision.

Step 3 is to confirm email, cell, and home numbers and address to make sure you can get in touch.

Step 4 is to send them a thank you card—not a thank you email—thanking them for their time and letting them know how much you are looking for ward to doing their job. (Once again, Sendoutcards.com will make this easy for you.)

Step 5 is to call back when you say you are going to.

Step 6 is to look for information regarding their job and send them email updates on products and maybe another reference letter. Send them a couple of emails with these updates.

Step 7, if they have not made their decision when you call back, is to set up another specific time to call back.

Step 8 and on is to repeat Step 6 until you have booked the job or they tell you to leave them alone.

Extra Credit: If you are in the neighborhood, drop by and say hello with a dozen donuts or some other treat you've learned your potential client enjoys.

NOW IT'S YOUR TURN

What does your ideal play look like? It is eleven acts? Is it seven? What are the steps in your sales process? From the moment you have contact with the customer to the moment the deal is closed, each of these steps needs to be outlined and practiced. Give it a shot. Write down your step-by-step process.

Act 1 _____

_____

_____

_____

Act 2 _____

_____

_____

_____

Act 3 _____

_____

_____

_____

Act 4 _____

_____

_____

_____

Act 5 _____

_____

_____

_____

Act 6 _____

_____

_____

_____

Act 7 _____

_____

_____

_____

Act 8 _____

_____

_____

_____

Act 9 _____

_____

_____

_____

Act 10 _____

_____

_____

_____

Act 11 _____

_____

_____

_____

Now that you have taken the time to write down your sales process, take to a few people who know you and your business well. Have them go through it with you and critique it. Do not be offended by any criticism. This feedback will help you define the process. Now rewrite it, memorize it, practice it, and train it.

Rehearsal

Actors rehearse their lines over and over again until the lines become burned into their memory so that they can perform without thinking about what to say.

Golfers, martial artists, and baseball players practice hour after hour on the same strokes, moves, and swings so that the movement gets burned into muscle memory, so that they can perform the action without thinking.

In *Outliers*, by Malcolm Gladwell, he talks about the main difference between musicians who were great, good, and okay. This difference was directly correlated to the number of hours they practiced over their lifetime. The top musicians had put in close to 10,000 hours, the good ones 6,000 hours, and the mediocre ones 3,000 hours or so.

The difference between okay and great is all about the practice time and not so much about a God-given talent.

You can relate to this in your own trade. There is a definite difference in someone who has logged 10,000 or 20,000+ hours in a trade versus the new guy who is in year two.

Experience Teaches Us Many Things

Salesmanship is no different than these musicians and athletes. You and your salespeople need to practice.

Go through your presentation until it is burned into your mental memory and you start saying it in your sleep.

Know and understand the common objections in your industry, and then write out the best answers and practice them over and over again with friends and family.

Rehearsal is required to get you from okay or good and make you great at sales.

Know Your Stuff

There is no excuse for not knowing the products you sell. How many of you have had this fun experience? You walk into a well-known electronics retailer and spend 15 minutes or so reading boxes trying to find out what new portable phone you should buy. Finally you get frustrated trying to figure out the differences between all the different makes and brands. Your head is spinning as you are reading about 5.8GHz versus 6.1 and those that have spread spectrum and Bluetooth versus those that don't even have a headphone jack. At long last a young man (or woman) comes along who is dressed like he works at the store so you ask, "Excuse me, but do you work in this department and can you help me?"

He looks at you and smiles, "Of course I can help you. What are you looking for?"

"A new portable phone, I just don't know which one is best," you say.

He keeps smiling as he picks up the boxes one by one and starts reading the labels the same way as you just did.

Frustrated yet? I know you are and I know you've had this same experience.

You have also probably had a different experience. One that starts the same way, but ends differently. This time when the young man walks up and you ask your question, he in turn asks you a couple of questions about why you need a new phone, what you liked and disliked about your last one, and which features are important to you. At the end of his questions he walks over to the shelf and says, "Based on what you just told me, I would recommend this model. I have been here for three years now and I have yet to see anyone return it to the store."

I know you have had both experiences and I'm confident that I know exactly how you felt after both. Don't let your employees be the first guy.

Be the Expert

Your customers want you to be the expert! They don't want to have to search for information online themselves. (Although they will do so if they feel like you do not have the answers to their questions or leave them with the impression that you are making things up.) We all want to buy from people who have the answers and who really understand their area of expertise.

Think about it for a minute. You are a business owner, you are a leader and you make decisions everyday leading your company. Isn't it nice to sometimes go to dinner or on vacation and have someone else make all the decisions for you? We all like to give up that control sometimes and are happy to do it when it is not in our area of expertise and we are dealing with a knowledgeable salesperson.

I am not an expert in home theater systems. If someone came to my home to set up a home theater system, I'd be at his mercy. If he obviously knew his business inside and out and could give me solid reasons why I needed my system set up a specific way, I would be very comfortable taking his advice. As long as he stayed within my budget, I would cede control of my home theater to him. If that another person came out to my home and could not answer basic questions in a thorough manner or left me with a feeling that he was being less than honest, then I would go into research mode. He would be gone. I, like you, would then research everything I possibly could about home theaters, including all pricing and installation options. No doubt I'd end up going with a different company.

"Don't Touch" Means "No Sale"

Consumers want to touch and test what they are going to buy.

If you really want to sell your service or product, your customers need to be able to touch, feel, and play with it. Would you ever buy a car without a test drive? Would you ever buy a bed mattress without first lying down and stretching out on it? If you want to sell your service or product, your customers need to see it in action.

Props Make All the Difference in a High-End, In-Home Presentation

Props, props and more props. All the world is a stage.

Every one of you have a few products that lend themselves to a little extra special attention and something that customers would be intrigued to touch, hold, or just watch on a video. Consider the following examples.

Window Replacement

Years ago we started a window replacement business in Illinois. It did not work out as planned (which could be a book in itself!).

I went to two days of training with our manufacturer in order to learn how to sell their product. I must say I was very impressed. I saw windows that reflected heat, were easy to clean inside and out and ones that had so much tint it could turn your house into a celebrity's limo.

My favorite demonstration of all was one where they pulled back a bowling ball on a rope and let it go, allowing it to swing right into this glass window without breaking the glass!

I loved this stuff.

The greatest thing of all was that for only $200 per salesperson, the manufacturer sold us these nice kits packaged inside of a small suitcase, ready for my salespeople to take out and do the same demonstration to our customers (the bowling ball, unfortunately was replaced by a hammer—yes, I was disappointed).

Those customer presentations were over the top!

Painters

There are some amazing products out there. One is fireproof paint. Although no one wants to watch a demo of paint drying, who wouldn't be riveted by a video of a room coated in this fireproof paint not burning after a Christmas tree, sitting in the middle of the room, is set on fire?

Now hand the customer a lighter and a stick covered with a coat of this amazing paint and ask him or her to try and light the stick on fire (preferably outdoors or over a fireplace).

Restaurants

I am always amazed that restaurants that want to push high-priced appetizers don't offer small samples from time to time. I understand the cost of food can affect the bottom line, however, if you have a repeat clientele, why not let them try some new options? The world is full of people who eat at the same restaurants on a regular basis and eat the same food every time they go there. Break those people out of their comfort zones and into a higher-priced overall ticket by giving them a taste of the good life!

Plumbers

Pex is an amazing product that is used instead of copper plumbing.

Hand your customers the simple blue and red tubing and let them play with the easy valve system. Show them how they can now control the hot and cold water from their attic or basement locations.

This is an especially cool product for new construction.

If you sell reverse osmosis water systems, the prop world is your oyster.

There are great props to show just how bad the water is that comes straight out of the tap (even out of store-bought bottled water).

Pet Stores

Samples, samples, samples. If you really want Fido to start begging for the new treats you are selling, invite him in for a visit. How about a dog day where owners get to come in and try out some new brushes for grooming and a variety of treats that you have in your bulk bins?

Electricians

There are almost too many ideas here to write down. Here is a simple one.

If you want to become a trusted advisor, bring a Phantom power meter to your next estimate.

Show your customers just how much electricity all of their TVs use when they are supposedly off. The easiest sale you'll ever make, after such a presentation, is pitching those power switches you have in your truck.

Dry Cleaners

What makes you different from your competition? What can you show your customers about your process that will make them say, "I don't want to go anywhere else"? Is it that the chemicals you use are green and better for the environment? Is your process and equipment newer and even gentler on clothing? Whatever it is, demonstrate it to your potential customers.

Website Designers

This is one of the easiest businesses to show your potential customers why your product is better than the competition's. The wonderful thing about websites is that their quality and effectiveness are so subjective. I have never met a website designer who (a) thought my website was up to snuff and (b) could not show me really cool designs that impressed me.

What are you currently doing to allow your customers to fully experience what you have to offer?

What are your competitors doing to allow *your* customers to fully experience what *they* have to offer?

What *should* you be doing to allow your customers to fully experience what you have to offer?

The Wow Effect

Props are only good if they have a *Wow Effect*.

Customers need to be able to look, touch, and feel your prop and say, "Wow, I've never seen anything like that before!"

YOUR BUSINESS: ASSESSING YOUR PROPS

List the props that you currently bring on your presentations:

1. _____
2. _____
3. _____

What is the Wow Effect from these props?

What could you use to create a Wow Effect?

Where To Get the "Wow Effect"—Suppliers

Products exist that have the desired *Wow Effect*.

Go to your trade organization shows and walk the floors.

Go have lunch with reps from different suppliers. Suppliers have teams of people who have spent years building kits for in-home demonstrations and are sitting around wondering why no one wants to use them. If you have a storefront, make sure you are pushing your supplier/manufacturer to give you special pricing on its product you are going to be using as a display model. Display models are, by nature, used and abused and both you and your manufacture win when customers get to play with the product.

Don't Over-Stock or Over-Prop

Customers want options but they don't need every option available from every possible manufacturer. Unless you are a big box retailer and have all the space in the world to store tons of these display models, you are much better off stocking about three levels of product from three different manufacturers, rather than five levels from eight manufacturers. It is important when selecting floor models and samples, that you hit the key price points that have quality options. When you stock every brand known to man, you are not maximizing your floor space and are making it too difficult for people to make a decision.

A word to the wise: you are better off having two or three really cool things that will deliver the *Wow Effect*, instead of eight things that will put your customers to sleep when you are giving in-home presentations.

Over-propping can kill a sale. How many props should you use? That depends on the customer's personality type, as mentioned earlier. This is another reason why it is important to read your customers and understand what they want to see and hear.

Sell More Product to the Same Customers

Is it more difficult to find new customers or to sell more products or services to your existing customers? It's easier to sell more to the same people who already know you and love you. It is absolutely amazing how many small and large businesses miss this opportunity. Successful examples of this are all around us. Let's take a look at a few.

Subway

Subway had 10 actual restaurants in 1974. They have been around for over 35 years and just recently decided that maybe, just maybe, they should offer breakfast sandwiches to its customers. For years, I have been going into customer-less Subway stores during breakfast hours while traveling and grabbing a turkey sandwich. Now I have to stand in line while others grab breakfast. Thanks a lot, Subway!

KFC

KFC has been slowly losing the chicken war over the past several years. Many people who could have or would have been loyal fried chicken fans have been opting for healthier grilled chicken. KFC did try an advertising campaign a few years ago touting how healthy fried chicken was, but to its dismay it was yanked from the airwaves. Everything changed in 2009 when KFC launched grilled chicken on the *Oprah Show*. The *Oprah* coupon was such a success that the local store in my area had to stop taking it during lunch hours as it could not keep up with the demand. Fast forward and KFC is now selling more chicken to fathers like me who can sit down to a grilled chicken breast (while my kids eat the fried stuff I wish I could have).

McDonalds

McDonalds is amazing at testing new products in different markets and not feeling the need to stick to a standardized menu. You can get beer in certain McDonalds in Europe. Different countries and states have options that are regionally specific to help sell more to the customers who love them.

My favorite McDonalds story revolves around something simple that it missed for years. Once it dawned on them to include premium coffee selections to its menu, McDonalds experienced a huge difference in its earnings. Earlier, McDonalds noticed (some would say, a little late in the game) that its share of the breakfast market was eroding. Interesting enough, it was eroding away to the relatively new kid on the block, Starbucks. People flocked to Starbucks in order to grab their coffee and breakfast. They went to Starbucks for the coffee, but with breakfast there as well, they grabbed breakfast, taking morning customers away from McDonalds. McDonalds eventually took notice and made some changes to its coffee menu. It started marketing the changes and, with the help of great tasting coffee and a little recession, people started flocking back to McDonalds for breakfast. McDonalds also did the same thing that KFC did by offering healthy alternatives. With healthier options for herself, more and more mothers are now willing to take their kids in for a Happy Meal.

Best Buy

Since its inception Best Buy has been a category killer. Best Buy came on strong, with a great selection and a well-trained sales team. Best Buy decimated Circuit City and anyone else who stood in its way. (Circuit City arguably killed itself by firing its well-trained commission sales force and replacing them with $9 hour kids who referred to the product labels to help customers with specs.) Radio Shack was forced to resign itself to be the store that we all go to when we need that unique electronics part we can't find anywhere else.

One of the best moves Best Buy made was to acquire Geek Squad. Best Buy always had a little place in its stores where you could drop off your computer or TV to get it fixed, but with the advent of Geek Squad it had the ability to do in home set ups and repairs. For many people, Geek Squad is the only option for home electronic repair. You have to ask yourself, "what's wrong with Radio Shack?" We all go to Radio Shack when things are broken. When will it step up and start to compete?

Starbucks

I don't know where to start or where to go with regards to Starbucks. It sells everything from music and books to maybe sparkplugs someday. Starbucks is not afraid to try new products.

Walmart

Walmart sells everything and anything. Have you been in a Super Walmart? I hear that some people actually park their RVs in the parking lot and vacation there.

Home Depot/Lowes

Both of these retailers have been known for being the one stop shop for home improvement "do it yourselfers". They have adapted to an aging population where fewer individuals have the interest and/or time to take on home improvement projects. They now have options for the "do it for me" customer. These companies now provided everything from carpet and blind installation, to roofing and painting.

Out of the Box Ideas: Some You'll Like and Some You Won't

Restaurants

Are you maximizing your kitchen space and time? One of my favorite examples of a restaurant that does this is a local place near my kids' school. The restaurant, already successful, decided to improve its profit by expanding into the catering business to, of all places, the school lunch program of my kids' school. My children would rather eat at school now than at home where they have to make their own lunch. The restaurant provides high quality and healthy lunches that the students love. To secure that relationship with the kids, the restaurant is constantly changing its menu based on the kids' suggestions.

Dry Cleaners

I have not yet seen a dry-cleaning business do this, but why not expand into the carpet-cleaning business? It may seem like a stretch, but think about it; how many hundreds of customers does a local dry cleaner have? Then, depending on the area, most customers are also homeowners. These homeowners, who are more likely to have clothes that require dry cleaning, also need to have their carpets cleaned. As a dry cleaner, you undoubtedly already have a friendly relationship. How difficult would it be to ask your customers if they want their carpets cleaned as well? I am not suggesting that every dry cleaner go out and invest $20,000 into a truck and hire a crew, but how hard would it be to set up a partnership with a quality carpet cleaner in your area and take a piece of the pie?

Landscapers

Why not expand into the pool cleaning business? You already have a trusted relationship with the customer. You know the yards, the dogs, and so on. And you're already making regular visits to your customers' homes.

House Cleaners

Why not expand into yard care? (Sorry landscapers.) You are already trusted in the house. Is it a big leap to take care of the outside as well? This of course assumes you can hire the right people.

Gift Card/Curio Shops

People are coming into your place of business to buy a card and perhaps a small gift for a friend or loved one. Why not invest in a small flower fridge and work out a relationship with a local florist who will provide floral arrangements to go with the "Sorry I Messed Up Again" card?

Day Care Centers

The majority of married couples with kids do not have a regular date night with each other. They know they should, but there are always challenges finding a babysitter who they can trust. How about offering a Friday or Saturday date night special where parents can drop the kids off and go out for a few hours?

Hobby/Craft Stores

Classes, classes, and more classes. Craft stores are generally pretty good at offering classes for first-time customers to get them hooked on a new craft and then selling them all the extra stuff they need to enjoy themselves. Hobby stores could easily do the same thing. There are plenty of parents who would take their kids down for a model building class on a Saturday morning.

WHAT CAN YOU DO?

Now that you have some stories from Big Business as well as some off-the-wall ideas from yours truly, it's your turn.

What is your current product or service offering?

_____

_____

How does this compare to your competitors?

_____

_____

What complementary products could you offer?

_____

_____

What complementary services could you offer?

_____

_____

Warning! Warning! You Can't Be All Things to All People

I know that I just spent the last few pages getting your head spinning about all the ways you can expand your business. Some would say that I just broke the Cardinal Rule of "Focus" and set shiny, tempting, and distracting objects in front of eager entrepreneurs. It's only fair to show you the opposite side of diversification. Here's a few examples of what can happen when you think you can be all things to all people.

Home Depot

Home Depot is a great example of what happens when you start believing your own hype. Home Depot expanded rapidly into services in the early 2000s. The "Do It For Me" mantra was heard loudly in the Atlanta boardrooms at "Fort Depot." Senior Executives believed wholeheartedly that as baby boomers grew older and the younger generation showed less and less interest in fixing up their homes, there would be more market for those who were looking for contractors. Home Depot decided to offer contracting services to their customer base in not just in a few specific areas, but in closer to 30 different categories. In theory, the strategy made sense. But there are many strategies that seem to make perfect sense in the boardroom, but don't translate well when executed in the field. The Home Depot Services, while arguably somewhat successful, never really became the growth engine that executives were hoping for.

Battle lines were drawn between the traditional retailers and the service teams that were vying for the same floor space to market. Advertising dollars were less than adequate and an antiquated CRM system meant that no one had any idea the effectiveness of the marketing dollars they were spending. (They *need* to read my book!) Home Depot outsources all services to small contractors around the country. Without proper oversight, the customer complaints started pouring in. Television news channels did exposés on The Home Depot Services and its unhappy customers. What began as an ultimately good idea turned ugly. Because of how poorly executed the program rolled out, by late 2007 The Home Depot Services started cutting services nationwide, thus alienating its small contractors who were told they were partners (most of whom shop at Lowes now!).

The Home Depot Services is still a part of the company, but not the hugely profitable division its executives thought it could become. The reality is the program may have done more harm than good. Disgruntled customers and contractor partners nationwide now shop elsewhere.

I do understand that this line of thinking is completely contradictory to my early comments about diversification. My purpose is to make you truly think through your decisions and remember that there may be a down side to diversification if it's not done properly.

From the Small Business Side

I was recently in Hawaii with my wife enjoying some time without the kids. One night we were wondering around and walked into a store with a larger than life size mechanical hula dancer. That dancer automatically made me think that this may be a good place to find some trinkets to take home to the kids. We found some cheap toys, but what I also found in this store were some high-end rocking chairs and decorative paddles made of KOA wood. The paddles were around $1,000 apiece and the chair was $2,400. Truth be told, the chair and paddles were amazing, the workmanship was first rate and I would be happy to have either piece in my home. The reality, though, is that I could not bring myself to spend that kind of money in a trinket shop with a large mechanical hula dancer in the window! I settled for a picture I took of the chair next to the hula dancer, which I use in my Business Boot Camps to illustrate what *not* to do. I also spent a half hour (to my wife's dismay) trying to convince the manager of the store why his business model was flawed. Aren't I just a blast to be with on vacation?

My Story

I have been successful at many businesses, but my partners and I have also failed at quite a few startups that we were confident were perfectly planned and would be successful. Our failure was the result of straying from our original business plan.

THE MORAL OF THE STORY

Diversification can be a great way to help your company grow. Selling more to the same people is a great way to grow. Before you do anything follow this simple plan:

- Survey your customers. What else would they want to buy from you? Can you offer what they want profitably with minimal investment?
- Test on a small scale.
- Track your results and your effect on your core business.
- Don't underestimate the challenges of adding new products and services
- Make sure the new products/services are within your skill/knowledge set.

Up-Selling

Up-selling is completely different from selling more and different things to your existing customer base.

Every customer has the opportunity to become a larger and more profitable customer for you—all the while providing a better experience for the customer.

The key to making this happen is to genuinely evaluate what your customers could need outside the average purchase.

Up-selling is generally thought of as moving your customer from one level of product or service to a higher level as well as adding the extras that they may not have thought of during the purchase process.

The Basic Up-Sells

The basic up-sells are the things that you are already doing (or should be doing):

- **Car washes.** The basic car wash becomes the complete detail.
- **Carpet cleaners.** Pre-treatments ensure those stubborn stains don't come back.
- **Stereo stores.** Higher quality equipment sounds better than the equipment they originally planned on buying.
- **Electricians.** Identifying faulty wiring or bad light sockets that you happen to come across while you are at the home means more profit.
- **Plumbers.** Checking sinks and fixtures and offering to replace or fix them makes for happy customers and increased sales.
- **Handymen.** The list is endless. What else needs to be done?
- **Painters.** Why not add an extra room or hallway to the job or suggest an accent color?
- **Landscape contractors.** You can quickly do a check of the sprinkler system and offer to replace sprinkler heads with more water-conscious options.

These are the simple things that everyone should do with every customer they have. Your business has something you can up-sell to your customer.

The average sale goes up and your customer has a much better experience because you were able to offer them an even higher quality product or service.

Everyone wins.

YOUR UP-SELL LIST

What are the five basic up-sells that you should be attempting to sell your customers? Consider how you can provide a higher quality product or service.

1. _____
2. _____
3. _____
4. _____
5. _____

The Quality Up-Sell

Everyone should have a good/better/best strategy.

Every customer is different and every customer decides to buy or not to buy based on his or her own set of criteria—not yours.

If you have not been offering a good/better/best option, you have lost work to your competitors.

Your competitor understood that this particular customer was not just looking for the cheapest price; they were looking for the highest quality workmanship and products.

In almost any business, there is a way to offer a "better quality" option by either spending more time or using different techniques, better materials, or simply offering the next step up in a product line.

For those of you who sell mainly products, this is a simple concept. Most manufactures already offer a good/better/best version of their product. Your job is to make sure you have all three available and that you are well versed in the differences.

Good/Better/Best Offerings

This first exercise focuses on a product offering. Remember, if you run a service business this exercise relates to the products that you use in your service.

YOUR PRODUCTS

Choose a typical product that you sell.

What are the three levels of this product that you are able to offer: good/better/best?

Good: _____

Better: _____

Best: _____

Now what are the key differences in each of these three lines?

Good: _____

Better: _____

Best: _____

The Good

Think about your typical service offering.

TYPICAL SERVICE OFFERING

What are the steps you would take to deliver a typical job?

1. _____
2. _____
3. _____
4. _____
5. _____

Time—How much time does it take to complete the project from start to finish?

_____

Pricing—What is the complete price of the project, including all labor, materials, overhead, and profit?

1. _____
2. _____
3. _____
4. _____
5. _____

The Better

For this option you need to take the same job and think about what would make it a better quality and longer-lasting finished product.

UPGRADES

Make a list of possible upgrades for the better job, including costs.

1. _____
2. _____
3. _____
4. _____
5. _____

Add up the cost of doing this "better" job and re-price the contract, taking into account the higher-quality materials and the additional time it takes to complete the revised project.

Obviously, this should be more expensive than the "good" job.

1. _____

2. _____

3. _____

4. _____

5. _____

The Best

Here is the fun one. This is the same good job, but with only the highest quality materials that you can get your hands on, as well as the proper amount of additional time taken to make sure the job is a work of art. What would you do to make this job absolutely the best job possible?

UPGRADES FOR THE BEST JOB

Make a list of possible upgrades for the better job, including costs.

1. _____

2. _____

3. _____

4. _____

5. _____

Now add the pricing for the "best" job, including the new materials costs, labor, overhead, and profit. This should now be an even higher price than the "better" option.

1. _____

2. _____

3. _____

4. _____

5. _____

Your Customers Want Options

Right about now many of you are saying, "Look, Jay, my customers will not pay for all these added things … all they ever care about is price."

Customers are not all driven by price, even though they almost always tell you that is the only thing that matters.

If price was the only thing that mattered then we would all drive the same type of car, live in the same style of house, and wear the same kind of clothes.

People make their decisions based on their different "hot buttons."

By only giving your customers the option you feel they asked for (usually the "good" option), you are not allowing yourself the opportunity to sell customers something more that they haven't yet considered.

You are also leaving bigger sales with larger profits on the table for your competitors to grab.

Green Options

Green is in! If you don't believe that, just turn on the TV and spend a couple of nights watching *The Green Planet* channel.

You will be amazed at all the different "green" options that exist.

Studies show that customers will pay upwards of 25% more for a green option.

The first step is to actually figure out what "green" means in your particular industry.

Your trade association magazines and websites are a great source of information for what your business is doing to be green.

Why Go Green?

Just in case you have been living under a rock and have not been paying attention to the news for the last 10 years, you need enlightenment: Everyone is doing it!

We, as Americans, have finally woken up to our perilous environment and all the harm we have been doing to it.

Going green helps save the environment for our kids and makes us feel better about our own contributions to the world.

It also allows us bragging rights around the water cooler. Believe it or not, it is cool to go green!

> **GOING GREEN**
> What are the top green options in your industry?
> 1. _____
> 2. _____
> 3. _____
> 4. _____
> 5. _____

Be an Energy Star!

Another great missed opportunity for contractors is showing customers how they can save money and help the environment, all the while spending more money with you.

Every industry has energy or water saving options.

Most customers have heard of the options, but don't have a great understanding of how they work or where to get them.

You can educate your customers on their different options and how they can buy them from you. The opportunities are amazing.

Here are a couple of quick examples of options that exist.

Electronics

More and more TVs, stereos, and other electronic components are being designed to "sip" electricity instead of devour it. Consumers are hunting down these options as the price of electricity goes through the roof.

Plumbers

Amazing opportunities exist for every plumber. Almost everyone would love to see their water bill go down.

The options are endless. Offer your customers dual flush toilets, low flow shower heads, tankless water heaters, and separate under-the-sink instant water heaters.

Buy Local

Consumers are more and more aware of the high cost of transportation. This means that many are more likely to buy products that are produced locally, therefore lessoning the carbon footprint and associated costs to send goods across the country.

Electricians

Most people have heard of compact fluorescent lighting, but the vast majority of households have not replaced all of the incandescent bulbs with these CFLs.

Many people have it on their to do list, but don't have the time to purchase and install them or understand what a great savings they could see on their electrical bill.

What if you always carried a supply of CFLs and offered to install them?

Simple dimmer switches save money, as do programmable thermostats, and more. The list goes on.

Take the time to offer a home energy audit and show your existing customers how they can save money on their electrical bills.

Organic

Check out your grocer's shelves—organic is in! Foods grown with no chemicals and pesticides are selling at a faster rate than others. Restaurants that buy locally grown organic produce are a winner!

Landscapers

The majority of people's water expenses come from irrigation.

Why not offer green alternatives, replacing older inefficient sprinkler heads and replacing or repairing drip irrigation or sprinkler systems?

Replacing grass areas with native drought-resistant plant areas can save your customers huge amounts of money on water bills.

YOUR BUSINESS: ENERGY SAVINGS

What areas can you save your customers money and make the job more profitable for you?

1. _____
2. _____
3. _____
4. _____
5. _____

Be a Trusted Advisor

Being an energy star is all about taking the time to find out how you can use your knowledge and trade to save your customers money and in turn make more money for yourself.

The side benefits are obvious. Customers will rave about you. Everyone loves someone who teaches and helps them.

You can also transcend being just another business and become a *trusted advisor*. A trusted advisor is someone who a customer will repeatedly go to for advice, not to just buy or fix things.

Of course, you will also feel pretty good about your contributions to the environment.

Being a trusted advisor is not just about being green. How you position yourself in the market is going to dictate your level of success. Consider these areas:

- **Electronics**—You are either the low price leader with razor thin margins or the only person I can trust to set up my home theater, teach me about digital photography, or educate me on how this darn computer works. All these options allow for a much higher margin.

- **Furniture stores**—You are welcome to be the place where I go to haggle about the price of a sofa my wife would like to buy. Or you can be the designer who picks out the perfect overpriced piece of furniture that my family cannot do without.

- **Insurance sales**—Far too many insurance sales people are simply order takers. Insurance is an important part of every family's planning. Are you really going to let them go online and get a quote or do you want to be one of the important people they call when making life decisions?

- **Landscapers**—Anyone can replace a sprinkler head. Very few can design a water-conscious garden that will help clients do their part in conserving energy and saving money.

The Fun Stuff Most People Don't Think About

What is new and cutting edge in your industry that you could offer to your customers that most of your competitors are not offering as an option?

Everyday, new products and materials are created that change the landscape of almost every business. Consider these examples.

Painting

Rustoleum® has a magnetic paint that can transform any wall in any room into a "refrigerator door" ready to tack up the kids' artwork. They also have a product that turns a regular wall into a chalkboard. Imagine the fun kids could have with that!

Electronics

3D television is now a reality. What does it take to tune a room for this new age?

Carpet Cleaning

New cleaning systems have changed the entire landscape of carpet cleaning. Are you on the cutting edge?

Electrical

Powersave has a product called the Powersave 1200®. When it is added to an electrical box your energy usage can be reduced by 10-15%. (It works! I have one.)

Landscapers

How about offering a satellite-controlled watering system that takes control of customers' outdoor irrigation system so that they don't need to adjust for warm or cloudy days?

YOUR BUSINESS: CONSIDER YOUR UP-SELLS

What kind of unique products exist in your industry as possible up-sells for your customers?

1. _____
2. _____
3. _____
4. _____
5. _____

Up-Selling Summary

By offering your customers choices and educating them on options that they never knew existed, you have the opportunity to change from being just a generic business to their trusted advisor. Trusted advisors have a different level of respect.

This added respect leads to increased average job size and profit. You will be able to leave your customer in a much better place than if you had just done the lowest-cost job possible. You will leave with greater profits.

Your most profitable and busiest competitors are probably doing this already! It's now your turn.

Chapter 6

Sales Management

The challenges related to hiring, training, and managing salespeople in the small business world is a company's single biggest roadblock.

The two limitations to growing a small business are:

- Marketing (see Chapter 2)
- Sales

You cannot grow your business beyond a certain point without having a sales force.

Think You Are Ready To Have a Sales Team?

Before you hire salespeople, you need to ensure that you are ready to have them onboard. Also, not wanting to do the sales yourself is not a good enough reason to hire salespeople.

No salesperson should be able to outsell the owner of the company. If you are not confident that you can outsell any person that you hire, don't hire anyone!

Instead, take the time to go back to your sales process and become great at it. If you are horrible at sales and you go out and hire and train salespeople, how good will they ever possibly be?

In the event that you are operating a retail location, you more than likely already have salespeople. If that is your situation, you still need to determine how many more salespeople you will need. The process for hiring salespeople is the same whether you decide to hire one or 10.

Do You Have a Strong Lead Generation Program?

Notice that I did not ask you if you understood your branding message or if you had a solid marketing program. I specifically asked if you had a strong *lead generation program*. If you are unclear what I mean here, go back and reread the lead generation section in Chapter 4.

If you have a strong lead generation program, you will know that you can generate a certain amount of leads weekly at a price point that fits your marketing model.

In other words, you know your numbers cold. For example, you know that it costs you $40 per lead and you personally can close one out of every four leads.

This results in a marketing cost per job of $160.00.

You also know that your salespeople will not be as good as you are out of the gate because of the "owner effect." You know that your business model still works when they close only one out of six leads.

You are confident that you are currently generating more leads than you can personally get to and that the trend will continue.

Production Capacity

Is your production team ready for the extra work that more sales will generate?

Will you need to hire extra people?

Will you need more trucks, extra equipment, and more physical locations?

Cash

Expanding your business and hiring salespeople can be a very expensive endeavor. The cost of hiring and training salespeople, including salary, expenses, and leads they will burn while getting trained, can add up.

It is not uncommon for new salespeople to need several months before they begin generating revenue.

Are You Going To Be Providing All the Leads?

If you are not going to be supplying all the leads (which isn't something you need to do—this topic alone could be another complete book), what are the activities that your salespeople will be doing to source more business? How do you know that these methods will work?

Have you personally performed these activities so that you can predict the expected results?

Hiring Salespeople

The best phrase I can think of to describe the hiring of a salesperson is *caveat emptor*, which means *buyer beware*.

I am always suspicious of salespeople when I interview them (after all, they are salespeople). It is sometimes difficult to separate the truth from the stories they may be feeding you in the interview.

They are prone to exaggeration and many will say almost anything to get the deal or the job.

Experience Is Great, But...

I have been in sales my entire adult life. I consider myself much better at marketing and sales than I do at actually working at the trade I chose.

Honestly, back to the book *Outliers*, I probably have well over 20,000 hours of experience in sales and management, but only a few hundred in my trade of hands-on painting.

Trust me…you don't want to buy any book that I write about painting, I am in no way qualified to author such a book.

I do, however, know salespeople. After more than 20 years of hiring salespeople, I am convinced that salespeople are one of the toughest hires out there.

It is still tough for me.

After all these years, I still consider myself fortunate if I am right 40% of the time. (Truth be told, I am probably wrong 75% of the time!)

Points To Keep in Mind

Why are they looking for work?

Assuming that you did not approach them directly and that they are not already gainfully employed, why are they looking for work?

Every employer in every industry understands just how valuable a top salesperson can be. One who truly delivers without an attitude is an amazing find.

Top salespeople are never let go, no matter how tough the economy is, without an underlying reason.

You need to find out what that reason was.

Organizational Fit

How will they fit in with your organization? A top salesperson who no one in your organization wants to talk to or even go near is not going to work out, no matter how great they may be at selling.

If you have a very team-oriented environment and your new salesperson is a prima donna or lone wolf, trouble is right around the corner.

If you have an organization where employees go home at 5:00 and never see each other after work and your new salesperson comes from companies where employees always hung out together after work for drinks and socializing, you will ultimately have a problem.

They're not going to enjoy the environment, will not be happy, and will start looking for a new place to work.

Will You Enjoy This Person?

Unless your organization is large enough to have a sales manager, you are going to be spending a lot of time with your sales staff.

Daily contact is essential for the "proper care and feeding" of a salesperson. I have a hard and fast rule about hiring salespeople. I have to like them as a person and I have to truly want to spend time with them. If not, this hire is doomed to failure and I don't hire them.

What Do They Believe?

What salespeople truly believe is more important than the actual truth.

There is no match if potential hires believe that in order to get a sale they must offer the lowest price no matter what.

If their version of follow-up and customer care does not match yours, you will have a problem.

If they believe that the world should revolve around the sales department and you believe everyone is equally important, trouble will brew.

If they believe that once the deal is sold, they're done and want their commission paid and you want them to service the job while it's in progress, they're not a good fit.

If they believe that it is your job to supply all the leads and you feel otherwise, they're not going to be productive.

You need to make sure that you are 100% aligned in all of these areas. This tact is the same as getting married and not having discussed with your spouse how he or she feels about having children.

Not being aligned on each of these points is a recipe for disaster!

Home Improvement Sales Is a Different Animal

Just because someone was successful in sales in one industry does not necessarily mean that the skill will transfer to your industry.

A skilled plumber is not necessarily a good mechanic or web designer. A successful software salesperson does not always make the transition to retail sales.

Take for example salespeople coming from an inbound sales organization. They are used to the phone ringing with customers excited to talk to them about ordering a product. Their sales may have been impressive, but their background and skills don't translate well in a sales environment where they must go into a customer's home and spend an hour and a half getting to know the homeowners.

How about salespeople who succeeded in business-to-business sales? It is still sales and they were successful, but what hours did they work? Monday to Friday, 8:00 am to 5:00 pm is not generally the best time to sell to home-owners.

If your business revolves around selling to homeowners and doing in-home presentations, your salespeople are selling primarily in the evenings and week-ends. If you are in retail, your hours are 9:00 am to 9:00 pm and in some cases seven days a week with maybe a few holidays off.

Making the transition from inside sales to retail sales can be very difficult. For example, imagine salespeople who spent 10 years selling cars. They are now looking for a change of career and so apply to your mortgage company. They are going from an environment where they are constantly walking around talking with people, very rarely sitting in one place for very long, to an envi-ronment where they are now forced to sit in a cubical all day. The activity of talking and selling is relatively the same, but the way in which they do it has completely changed.

That isn't to say that it is impossible to have salespeople change industries. But there are potential challenges. Make sure you spend some time asking the right questions so that the person you are about to hire is a perfect fit.

Understand the Sales Role

Be sure to define is the actual sales role that you are hiring. In your industry, what does someone really need in order to be successful? Here are some examples of different types of salespeople.

Retail: Consumer Goods

The perfect retail salesperson should always be smiling, have a "I will help you" attitude, and know when to be available for questions and when to "hang back" and let the customer browse. They understand the hours are grueling and that weekends and holidays are not necessarily their own.

Consumer: Inside Sales (Telephone)

The perfect inside salespeople love to talk on the phone. They are content and happy in a cubicle. They don't need to be face to face with someone in order to establish a connection. They understand that, depending on the business model, they may be working at nights and on weekends and they are happy to do it. Above all, they have the perfect phone voice.

Business-to-Business: Inside Sales (Telephone)

Inside business-to-business salespeople are very similar to consumer salespeople.

The differences revolve around "getting past the gatekeeper." Business-to-business salespeople need to have the special added skill of getting past the receptionist in order to get to the decision maker.

Business to Business: Outside Sales

The trickiest group of salespeople to track is the outside salespeople who call on businesses. They are constantly on the road driving from place to place. They generally have to be happy driving, being by themselves, and stuck in traffic for a chunk of their day. They need to have a high degree of self-motivation. In order to allow these salespeople out of your sight, you need to have a high level of trust and systems in place for accountability. When outside salespeople go bad, they really go bad!

Technical Sales

Technical sales cross over into all of types of sales. You could also argue that every type of sales has a technical aspect to it. For the sake of this argument, let's say that even though door-to-door vacuum sales might have a technical component to it, the training does not equal that required of an electrical engineer. Sales engineers are very tough animals to find. In 90% of cases, engineers and salespeople are the exact opposite of each other. Sales engineers require a much more thorough interview process, as they will need to sit with both the sales team and the engineering team separately in order to ascertain their qualifications. They will also need two mentors, one from sales and one from engineering, in order to make sure they are up to speed with everything they need to be effective.

What Kind of Salespeople Do You Need?

Take a few minutes and think about the role your salespeople will fulfill. Are they primarily inside salespeople? Outside? Retail? In home? Business to business? How technical is the sale?

SALES FORCE ACTIVITIES

Write down the activities your salespeople will be involved in during a typical day.

7am-8am _____

8am-10am _____

10am-12pm _____

12pm-1pm _____

1pm-3 pm _____

3pm-5pm _____

5pm-? _____

If you are struggling with how to fill this out, here is a sample of a typical day for an outside business-to-business salesperson.

7am-8am—Plan day, send email confirming appointments; 7:30am morning conference call with the team

8am-10am—First set of appointments (depending on proximity and length may be one to five appointments)

10am-12:00—Strategic cold calling/marketing around first set of appointments

12pm-1pm—Lunch with a client or lunch with Wi-Fi in order to get caught up on email

1pm-3pm—Second set of appointments

3pm-5pm—Second strategic cold calling/marketing session of the day

5pm—End of day conference call recapping successes of the day

5:30pm—Email, proposal writing, organizing next day's activities

---

Are They Salespeople or Just Marketers?

For years, I have had an argument with a friend in the pharmaceutical sales industry. He has worked in the pharmaceutical business as either a director of sales or as the VP of sales capacity.

He would tell me about his salespeople. I would, in turn, argue that if somebody is not closing a sale, he is not a salesperson, but a marketer.

A salesperson, in my mind, is someone who actually is required to "close the deal." They are required to bring home a signed contract or make a sale in order to get paid.

If they don't do this, they are not salespeople, but are simply promoting the product—they are marketers. (The great thing about writing your own book is that you win all the arguments!)

Salespeople Are Pack Animals

You will never be finished hiring salespeople. It is a huge investment and one that has the capability of taking your company to the next level.

It is also a project that never ends.

You have about a 25% chance or so that the person or people you hire will work out. You need to be constantly on the lookout for more applicants.

Never hire just one salesperson. It is much easier to manage a group of salespeople who now are forced to compete with each other than it is to manage just one, who might start to believe after a few sales, that you need him or her more than he or she needs you.

Salespeople need to be around an exciting and fun environment. They need to be with others who are the same as they are. You should not leave them alone and they should not be left to their own devices. Top salespeople feed off of each other. They can't wait to tell each other their stories of their latest sale. Given the opportunity, they would love to team up with another member of the pack to close a deal!

If you decide to ignore my advice and run with a "lone wolf" salesperson, don't be surprised when this person decides to jump ship and join a company that has a full sales force.

Proper Care and Feeding: Assembly Required

Salespeople need to be trained not only in your industry but also in how your company operates.

There simply are no out-of-the box, ready-to-work salespeople.

New salespeople require more than just "some assembly." Full assembly required is your task (and batteries are not always included).

Every company and culture is unique and your new salesperson needs to be brought up to speed on all the nuances of your organization.

Shadowing

You need to be willing to commit to shadowing the first 10 or more customer visits with new salespeople in order to make sure they are effectively communicating your company's message.

Are they communicating your company's message exactly the way you scripted it or are they adding their own spin that contradicts it?

After making sure that they are doing things the way you want them to, you still need to be prepared to shadow them once a week for the first year and once every two weeks until you retire.

Ask a Veteran

Ask any veteran sales manager what it feels like going out in the field with their people and they will all tell you the same thing, "I wish I could be out there every day."

It is absolutely amazing that no matter how much you train people before they go out into the field, that when they're out there on their own, they will say the wrong thing. You can't know that unless you are out there with them and hear them say it. Your correction after the fact will always be remembered by that salesperson who uttered the snafu.

If you plan on hiring salespeople and then retiring to your office to surf the Internet with your feet up on the desk, this might just be the beginning of the end of your business.

Training

Always commit half a day a week to in-office sales training. Obviously this makes the most sense with an outside sales force. In the event you have an inside sales force or a retail location, take advantage of the downtime between customers to role play and hone your salespeople's skills.

Take the time to review every deal with them from the previous week. Spend time "role playing" objections and rehearsing different acts from the play. Listen to them on the phone while they are talking to customers. Watch them in action in your shop.

This is arguably the most important time of the week.

Talk to Your Salespeople Three Times a Day

Salespeople need lots and lots of contact.

As a sales manager (you), you need to know what is going on at all times. This isn't because you don't trust them, but because you want to make sure their days are planned properly and that they are making the best of their time. You want to be available at all times to celebrate the successes and to pick them up and brush them off when things go badly.

THREE CHECK-INS A DAY
1. Start the workday with a check-in to review the day's plan.
2. Check in around the middle of the day to see how things are going.
3. Check in at the end of the day to review the day's accomplishments.

This may sound like overkill, but the constant contact is vital. After 20 years in business, I still run a sales force this way.

Sales managers need to talk to their people three to five times a day. I still drop in unannounced occasionally to the morning and end-of-day calls just to make sure they are happening.

Still Want Salespeople?

If you are not prepared to do all of these things, you really should not be spending the money to hire salespeople.

If you don't follow these basic steps, your sales program will fail.

If you are, however, prepared to follow all of these steps and understand the serious commitment that is required in setting up a sales team, you can begin to create your best opportunity of company growth and success.

Chapter 7

Employees:
Hire Slow, Fire Fast

You can't do all of the work yourself, right?

Yes, you can. You can do every job yourself and you can do it better than anyone you could possibly hire.

But, is this really what you had in mind when you told your family and friends that you were starting your own business?

When you left your job and its accompanying paycheck, was your goal to be doing the same thing you did before you left, only now with the headaches of being responsible for finding the business and managing the cash flow as well?

That wasn't your plan.

So What Happened?

Every time I ask that question the answer is pretty much the same.

Everyone starts telling me how hard it is to find good people who know how to do the work or they launch into the story of how badly the last guy messed up.

Good people are hard to find.

A lot of the people available to work are not people who you want to have working for you.

NEEDLE IN A HAYSTACK

In my experience, the players in the labor pool break down something like this:

F—Not the least bit interested in having a job (5%)

D—Will work when they are broke and need money, but do a bad job (10%)

C—Barely willing to put in a day's work, but do so only because they need the money and the job (20%)

B—Will work when told exactly what to do and when followed up on hourly (30%)

A—Able to work independently and to solve problems as they arise (25%)

A+—Able to run the business while you are on vacation (7%)

A++—You (3%)

This very unscientific study is very hard for anyone who has ever had to do a lot of hiring to argue with.

The challenge that most small business owners run into when hiring help is their unrealistically high expectations. They assume that everyone they hire will treat the job, the customers, and their place of business with the same respect and dedication that they do.

Unfortunately, that is just not in everyone's genetic make up.

If it was, everyone would have a business and there would be no one left to hire.

The Employee Groups

The "F" Players: Hurricanes

We all know at least one of these guys. In some cases, we have them in our family or maybe they're a good friend who is great to go have a beer with (as long as you are buying).

Some people have no interest in doing anything productive. They just don't want to work. In extremely rare situations, when their backs are against the wall, they will work for short periods of time.

These people are referred to as "hurricanes" because of the rarity in which they show up at work, as well as the damage they leave behind.

These natural phenomena rarely occur twice in the same location, as these wonders of Mother Nature are never invited back to work again.

One of the most important things to remember about "F" players is that they are hired because they are generally charismatic folks who people enjoy being around.

They have plenty of time to come up with stories to explain the large gaps in their employment history. They will infiltrate your organization and lay waste to your business and to customer relations if you don't cut them off quickly.

The "D" Players: Tropical Storms

These folks are generally employed regularly throughout their life.

They can easily be spotted by their general lack of caring and their colorful work history spanning multiple companies and industries.

Chances are you have employed or do employ one or two of these "D" players now.

These are the people who, no matter how many times you tell them to double-check their work, always seem to miss something. They not only watch the clock, but also make sure they start packing up for a break, lunch, or the end of the day a good 30 minutes early just to make sure that nothing cuts into their time.

Left to their own devices, they will mess something up eventually.

These are the people who you yell at daily because you have tried everything else and nothing works.

These are also the people who you keep around because you gave up finding anyone else.

Tropical storms do not do as much damage to your business as the hurricanes, but will generally leave a good-sized mess that needs to be cleaned up.

The "C" Players: Occasional Showers

The "C" players are those who most small business owners end up with. (We will get into the reasons for this in a couple of pages.)

For the most part, these people will get the job done, but only with maximum supervision.

They don't disappoint as often as the "D" players do, although they do have a tendency to show up late from time to time and don't do what they say they are going to do.

The "C" player is the reason why most small business owners have the feeling that there just aren't any good workers out there. These players will be doing just fine for weeks on end and then, almost like clockwork, they will have an issue at home or with a customer that mushrooms into a major issue. At those times, you begin to question why you started your company in the first place.

This group tends to be the biggest disappointment, because for many of us, this quality of employee is as good as we get.

Your days will be going along just fine, when out of nowhere comes this rain cloud that drops crud all over your day—maybe not enough to ruin your week, but surely enough to mess with your day.

The "B" Player: Sun Showers

These "B" players are often confused for "A" players, mainly because many of us have never actually had an "A" player working for us and therefore have nothing to compare them to.

The "B" player is hard working and gets the job done. They are conscientious and genuinely care about what you think of them and the job they do.

The only challenge with "B" players is that they need constant direction and don't think very well on their feet. When a problem arises, they call you and need specific direction to solve it.

"B" players, though, are much better than the "Cs" and "Ds," who either don't recognize the problem or don't care.

"B" players are the largest percentage of today's work force and they are the reason why "management" exists.

Management is not only there to fire the "Ds" and "Cs," but to make sure the "Bs" know exactly what to do every step of the day.

This is how the majority of the work gets done.

Sun showers will pop out of nowhere, as a little problem now and again, but generally, everyone works through the issue without lasting effects.

The "A" Players: Rarely a Cloud in the Sky

These are the people you dream of having at your side.

An "A" player is the kind of person who does not freeze up in front of a customer.

They are those who you can give a job to and almost forget about it. You only need to check in by phone and drop by to say "hi" and share a joke or two.

They are the kind of people who will manage and motivate the "Bs," while isolating the "Cs" and firing the "Ds."

Stay tuned as to where to find these mystery people and, more importantly, how to keep them.

The "A+" Player: Sunny Days Are Here Again (Your Vacation Players)

I like to call this group the vacation players.

These are the ultimate people to have in your business. Many of you have never had one.

They are like trying to find a glimpse of a tiger in a dense jungle. They are elusive, but when you see one in its natural habitat, it is amazing to watch.

The vacation players are so named because these are the people who make your vacations possible.

The "A+" players are the ones who make all your problems go away. They treat your business as if it was their own and are the single most important group to have in your organization if you ever want to grow it.

The "A++" Player: The Weatherman

This is you. The risk taker. The person who had the vision to start a business in the first place.

You are the one who cares most about how things work out.

The key thing to remember about "A++" players is that if you are looking to hire people just like you, you are going to be disappointed.

They already have their own companies and are not looking for a job.

You create your own weather and show others how to navigate through the challenging storms.

A CEO's Responsibility

One of the most important roles that I have as a CEO is to make sure that my organization is staffed with the best people possible. Without "A" players and above, an organization will not be able to grow. In fact, it will be doomed to make the same mistakes and will never be able to achieve the owner's goals.

My responsibility as a CEO is to make sure the systems and processes are in place to guarantee that the best people are being hired at all times.

In the beginning, you have the ability to be part of the decision process on virtually every hire in your organization. You can take the time to search out talented individuals and perform every interview yourself, call the references (and you should), and make sure that every hire is top notch.

As you grow, you can't be personally responsible for every hire; however, you should draw a line in the sand that says "for hires at this level and above (including salespeople)," you personally sign off before the person comes on board.

The True Cost of a Bad Hiring Decision

The true cost of a bad hiring decision is much higher than most people think. Most business owners simply think a bad employee costs them that person's salary and benefits. There are some more expenses to include in the total price that person you just fired cost you.

Just to make the point, think about your last hiring mistake and add up the dollars he or she truly cost you.

The Interview Time

How much was the total cost for the time you and your team took to go through and interview *all* of the candidates, not just the one candidate you hired? How much time did you take with your team to talk about the candidates and to make the final decision? How many hours have actually gone into that one hire? Add those hours up and you will be surprised.

Your time in hours   _____
× Your hourly value $_____
                              Total cost = $_____

Your staff's time in total hours   _____
× Your staff's hourly value $_____
                              Total cost = $_____

                           Total wage cost = $_____

Cost of Ads

This is a simple one. What is the total cost of the employment wanted ads that you ran (assuming that you did) in order to get the hire?

Total cost of ads = $_____

Salary and Benefits Costs

What was the total salary and benefits cost of having this person in your organization?

Compensation cost = $_____

Training Costs

Add the total hours that you and your staff spent actually training this person.

Training hours and dollars = $_____

Frustration Hours

How many hours did you spend having conversations with your spouse, your other employees, and yourself about whether this person should be involved in your business?

This piece of the hiring cost in generally overlooked, but since most small business owners "hire fast and fire slow" (you need to do the opposite, but we will get to that in a minute), they tend to spend hours and hours talking and thinking and giving that troubled employee third and fourth chances. If you are able to add up these hours and apply your dollar amounts, you will be truly shocked.

Frustration hours and dollars = $_____

Lost Business

So you think that bad employees don't cost you business? Really? Think again. Bad employees are costing all of us business every day. Customers are leaving all of us because of their interactions with our hiring mistakes. In many cases, you will never know why a customer left, but you also will never see them again.

Take a guess at the business lost due to this employee; whatever you guess, it is probably low!

Lost business = $_____

Opportunity Cost

Where else could you and your team have been spending their time if you were not agonizing over what to do with your mistake? What additional business would you have obtained?

Opportunity cost = $_____

Employee Morale and Productivity

Bad employees have a detrimental effect on all of your employees. They bring down morale. They lower the bar. Others who are forced to work with the bad employee become resentful that you are keeping this guy around even though he is obviously working at a substandard level.

Your entire workforce becomes just a little slower, knowing that since you put up with the substandard employee, they have nothing to worry about. The bar gets lower and lower the longer the guy is around.

Take yet another guess. What does this lower productivity cost you?

Low morale and productivity loss = $_____

Add It Up

Okay, now go back and add up all of the numbers. Now double it (because I am confident most of us will have dramatically underestimated the actual expense). The total number that you came up with is the actual cost of a bad hire. Simmer on that number for a while. Please tell me you are now more committed to making sure you hire the right people.

Finding People

Now that we have identified the different players in the game, and the importance of hiring the right people, we need to figure out how to get them.

Scouting: Always Be Recruiting

"A" players are very difficult to find. They generally are not looking for work.

They are employed by someone else and if their bosses are smart, they recognize who they have working for them and will do anything to make sure that they don't lose them.

Lucky for all of us, most employers are not sharp enough to see the true value in an "A" player and, consequently, there will come a time when they are ready to change jobs.

"A" players can be found just about anywhere, not only in your trade. In most trades, they can be taught and will learn the nuances of your particular trade.

The skills an "A" player brings to the table are skills they are born with, not taught while on the job.

Constantly be on the lookout for people who amaze you. Look everywhere: the grocery store, fast food places, and other job sites.

You need to think of yourself as a talent scout. Always carry business cards, your calendar, and a pen. Walk up to people and get their names and phone numbers. Ask if you can call them. Sit down and talk with them about a new opportunity.

Your Favorite Sports Teams Do It

Don't doubt yourself. Don't be tempted to tell yourself, "I can't do that. I can't go and hire away someone who is working for another company. It's just not right."

If that's the case, prepare to be very frustrated and unable to grow your company.

Just like a top sports team cannot get any better without constantly attracting top athletes, your company cannot grow without its "A" and "A+" players.

And don't count on attracting these "A" players through the Want Ads of the local newspaper. Why? They are already working for someone. You need to go find them!

"No" Does Not Mean "No" (In This Case)

Persistence pays off.

Most "A" players are not willing to leave their jobs on a whim. They are generally being treated well and don't see a need to leave.

The timing needs to be right. In many instances, it might take you months to get a great player to come join your team. It can be quite the task—phone calls, lunches, dinners, and more.

The time will come when the door opens for you if you've been persistent in recruiting the "A" players. Work slows down from time to time. Many of their employers, who don't recognize how lucky they are to have that "A" player, don't hang onto them during these slow times for one reason or another.

If you stay in touch with these "A" players, you can always count on a time when they will have something happen at work that will cause them to want to entertain other offers.

Keep Your Roster

In my own business, I have always kept a list of people who I stay in touch with in order to be ready to have them join us when the timing is right. There will come a time when the right opportunity comes up for both of us and the "A" player is ready to listen.

Patience is the key.

Danger, Will Robinson!

Don't be naïve. Your own "A" players are being stalked by your competition. People offer them jobs once every month or so.

Sometimes they entertain these offers and sometimes they don't.

Their decision to listen or not is 100% determined by how you are treating them.

Are they well compensated? Appreciated? Challenged? Do they see a long-term future in your organization? If not, chances are they will be leaving you soon.

Recruiting the Normal Way

Craigslist

Craigslist is simple and it's free. It is a great way to gather a bunch of names of people who were sitting at home looking for work.

Keep in mind, though, that if there are 50 people applying for the job, there are only 10 who are probably worth talking to and only two or three who are worth hiring. Those two or three worth hiring may not want to work for you.

Newspapers

Do newspapers work for recruiting? The answer to that is, "it depends." It depends on your local area and culturally where people go to look for jobs. For example, when I was a partner at Platinum Capital, a nationwide mortgage bank, we would run ads in the *Orange County Register*. Why? Because everyone in that industry looked in the *Orange County Register* to find a mortgage job. Because it was that newspaper where the applicants looked for jobs, there was a war among all the major mortgage companies to see who could make the biggest and best employment wanted ad.

Depending on where you are located, advertising in classified advertising sections in newspapers can result in you obtaining responses from a long list of people who say they are willing to work for you. These ads can be expensive and, just like Craigslist, may require a ton of energy because typically only 1 in 50 people who apply are worthwhile enough to interview.

Here are a few points to keep in mind about newspapers:

- **Geography**—What is the geography covered by the newspaper? San Diegans can get the *Los Angeles Times* delivered to their door, but that does not mean that you should advertise your San Diego restaurant job in the *Los Angeles Times*? There are simply not enough San Diego *Los Angeles Times* readers to make it worth your while. And, maybe even more importantly, San Diego job applicants are not looking in Los Angeles newspapers for San Diego jobs.

- **Demographics**—The *Wall Street Journal* is a great newspaper. Based on the readership of the *WSJ*, you may be wasting your money to advertise your construction job there.

- **Employment sections**—Check out the employment sections of the newspaper you are considering using. If there is a large section for retail jobs, chances are this may be a place where others have had success advertising for retail positions. If there are no postings for your type of job, choose another course of action.

- **Small local newspapers**—If your business serves only the community in which it is located, try your local community newspaper first. These local papers are typically read cover to cover by members of the community.

Career Websites

Career sites are best suited when hiring for jobs that require a college education.

They tend to be expensive and the results are similar to what you'd expect to receive from Craigslist, newspapers, and the like.

Here are some of the most common career sites as well as some unique, specialized sites to illustrate just how varied career sites have become.

Monster.com

Monster.com's job postings allow employers to:

- *Post a job in minutes:* Fill out a simple form with key criteria, enter your job description, and submit!

- *Reach qualified candidates:* Leverage the power of Monster—17.9 million adults age 18+ in the United States have used Monster to search for jobs at least once per month.

- *Drive targeted, local traffic to your jobs:* Monster has newspaper partnerships with more than 420 daily and weekly papers in the United States, doubling job seeker reach in local markets. Newspaper partners have a combined readership of over 17 million people and over 40 million unique website visitors each month.

- *Filter responses online:* Monster's free hiring tools help you filter and rank your responses so that you can focus on the most qualified candidates first.

- *Add screening questions:* Do you have a must-have requirement? Qualify your candidates through Monster's free screening tools that display your custom questions to all applicants.

- *Manage candidates online:* Use Monster's free résumé-management tools to manage, contact, and track candidates online.

Purchase options

Purchase as needed: Purchase your online job posting and publish instantly.

Purchase in advance: Save by purchasing multiple job postings at once—jobs are good for one year from the date of purchase.

Power Résumé Search

Monster's Power Résumé Search feature precisely matches job seekers to your opportunities as it:

- Interprets the meaning behind words and concepts rather than relying on narrow, literal meaning of keywords

- Prioritizes candidates with the most recent experience

- Sorts and ranks candidates with the best matches on top

- Displays candidates side-by-side for quick comparisons

- Provides flexibility to easily broaden or narrow search criteria

- Integrates with Monster's powerful candidate management tools

CareerBuilder.com

More than 9,000 websites make up CareerBuilder's partnership network, including 140 newspapers, numerous niche and diversity sites like Univision, BlackCareers, and DisabilityJobs.org, and broadband sites like MSN and AOL, which feature CareerBuilder's proprietary job search technology on their career sites.

Additionally, partnerships with social networking sites such as Facebook and YouTube, a widespread presence on Twitter, and CareerBuilder's own talent community, BrightFuse, further CareerBuilder's reach in a rapidly growing social media landscape.

Wide Reach

CareerBuilder offers a vast online and print network to help job seekers connect with employers. It offers direct, real-time access to more than 24.8 percent of the U.S. work force and 98 percent of the Fortune 1,000.

Industry Specialization

CareerBuilder employs experts in a wide range of vertical markets such as construction, education, engineering/science, finance, insurance, banking, healthcare, hospitality, HR/diversity, IT/telecommunications, legal, manufacturing, oil and gas, public sector, restaurant, retail, sales, and transportation. These experts know which trade publications, niche websites, and other forms of media the candidates in your specific industry are using to search for their next opportunity.

But Wait, There's More...

Career/job websites have multiplied like rabbits over the last few years. They have started to become sites that cater to specific niches. Here are a few of them.

TheLadders.com

Looking to fill a job that pays over $100K or want to hire someone who thinks they are worth that much money? Try TheLadders.com.

Snagajob.com

Looking to hire someone for your restaurant? Try Snagajob.com.

Foodservice.com

This is another fun site for restaurant employee hiring.

Hcareers.com

This site specializes in jobs for hospitality workers.

WorkInRetail.com

Whether your goal is to successfully staff stores, fill management positions, or hire corporate leaders, WorkInRetail.com has the retail candidates for you. (Can you tell this is directly from its website?)

AllRetailJobs.com

AllRetailJobs.com is the largest career and recruiting board designed for retail. AllRetailJobs.com is appropriate for hiring and recruiting top-quality corporate/district/regional executives, store and assistant store managers, buyers, merchandisers, as well as sales and part-time associates.

AllRetailJobs.com is user friendly and has one of the most advanced search engines on the Internet. AllRetailJobs.com is the only retail job board selected by Weddles, the recognized expert on Internet recruiting sites, in its list of best sites for every year from 2002 to 2010. Over 12,500 employers and recruiters have registered for advertising and recruiting services on AllRetailJobs.com.

AllRetailJobs.com provides unique recruiting tools, including Job Cloning and Candidate Tracker, which reduce time in posting jobs and in reviewing and managing applicants' résumé responses.

MechanicJobs.com

This site attracts top Mechanic Services professionals by offering the most relevant career opportunities in their field. Connect with this highly-specialized audience with MechanicJobs.com's comprehensive recruitment solutions.

ConstructionJobs.com

ConstructionJobs.com is the nation's premier employment job board and résumé database built exclusively for the construction, design, and building industries.

The site provides targeted candidate searches by geographic region, specific industries, job titles, education, and experience. It is free to job seekers and available to employers at various subscription fees.

Dice.com

Dice.com is the leading career website for technology and engineering professionals and the companies that seek to employ them, in the United States.

This site is designed for the specific needs of technology professionals, enabling them to perform highly targeted job searches based on specific criteria, including location, type of employment, skillset and keyword. Dice.com also provides job search tools such as search agents, résumé posting, and career-related content. The job postings available in the Dice.com database, from both technology and non-technology companies across many industries, include a wide variety of technology positions for software engineers, systems administrators, database specialists, and project managers, and a variety of other technology and engineering professionals.

Dice.com provides specific tools and resources to help recruiters and human resources managers improve the effectiveness of their recruitment processes. The résumé database search capabilities allow customers to quickly and efficiently find candidates with specialized skill sets that match desired criteria. Due to this site's exclusive focus on the technology industry, employers can find results faster and easier than on other, less targeted services.

Fishing-Jobs.com

This site is focused entirely on jobs in the commercial fishing industry. This site provides advice on a range of issues such as:

- Details on the processes of commercial fishing
- Information on working conditions and salaries
- A broad listing of fishing industry employers, along with details on training requirements and training recommendations to ensure you meet the entry-level requirement
- Instructions on what to do next to secure a job as a Commercial Fishermen

Get the Point?

Basically no matter what industry you are in, there is a dedicated website set up for hiring. I am not by any means endorsing any of these sites. This is meant to show you how recruiting on the web has evolved.

Here are a couple of points to keep in mind before you use the web as a recruiting tool.

Research

Don't be fooled by a slick website (you probably have one as well…). Do your research, talk to industry partners, and see what has worked for them. Utilizing your local industry association to do this research is one of the great values you, as a member, receive from it.

Price

Compare prices and ask for a deal! These sites can be very expensive and, depending on the economy, may be willing to cut you a deal.

Is Bigger Better?

Big-name sites might not have the local reach that you need. Test their résumé search to give you an idea of how many people are using the site from your location.

Expect a Flood

A lot of online job searchers will simply email a copy of their résumé to every posting in their local area (their motivation, sometimes, is just so they can get on CNN and say, "I have applied for 2,000 jobs and only got four interviews). Be prepared to weed through hundreds of résumés from people who don't fit the bill.

Needle in a Haystack

This is a long process. Don't skip any steps. Online recruiting can be like searching for a needle in a haystack. All of that said, I have successfully hired people from many of these sites. (Well, except for the fishing-jobs.com site, but after all I do own a painting business!)

Friends of Friends

My favorite way to find future employees is to talk to friends or to people who are already working for you. They may know someone who is looking for a job in your industry.

If your employees enjoy working with you and feel like the company has a future, they are generally willing to refer you to their friends.

Offering a hiring bonus of $200 or so is a nice incentive to have your people start thinking about whom they know. Make sure the bonus is paid only after someone has been with you for at least 90 days.

These referrals are pre-screened. Your employees do not want to embarrass themselves by having you hire one of their lazy friends.

Now, if you are getting referrals from your "D" and "F" players, all bets are off. Guess what caliber of worker they're going to recommend?

Screening Applicants: Hire Slow, Fire Fast

Hiring the first person who responds to your advertisement is generally a bad idea.

If you're doing this, go back and re-read the title of this chapter one more time: "Hire Slow, Fire Fast." Remember the dangers and costs of a bad hiring mistake?

Take the time to properly screen all of your qualified applicants. Do not allow yourself to get rushed by an applicant who says he or she has another job offer. It is better to take the time to make the proper decision and risk losing one candidate than to rush to judgment and make a poor hiring decision.

The Screening Process

Here is a simple process to help you screen applicants.

Résumé Screening

In many cases, you will have hundreds of résumés. Here are a few tips to get you through the pile.

Relevant Experience

Do the applicants have relevant experience to the position or are they just sending out résumés?

Gaps in Employment

Do the applicants have large unexplained gaps in employment that would cause you to have questions about their consistency and reliability?

Job Jumping

Look to see if the résumé shows a new job every 8-24 months? Toss these people on the side, for now, as well. Even though they may have a good story as to why every job has not worked out, you can get back to them later. There is no need to take the chance on the same thing happening to you since you have this huge pile of résumés.

Typos on the Résumé

If the résumé has typos or spelling errors, and is generally disorganized, toss it aside. This should be telling you volumes about this person's attention to detail and desire to impress.

A/B/C

Sort the pile of applications into smaller piles of As, Bs, and Cs (evaluating each as to their worthiness of an interview).

Go through them one more time. Write notes and questions on the résumés.

Have someone else sort the pile as well and see what they think about your picks.

Narrow it down to 15 or so prospects.

Top 15: Phone Interviews

Pull out your top 15 applicants from the A pile. Put together your list of questions and call each 15. Your goal is to screen this list down to seven or eight people who you are willing to meet in person.

Think about the job for which you are hiring. Ask questions that are relevant and simple. Save the life and career questions for another day. Ask questions based on their résumés and job relevance. Listen carefully. If the person can't carry on a coherent conversation on the phone and you are hiring for sales or customers service, don't bother with an in-person interview.

In-Person Interviews

Once you have narrowed down your list of applicants to the top seven or eight individuals, it is time to call them in for in-person interviews.

Where?

In-person interviews can be held at your office or at any coffee shop in town. You just need to make sure that the environment is quiet enough and not too distracting to allow for a real conversation.

How Long?

Each interview will last anywhere between 30 minutes and two hours, depending on the job.

Hourly wage jobs may not require as much time, but if you are looking for people who will have positions of responsibility, you will want to take a greater amount of time.

Salespeople and other management roles require multiple interviews by different managers in your organization. In our organization, all positions require applicants to be interviewed by at least two people. In the cases of management or sales positions, they may be interviewed several times by as many as four different people.

Questions

There are dozens and dozens of books and websites that outline what questions to ask during an interview. There are also many schools of thought on how and what to ask. Do your research and find out what best suits you. For those of you who would prefer an easy roadmap, the sidebar outlines what I use.

> **TYPES OF QUESTIONS**
>
> *Last job questions*: These questions are tailored around what they liked and did not like about their last jobs and, more importantly, how they liked their last employer and co-workers.
>
> *Skills-based questions*: These are the basic nuts and bolts questions that allow you to ascertain if they know how to do the job for which you are hiring.
>
> *Motivation questions*: The "what makes them tick" questions. These are designed to see what they want out of life and what their goals are. For example, if someone's goal is to be a police officer and they are applying for a sales job, does it make sense to hire them and invest in training? The second they get accepted to the police academy, they will be gone. It pays to find this out in the interview, not two months later when they're off to shoot guns.
>
> *Open-ended questions*: All of your questions should be open ended; meaning they should not be able to be answered with a simple "yes" or "no" response. Each question should require the applicants to have to think and explain themselves.

Listen Carefully

Every answer that an applicant gives you holds the clue as to what to ask next. If you listen closely enough, you will be able to find something about the answer that will lead you to another question.

An interview is just like peeling the layers of an onion.

It's a Two-Way Street!

An interview is a two-way street.

Why should this person come to work with *you*? What makes you and your organization special? Why do your customers buy from you?

Part of the interview is to present them with your company commercial. Once you feel comfortable that you are sitting in front of someone who you want to hire, be prepared to sell them on why they should join you. You want them leaving the interview with a great desire to join your company.

No matter how bad the economy is, A players will not be out on the street for long. They will always have options.

You are not the only one who is hiring right now.

Regardless of what you see on the evening news, companies are still hiring and the best of the best have options.

Offsite Interviews

If you are hiring for a management or sales position, you should conduct the interview away from the office. Choose a location that will allow the candidates to relax and be themselves. A golf game for some works great. Meeting for lunch or dinner at your favorite restaurant usually provides the right atmosphere.

The goal here is to get the individual to drop their "interview guard" and be themselves. I could bore you (but I won't) with countless stories of how these offsite meetings have saved me and many of my friends from making the wrong hiring decision. It is amazing what you learn over a casual dinner and a glass of wine.

On-the-Job Trials

Every top candidate for your key jobs should spend a half-day on the job with some of your key employees. In our sales group, for example, all prospective salespeople are required to go on a half-day ride along with one of our top salespeople.

Doing this serves two purposes. First, your top people will give you valuable input as to the overall ability of the candidate. And, second, the candidate will get a real sense of whether they are a fit for the job, and if they will enjoy it.

Résumé Checks

For many years, I did not believe in résumé checks. However, now, after doing some checks of applicants, I am a huge believer.

Reference Checks

Many people, who seemed so great in the interview, are not really as great as you thought. They may show well, but have no substance to back them up. These people will have difficulty supplying you with "glowing" recommendations from anyone other than their mother.

Everyone should be able to give the names of 10-20 people who they have worked with or have known over the years who can give recommendations about themselves. I truly believe this. Think about it for a minute. If you are like me (and you probably are), if someone asked for a reference I would say "sure, how about I give you 20 and when you are done with that list, I will give you 20 more." I can play the game until they get tired of asking. "I do not even need to call and prep these people, just call them and say that you know me. They will chat with you."

Most of you who are reading this book would be able to do the exact same thing. So why is it so hard to for some candidates to come up with three people for you to call? I think you know the answer!

When checking references, I am always surprised when someone says, "Hey, he is a great person, but I don't see him in that type of role." It happens more often than you would imagine!

Employee Screening: Background Checks

Criminal Checks

Do a criminal background check on everyone you hire. There are plenty of sites on the Internet that will allow you to run a background check for as little as $40. Pay the $40 and don't make the mistake I had to learn the hard way.

Credit Checks

If you are hiring someone who will be handling your money, it is not out of the question to require a credit check. After all, do you really want a bookkeeper who is down on her luck and behind on her mortgage? Those cash-filled tills are simply too tempting for those desperate to keep the water turned on at home.

Driving

In the event you are hiring someone who will be driving a company vehicle, make sure you get a DMV report. You cannot afford to have bad drivers behind the wheels of your company vehicles.

Drugs

Drug testing can be beneficial and many companies do it. Some of those doing the hiring simply don't want to know whether this great applicant has dependency issues. Depending on the job you are hiring for, though, it may be critical to make sure your employees are drug free.

Talk to Your HR Professional

Keep in mind that there are many questions that you cannot ask and some tests that you cannot do when making hiring decisions. Talk to your HR professional to make sure you know and understand the laws in your state.

To Summarize

One of the most important roles that you have as CEO of your business is to make sure that you have "the right people in the right seats" (to steal a line from *Good to Great*, one of my favorite business books).

It is your responsibility to hire correctly or to design the system that everyone who does the hiring will follow. This will ensure that you are hiring top-notch talent who will be happy within your organization and produce to your satisfaction level.

Remember: Recruit, don't hire! And hire slow, fire fast.

Chapter 8

It's Your Time, Use It Wisely

Delegation is the key to a happy life.

Delegation can be broken down into two important categories:

- Realizing your weaknesses
- Getting help when you need it

Realize Your Weaknesses

There are things that you should not do because others can do them better.

Realizing your weaknesses is as important as understanding where your talents lie.

For instance, I am not detail-oriented; therefore, it is important that I surround myself with people who are great with details.

I have tons of new ideas; just don't ask me to implement them without a team of people to clean up after me.

I am not very good with money, so I have a top-notch CFO, controller, and accounting team (not to mention how I'd be a credit nightmare if my wife didn't manage our household bills).

Spend the time to figure out what you are really great at and, then, where your weaknesses are. Surround yourself with people who can fill in the gaps where you are lacking.

Get Help

There are things you should not do because it is better to hire someone else to do them.

We all know how this works.

Should you be sweeping the floors at the close of business when you can pay someone less than $10 an hour to do it?

No one can do it as good as me!

This is one of the main reasons why small businesses stay small. The owners truly believe that no one can do the job as well as they can.

You may be right. No one can do the job better than you. You win! Your prize is a lifetime of having a one-person business that may not allow you to ever take time off to spend with your family.

It may be that you actually have a couple of employees, but you still want to be on top of every little detail. You just don't trust your people to do much more than take out the trash (and that is only when you are supervising). This scenario means you are working 80-hour weeks and are not enjoying a balanced life. Congratulations! If you listen carefully, you can hear a very tiny violin playing just for you.

It is hard to watch someone mess up something that you would have done perfectly. Your new employees will invariably make mistakes that you would never make. You have based your business reputation on the quality of your product or service. Regardless, you just must take the steps to give up some of the things you are currently doing. Some of these tasks are things that you enjoy doing and some that you don't think people can do as well.

The Delegation Process

1. The Easy Stuff

What tasks do you know of right now that should be done by someone else in your organization?

Make your list:

1. _____
2. _____
3. _____
4. _____
5. _____

2. Daily Log

List the tasks that you do on a daily basis in a basic log:

Monday

7:00 am: _____

7:30 am: _____

8:00 am: _____

8:30 am: _____

Continue for each hour of your work day. Repeat this for each day of the week.

You get the point. Create a diary of your activities for a minimum of one week (ideally for two weeks). Be fanatical about writing down everything that you spend your time doing.

3. Analyze Your Diary

Now take your week or two of information and go through the pages. Be objective. How do you really spend your time? You're probably a little surprised. Are you starting to see a pattern? Are there tasks you seem to do more often than you thought that might be better assigned to someone else?

4. Highest and Best Use

What is your highest and best use as a business owner? If you had all the right people, what would you be spending your time on? (Vacation is not the correct answer for this one.)

Make a list of the five top activities that you should be spending more time on in your business. (Here's a hint: The "Big Five" are in this book!)

1. _____
2. _____
3. _____
4. _____
5. _____

5. Give Up Something: Baby Steps

This part is tough. Give up something you do all the time that is not your highest and best use, but is something you don't think others can do as well as you. Don't give up something that is of critical importance to the business, just something that you are holding onto because, well, you are just holding onto it.

6. It's All About the Hand-Off

Many attempts at delegation fail because instead of actually taking the time to hand off the task with proper documentation and training, business owners simply give the task to their employees and walk away. This type of delegation invariably fails. The owners pull back the task and gloat about being right; no one can do things as well as they can and delegation does not work.

Take the time to document the steps in the task or project that you are handing off. Spend the time to train your protégée. Watch them do it and give them feedback.

7. Walk Away

Once you have documented the process and trained the employees, you need to walk away and let them do the job you trained them to do. Give them some space. Of course, you will come back to check on their progress from time to time—just no hovering!

8. Expect Mistakes

Those with the delegated tasks, in the beginning, will not be able to do the task as well as you can. They will make mistakes. Some of these mistakes will cost you money. Try to remember back when you were just starting out. How many mistakes did you make?

As these mistakes are being made, evaluate whether they are making the same mistake over and over again or are making new mistakes.

If they are making the same mistake over and over again, it is either a training issue or an issue that you delegated to the wrong person. If this isn't working, the issue isn't that you should not have delegated the task, it is simply that you may have delegated the task to the wrong person. If it is not one of your Big Five, someone else should do it.

If they are making different mistakes each time, you are on the right track. Eventually they will run out of new mistakes that can be made and they will be ready for a new task!

9. Repeat

(Some important lists only go to nine, so pay attention!)

Now that you have taken your first baby step, it is time to take another task off of your plate. Keep repeating the process until you spend your time either training or working on your Big Five.

Steps to Freedom

For those of you who need a little more convincing, here is another way to look at the reason you need to delegate.

First...

Figure out how much money you believe you should realistically make or want to make during a 12-month period.

Let's say the number is $100K, or maybe $250K.

Second...

Take that number and divide it by 2,000.

This will give you a very close approximation to the hourly wage that you are worth. $100K per year is roughly $50 an hour and $250K is roughly $125 an hour.

Third...

Here is the easy step. Hire people to do the jobs that are not up to your hourly wage.

In other words, if the task would cost you $25 an hour, you should be paying someone else to do the job.

All of this is simple and is obviously not the first time you have heard it. It's the fourth—and most important step of the process—that most people mess up.

If you don't do the fourth step perfectly, you will end up making a lot less money than the people you are employing for $10 an hour.

Fourth...

You need to make sure that your time is being spent doing the tasks that warrant your decided pay level.

Tasks that are worth the bigger bucks are generally tasks that have to do with driving your business. Jobs like marketing your business, making sales calls, managing multiple crews, and developing your business.

Tasks that will quickly have you making less than your employees would be things like surfing the Internet or napping in your office and thinking about how you should really get out there and do something productive today.

Remember, in order for all of this to come together, you need to spend 40+ hours a week on real tasks that drive your business.

Your business will fail if you do not have the discipline to spend your time on the larger priorities in your company. Simply hiring people so you can do less is a surefire recipe for failure.

As a business owner, you need to have the discipline that your employees may not have. You need to have the drive that others don't.

You need to be focused on what's important while others are playing or not paying attention.

If you don't think you can do this on your own, go get a job elsewhere and save yourself a trip to bankruptcy court.

Your Organizational Chart

Now that you have mastered the art of delegation, it is time to move on to the big leagues. It's time to think about your organizational chart. Your *org chart* is essentially a chart with all the people who work in your company and who they currently report to. You, of course, will be on the top of that chart.

Figure 8.1 shows an example organizational chart.

Now, think about your organization as it stands today. What does your org chart look like? Take a moment and sketch it out. It doesn't have to be pretty. Pencil on napkin works fine at this stage.

Take a look at your organizational chart. In some cases, it may just be you all by yourself in a square at the top. In other cases, it may be you and just a few other people. Adding boxes is the natural evolution of any business. In still other cases, the chart is you and 10 or more other people. That chart could contain several layers of management while other businesses may have everybody reporting directly to you.

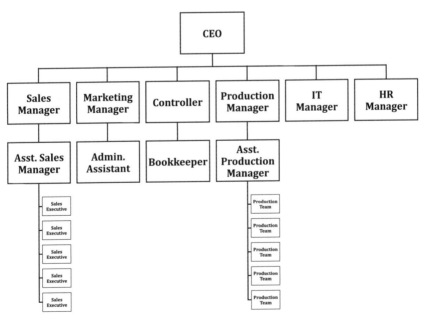

Figure 8.1 *Sketch out your company's org chart—pencil on napkin will do at this stage.*

However your org chart looks, it is intended simply to be a snapshot of how your business looks today. It does not mean your business will always look like this. That choice is up to you. Here are a few things to think about in your organization.

Think About Delegation

Are you doing too many things? Are your fingerprints all over everything in the business? Does everything require your approval before it gets finished?

How Many People Report Directly to You?

One of the major challenges with businesses as they grow is that the owner/founder has too many direct reports. There are many studies done on the optimum number of direct reports. The optimum number can vary from industry to industry. In general, most people can properly manage five to eight direct reports. When the number starts to go over eight, your time becomes too stretched and it can become difficult for you to give your people the time they need.

Having no more than eight direct reports tends to be most efficient, however, there is some sway in the number. For instance, if all of your direct reports are A^{++} players, you could, in theory, have 10 or more direct reports. A^{++} players don't need to be micro-managed and therefore do not need as much of your time. However, if you have the other extreme and have loaded your team with C, D, and maybe F players, you can end up with two direct reports and no time to get anything done.

Take a Look at Your Direct Reports

You have already graded them in Chapter 7, but when you see them in the org chart, do you feel the same way about how you graded them? If you do, great. If not, it may be time to start recruiting.

The Fun Part: Looking Ahead

Think about your business and what it will look like two years from now.

This is sometimes hard to do, but give it a try anyway. Be realistic. How much business do you think you will do in two years? Got a number? Good. Now look at your existing org chart. Can the structure you created there support that amount of business?

There are two possible answers to that question.

Yes

If you answered "yes," you have one of two challenges. You are either over-staffed today or you are not growing your business.

If you are overstaffed, take a hard look at your business model and profitability. Make sure you are staffed at the appropriate levels for the amount of business that you are doing.

If you are not planning to grow, heed this caution. Businesses rarely stay the same. They are constantly in motion. They either expand or shrink; they typically do not stay the same. In the event that your revenues do stay the same in two years, it is unlikely that your profits will remain the same as well. They usually shrink.

No

Congratulations. "No" is the correct answer. If you are in the early stages of growth in your business, it is reasonable to say that as you grow you will need to staff accordingly. (You will reach a certain point as your company matures where your goal will be to do more with the same or less people, but that is a little later down the road.)

Future Staffing Needs

Now let's get back to the org chart. What does it need to look like in two years for you to hit your goal? Do you need:

- More salespeople?
- A bookkeeper or controller?
- An assistant manager?
- A manager?
- New front-line people?

What kinds of employees do you need in order to take the company to the next level?

Where do your existing people fit in? Will they be in the same roles they are in today? Will they be promoted? Do they fit in at all?

When do you need to have the new people in their new roles? Is it three months? Six months? Nine months?

What trigger points would cause you to say, "Yes, things are going right and I need to take the next step and hire the next person?"

Next Steps

Now that you have taken the time to design your organization and forecast its look in two years, it is time to do the same exercise in four years and six years. You may view this as a bit of a stretch, but if you spend the time and update your org charts every three months, it will make planning for your future a much easier process.

Summary

Your business will not grow if you try to do everything yourself. The overall growth and success of your business depend on your ability to delegate tasks to your employees as well as your ability to plan for the employees you will need in the future.

Chapter 9

Customers

For far too many small business owners, the customer is the biggest hurdle that stops them from enjoying their favorite pastime—running their businesses.

Now, of course, not everyone looks at their customers this way, but let's be honest—we all have had those days or weeks when it feels like those pesky people just get in our way.

Every Customer Has at Least One Friend

The most successful small businesses understand that they have failed to fully satisfy a customer if that one customer interaction does not turn into two or three referrals.

Just drive down your street.

How many of the people in your neighborhood will need your service or product in the next year? If you really think about it, the majority of people in your own neighborhood need your product or service now or will need it in the future. They are going to buy; the question is will they buy from you?

We have already covered the importance of referrals in your marketing mix, so let's talk about how you make sure you get them.

The 11 Rules of Customer Service

1. Call Me Back, Please!

The most important reason why customers lose that loving feeling is because you don't call them back in a timely manner.

The most important thing to remember here is that you respond *immediately* when a customer calls you, emails you, or texts you.

It is no longer acceptable to wait until the end of the day or end of the week to respond to a customer's inquiry. In today's day and age, our customers are used to getting the answers to their questions instantly.

If Google can tell them how many penguins live on the South Pole in 2.6 seconds, they feel you should be able to return their phone call, email, or text within at least 30 minutes.

Yes, You Do Need To Be Able To Text

One of the keys to amazing customer relations is communicating in a format that makes your customers most comfortable.

Texting is not just for teenagers anymore. Texting has been around for enough years now that a bunch of those teenagers are now young home-owners. And many of the parents of those teenagers found it a great way to stay in touch with their children. Having discovered texting, adults now use it daily to communicate efficiently and effectively with friends, family, and co-workers.

Texting a customer who loves to communicate in this manner is like speak-ing the native language to those we meet on foreign vacations. It makes a very favorable impression.

Communication is vital. Find your customer's preferred method of commu-nication and embrace it! Some prefer email, in-person daily chats, phone calls, texting, or a combination of the aforementioned.

Be ready and be aware.

Communication Is Key

A key to a happy customer relationship is communication. The more you talk to your customers and the more you keep them informed of what you are doing the happier they will be.

It isn't possible to over-communicate with your customers. If they ever feel you are making too much contact, they'll not be shy about telling you. But, that almost never happens. Feel free to email me and tell me that someone actually told you to stop keeping them informed about the progress of their project.

2. Liar, Liar

Your customers know when you and your employees are not telling the truth. Even if you are a world-class poker player, you will get caught fibbing to your customers if you lie. "I'm sorry, so and so is not in right now" or "We are out of that product, but we do have this more expensive version available." All the little white lies that tend to become common practice are a slippery slope to the bigger damaging lies that lose us customers. Create a zero-tolerance policy for lying in your organization. If need be, make an example and fire someone for breaking the rules.

3. Do What You Say You Are Going To Do

Keeping your promises is what customers want to see and hear. If you say you are going to deliver a product on a specific date, do it. If you have something special on the menu, don't run out of it! Customers will remember something as simple as "The last time I ate at that Mexican restaurant they ran out of tortillas! Let's try this one instead." Customers treat your menus as an implied promise or contract. Or, "The dry cleaner promised to bag all my shirts separately; what's this mess?"

Don't underestimate the negative effects of broken promises.

4. Everything Rolls Down Hill

Your employees will treat your customers the way that you treat them. If you treat your employees with respect, that is how they will treat your customers. If you treat them poorly, do not be surprised when they do the same thing to your customers.

5. The Best Generals Are on the Front Lines with Their Men

If you want to provide the best customer service, you and your managers must accessible to your customers.

The job of your "front line" employees is not the same as the job of a "front line" infantry soldier. Their job is not to keep the enemy from breaking through and getting to you! Remember, very few issues will frustrate customers more than their inability to get to someone with real decision-making power.

Think about the last time you were on the phone with your mobile phone service. How many times did you get passed from India to the Caribbean and back again, still without a solution to your issue? You have spent a half hour with all of these folks and you're still stuck having to leave your name and number for a supervisor who you can only hope has the authority to make a decision.

Remember, lead from the front. Show your employees how to disarm and take care of a challenging customer. Don't let your management team hide from customers. You and your senior team should try taking turns on the front lines, just to make sure you still truly understand the issues that your customers face with your company.

6. Show You Care

You may not be able to fix the problem in every case, but you can do something to show you care.

Most customers just want to know that they were heard and that you have offered something to show that you care. In the ideal world, we would all be like the Ritz Carlton hotel chain. Their employees have the approval to spend up to a certain amount of company money in order to make a customer happy. You can only imagine how high that pre-approved limit is for Ritz employees. It may give you heartburn to match that amount in your own business.

How about Nordstrom? We have all heard the stories (possibly myths) that Nordstrom will take back any product no matter how much time has passed since the "purchase." They'll take back items they didn't even sell you just say, "I bought it here and I don't like it anymore." I have heard the stories of people taking back 10-year-old shoes in exchange for a new pair. My personal favorite is the fable about a guy who returned a set of tires (Nordstrom does not even sell tires) and getting store credit to go buy something else. Thinking about having a similar policy at your store may also give you heartburn.

Heartburn

Here is a story that gives me real indigestion. I was in South Beach at a local restaurant. I was having dinner with 10 of my top people. We were having fun enjoying the Miami atmosphere when our meals arrived.

I had ordered a meal with shrimp. When I took the first bite, the shrimp tasted very fishy—it just did not taste very good at all. I called my waiter over and complained. He responded by shrugging his shoulders in the universal sign of all poorly trained front-line folks and responded by saying it seemed fine. I, in turn, asked him to send over the manager.

A few minutes passed until the manager came over, obviously annoyed that I had interrupted her evening. I explained to her what my issue was and she said, "I had the shrimp earlier tonight and there is nothing wrong with it." I looked at her as if I had seen a ghost (which, if she worked for me, she would have immediately been the ghost of employees past) and told her once again that the food was unacceptable. She made a little huffing noise and said she would be right back.

I continued to steal food off of my friends' plates as about 10 more minutes passed. Eventually, I flagged her down again and she reluctantly came over to the table. This little disagreement now digressed into a small melee as she told me there was nothing wrong with my meal and I told her she was the absolute worst restaurant manager that I had ever met. Using your wildest imagination about the rest of the conversation gives you a picture of what the rest of the "discussion" looked like.

What did this manager have to lose by simply replacing my meal with another? The lost tip alone was much more than what it would have cost her to toss the shrimp and bring me the pasta. And the others in the restaurant could not have been impressed with the way we were being treated. What an incredibly absent-minded approach to running a business. This story still gives me indigestion.

Please the Customer

Even if you cannot afford to be the Ritz Carlton or Nordstrom, you can still find a way to efficiently take care of your customers and show them that you care about the inconveniences that you may (or may not) have caused.

I was at a Denny's for breakfast with my family. We had been in San Francisco all week and the seven of us (yes, I have a big family) were grabbing breakfast before making the eight-hour drive home.

Our breakfast took almost 50 minutes to arrive at the table. Multiple groups who had been seated after us had been served, had already eaten, and had left. When our food arrived, I told our waitress how disappointed I was. She immediately apologized and went to get the manager.

The manager came right over and said, "Sir, I am sorry for your inconvenience, while I cannot give you the time back that you lost here today, I do want to apologize and take 50% off your bill as a gesture of our appreciation of you as a customer."

She was right; she could never give me back the time that my family lost in that restaurant. However it's not like I had a horrible time hanging out with my wife and kids (the eight-hour car ride is another story).

The point is that Denny's and this manager made an effort to satisfy us and they apologized. People make mistakes. Most reasonable people in the world recognize that. They are willing to forgive and forget—especially if the one who erred is congenial and offers some sort of simple gesture.

I will eat breakfast again at Denny's with my family. I, however, will never, ever step foot in that South Beach restaurant.

As in the Denny's story, it does not take much effort to change someone's negative impression of your business.

SOOTHING DISGRUNTLED CUSTOMERS

What do you currently do to sooth customers who have had a poor experience at your place of business?

When something small happens?

1. _____
2. _____
3. _____

When you really mess up?

1. _____
2. _____
3. _____

How about having on hand something like:

- A Starbucks gift card
- Movie tickets
- Blockbuster gift card
- Free oil change
- Flowers
- Dinner out on you

Do all of your employees know that they have the authority to take care of customers in this way without needing to ask for approval?

---

7. The Job Site: Hey! Someone Lives Here!

I am constantly amazed by the way some service companies forget that their job site is actually someone's home.

That home is also one of the most important things in that family's life. In fact if you had to rank their most cherished things it would go something like this:

1. Kids
2. Spouse
3. House
4. Pets
5. TV
6. Car
7. Etc.

There are even some people who put their homes as number one on the list, cars as number two, and, well, you get the idea.

If a service business misses this point, they'll definitely not do not do a good job of getting their employees to treat the job site as someone's castle.

Off with Their Heads!

Everyone on your crews must understand that one of the top five career-losing moves is to disrespect your customer's home.

Everyone from you, the owner, to the helper who sweeps up at the close of the day must not treat the job site as they would their own home (we all know why this is a bad strategy).

In keeping with the "castle" theme, they must treat it as if a King or Queen lives in that castle. If they disrespect the space in any manner, it will mean the gallows for them.

A Mess by Any Other Name...

A mess is a mess is a mess—all grounds for firing.

KEEPING THE JOB SITE TIDY

1. All tools and supplies that are brought into or around a customer's home must be clean and organized.
2. Drop cloths should always be placed on the floor or ground, with all tools and supplies on top.
3. Paper booties need to be worn at all times in a customer's home.
4. All debris is to be cleaned up immediately, placed in trash bags, and taken off-site. Do not use the customer's trash containers.
5. Never leave lunch or snack wrappers, pop cans, and so on, at the job site.
6. Always perform a full clean-up at the end of every day. No exceptions.
7. Don't leave the little stuff until the end of the job; clean up as you go.
8. Always ask first about using bathroom facilities. Do not assume you can use them.

Job Site Cleanliness = Job Quality

Customers will always make the assumption that the cleaner, neater, and more organized the job looks during the work process, the better quality the job is in the end.

When customers see a disorganized mess of a job site, they automatically assume that the quality of the job is in question and therefore they must "micromanage" the process themselves.

When this happens, your customers suddenly seem to be around a lot more than they were at the beginning of the job, they ask a lot more questions and seem to be asking for a job that was not the same one that you thought you signed up for. All of that can be avoided. Keep the place clean and organized!

SHARP-EDGED TOOLS AND OTHER DANGERS TO THINK ABOUT

Sometimes it is the simple things that get missed.

- Leaving tools lying around the job site where kids and pets can reach them.
- Chemicals left with the lid off for easy access to crew members and "Fluffy," the family cat.
- Ladders left, leaning against a wall, for just a moment while you run out to the truck.
- All things that are tons of fun for kids and pets, but not for you after those kids and pets discover them.

Magnifying Glasses

All customers own a huge magnifying glass and a set of binoculars that they choose to use or not use depending on how you treat their home throughout the job.

The minute customers feel that you are not to be trusted or that something is amiss in their home, they will go and grab their high-powered microscopes and turn them directly onto your job.

There isn't any project that can withstand that level of scrutiny.

If, by chance, your only crime is a messy job site, the next step is your customer questioning everything that you did or did not promise.

Lose, Lose

You will never win the battle of the messy job site. Your customers are right. They deserve a clean and neat home during the service process.

You will either stand up to this level of scrutiny or end up paying for it in the end. You'll end up with an unhappy customer who will not give referrals and/or spend money out of your own pocket to make the customer happy.

Either way you lose.

Remember: if your staff and crew do not understand this to be a top priority within your business, then "off with their heads!"

8. Say "Hello"

Customers want to feel welcome when they enter your place of business. Teach all of your employees (and yourself) how to say, "hello."

This may sound pretty basic; however, in many cases as we get busy with our day, the basics are the easiest to forget. Here are a few tips.

Keep Your Distance

Say hello from a distance. There is no need to infringe on personal space. If someone wants to shake your hand or give you a hug (doubtful), they will walk right up to you and make it clear.

Smile, Baby, Smile

I don't care how bad your day is or how challenging that customer may be that you are dealing with. Smile when you say hello!

Stop What You Are Doing

Even if you are right in the middle of something or with another customer, take a moment, say "excuse me" to the person you are with, and take two seconds to say "Hello, welcome to…." The customer you are dealing with will understand and will certainly not be offended.

Look at the Customer When You Say "Hello"

Don't stare at the floor, at the phone, or at the product on the wall when you say hello. Look at the customer and offer a genuine smile.

Practice

Practice in a mirror saying hello and thank you with a smile until it becomes second nature. Teach your employees to do the same.

9. Follow Up

If you tell customers you are going to email them some specification on a product they are interested in, or if you say you will call them back at a specific time, do exactly that. Most of us have such low expectations of customer service that we will not be surprised when you don't call back, but we will be amazed when you do. And isn't having amazed customers the thing that will make your business explode?

10. Take Notes

Taking copious notes when your customers are talking shows that you are really paying attention to what they are saying. Customers have much more confidence in you when you write down the details.

This is particularly true in the restaurant business. There are far too many restaurants that pride themselves on the fact that their wait staff does not need to write anything down. These waiters want to impress by making their customers believe they can remember the specifics of the six people at the table. Here comes the rant. Are you serious? Do you have any idea what we are all thinking at the table, as you *don't* write down our orders? Let me give you some insight. We can't wait to see whose order is screwed up this time. Sometimes we all take bets.

The feeling of wondering if my meal will show up as ordered is not what I want out of a dining experience. If you are that great with your memory, go ahead and join Mensa and impress your friends. Chances are that you are not that great, and taking orders by memory is just your own version of Sudoku or some other memory-improvement game. Please play with your memory on your own time, not during my night out.

End of rant.

I must say that little rant made me feel much better. Seriously though, no matter what business you are in, customers do not believe that your memory is perfect. They will much more confidence that the job is going to get done correctly if you write down the details.

11. Create a Customer Bill of Rights

Take the time with your team to design a *Customer Bill of Rights*. Write out what your customers can and should expect from you.

Consumer Bill of Rights

In 1962, President Kennedy created the consumer bill of rights. Here are the basics, once again thanks to our friends at Wikipedia.

The Right To Be Safe

The assertion of this right is aimed at the defense of consumers against injuries caused by products other than automobile vehicles, and implies that products should cause no harm to their users if such use is executed as prescribed. The Right was established in 1972 by the US federal government, the Consumer Product Safety Commission (CPSC) has jurisdiction over thousands of commercial products, and powers that allow it to establish performance standards, require product testing and warning labels, demand immediate notification of defective products, and, when necessary, to force product recall.

The Right To Choose Freely

The right to free choice among product offerings states that consumers should have a variety of options provided by different companies from which to choose. The federal government has taken many steps to ensure the availability of a healthy environment open to competition through legislation including limits on concept ownership through Patent Law, prevention of monopolistic business practices through Anti-Trust Legislation, and the outlaw of price cutting and gouging.

The Right To Be Heard

This right asserts the ability of consumers to voice complaints and concerns about a product in order to have the issue handled efficiently and responsively. While no federal agency is tasked with the specific duty of providing a forum for this interaction between consumer and producer, certain outlets exist to aid consumers if difficulty occurs in communication with an aggrieving party. State and federal Attorney Generals are equipped to aid their constituents in dealing with parties who have provided a product or service in a manner unsatisfactory to the consumer in violation of an applicable law. Also, the Better Business Bureau is a national non-governmental organization whose sole agenda is to provide political lobbies and action on behalf of aggrieved consumers.

The Right To Be Informed

This right states that businesses should always provide consumers with enough appropriate information to make intelligent and informed product choices. Product information provided by a business should always be complete and truthful. Aiming to achieve protection against misleading information in the areas of financing, advertising, labeling, and packaging, the right to be informed is protected by several pieces of legislation passed between 1960 and 1980.

The Right to Education

The right to have access to programs and information that help consumers make better marketplace decisions.

The Right to Service

This includes the right to convenience, to be treated with courtesy and respect, to responsiveness to needs and problems and to refuse any services offered.

Now It's Your Turn

What rights are you going to insist that your customers have? Be brave, write them out, and post these rights in your place of business. Ensure that your employees adhere to the rights on your list and evaluate them accordingly.

CUSTOMER BILL OF RIGHTS

Our customers have the right to: _____

_____

_____

Our customers have the right to: _____

_____

_____

Our customers have the right to: _____

_____

_____

Our customers have the right to: _____

_____

_____

Our customers have the right to: _____

_____

_____

Our customers have the right to: _____

_____

_____

Remember, all good lists go to eleven!

Chapter 10

Technology

Many small business owners try to run and hide anytime someone brings up technology. They're not interested in the latest gadget. The same cell phone they have had for the last six years works just fine, they keep telling themselves. Most of that cell phone's buttons still work (do they really need to call people whose phone number has a three in it?).

The first step into the 21st century is to stop being afraid of new technology. You are not too old or too set in your ways to learn how to use technology.

We live in a day and age where customers expect to have their phone calls, emails, and even their text messages returned immediately.

Customers simply don't understand why it would take more than a couple of hours to call them back or return their email.

The Technology Basics

Cell Phone

You need a good cell phone with all the basic options and you need to know how to use them.

Voice or Speed Dial

Keep your office phone numbers, including key employees, in your speed dial numbers. Also, if you have just a few clients, rotate your current customers into the speed dial numbers. The speed dial feature on your cell phone makes it much easier to call while on the road.

Camera

By having a cell phone with a built-in camera, you can easily snap a picture of work-related issues. From a problem area you want to show a customer to the finished project, you can quickly have it on "film".

Even better is a quick video of a finished project that you can send to a potential client's cell phone.

How about a video testimonial from a happy customer just to put up on your restaurant's website or Facebook page?

Text Messaging

Text messaging is not just for your teenage kids. It is a quick and easy way to communicate with your crews and customers.

Not all your customers text, but if they do, you better as well! You can pretty well assume that if they have a cell phone, they are capable of receiving texts. When you get customers' cell numbers, ask if they would like to receive text messages about their projects.

Many small businesses are now using texting as a way to market to their customers. For instance "Text 848 to 555-555-5555 for a coupon for 10% off your next purchase." These kinds of text ads are being promoted across many different industries. It fills the dual purpose of marketing for today and also gathering phone numbers of potential clients. However, always ask customers to opt in before sending out any marketing texts. Some cell plans charge for each text message so you do not want to assume that every customer wants to receive weekly text offers that will cost them as much as your coupon.

Having a slow lunch day? How about texting to your database a "free appetizer for today's lunch only"? What if you were to text an offer to your clients for a free upgrade on all oil changes, today only? The possibilities are endless.

Email

A good email address should consist of your name (first initial and last name or just first name, if possible). You don't want a series of numbers behind your name or something relating to your spare time like fishingguy@com. You want to look like a professional company, not a weekday hobby.

Be @yourcompany.com

Gmail, Yahoo, AOL, and others are great providers of email, but do not give the image of someone running a real company. When your email address is not *@yourcompany.com*, you give the impression that you are running a small, disorganized, out-of-the-back-of-your-car outfit. This is not the image you are trying to achieve (after all, you are reading this book).

Make It Easy To Remember

The easier to remember and the shorter your email address is, the better. Ideally, you should be able to tell potential clients your email address on the phone and they should have no trouble writing it down or remembering it.

Mobile Email

If you don't already have a Blackberry, iPhone, or equivalent PDA, go buy one right now. Seriously. Put down the book (it will be here when you get back) and go buy a smart phone. These phones allow you to read and reply to email as easily as if you were at your desktop computer.

Email has become a significant part of our daily work routine.

People expect their emails will be returned immediately, just like a phone call or a text. If you're busy, at least you are able to reply immediately with a quick note saying, "I will respond in detail tomorrow."

Choose your poison, but mobile access to email is just as important as a cell phone.

Smart Phone Options

Blackberry

Upside: The Blackberry PDF is the workhorse of the mobile email crowd. It is simple to use, has a keyboard, and has years of history. It is capable of saving thousands of emails on the device. The long battery life means that if you forget your charger, you will still make it through the day. The Blackberry is also available from most wireless carriers.

Downside: If you want to surf the web, play games, and see what cool new apps are out there, you are out of luck. Blackberries are a business-first device.

iPhone

Upside: The iPhone has web access and has access to tens of thousands of free or very inexpensive "apps." These apps range from business productivity applications to games, puzzles, and newsreaders. The iPhone is definitely great for entertaining yourself on airplanes or while waiting for meetings. It also has the "coolness" factor.

Downside: The iPhone has a couple of challenges. It has a short battery life, which means you always need to have a charger nearby. The lack of a physical keyboard can be a downside to some. Its email saves only 200 messages on the device, which means saving and searching past messages can take a little longer as the iPhone has to reach out to your email server to search old messages. The final downside is that the iPhone is currently only available on the AT&T network (although this will probably change soon).

Droid and Other Smart Phones

There are far too many smart phones on the market today for me to offer a full review of each one. New smart phones hit the market on an almost daily basis. Keep in mind that your primary need for a smart phone is mobile access to email—anything beyond that is for your personal enjoyment.

Email: More Basics

Signature Line

A surprising amount of business people forget to add a proper signature line to their emails. A signature line is another opportunity for you to market your company and make sure it is front and center in your customer's minds. It is also where many people will go to look for your phone number if they don't already have it saved somewhere. When your email sign off is just "Joe Smith," you are missing an opportunity.

SIGNATURE LINE

A good email signature line will have:

- Your name
- Your company name and preferably the logo too
- Your title
- Your cell phone, office phone, and fax numbers
- Your company's tagline

Spell Check

I know, I know…some of you are thinking, "Is he really going to tell me to spell check my emails? Is he running out of things to write about?" Yup, I am going to insist that you spell check and review your emails.

A day does not go by when I don't receive an email full of typos. Email typos are just as bad as poor-quality product, food, or workmanship. It makes you and your company look horrible.

If you are grammatically challenged like me, make sure you spell check every email before you send it.

Computers

Even though I am old enough to remember when computers were not on everyone's desk, I still find it hard to remember what life was like without one. I may be slightly eccentric when it comes to technology. I have *three* laptops. One is a desktop replacement, one is a small inexpensive mini-notebook, and the other is a MacBook. I don't find having these three laptops odd in the least. I use each of them for different purposes and I always feel the need to be no further than 20 feet from a computer at all times. (You just never know when a question will come to mind and I will need Internet access.)

So you might have questions about what type of computer you should buy for your business. Here are my simple thoughts to help you with your decision.

BUYING OFFICE COMPUTERS

Consider these points when deciding which computers to buy:

Portability: Do you travel? How often? The more you travel, the lighter you are going to want your laptop to be.

Battery life: Are you always near an outlet or are you taking long flights where battery life is important?

Screen size: How are your eyes? Do small screens bother you for extended periods of time?

Keyboard size: Do you have large hands and need a full size keyboard?

Apple or Windows: If you are used to one, switching can be a bit of a learning experience. If you're leaning toward purchasing an Apple Macintosh, make sure your business software is compatible with an Apple computer. (You can also now run Windows on a Mac.)

Speed: How intense are the applications you are running? Do they require a fast processor? Do they require more RAM (memory chips)?

Entertainment or business: How much of your computer time will be business related and how much will be for entertainment, such as movies, games, and so on. The answer to this question can impact what you want to buy.

Memory: How many "gigs" of pictures, movies, and work stuff do you have to store on your computer? If you are like me, it does not seem to matter how big a hard drive is, you will fill it up. If you have lots of big files (movies are particularly big memory hogs), make sure the computer you purchase comes with a bigger hard drive.

Software

ARRR is the sound that make-believe pirates utter seemingly in every-other sentence. Real pirates exist off the coast of Somalia and, in many cases, right there in the office or the business next to you.

Software piracy is stealing. It is unethical and bad business. Software piracy is not only wrong, but can land you in a lot of hot water. In major cities all across the US, the software alliance is running radio ads, asking for people to turn in companies that they know are pirating software. Both your past and present employees and customers can receive a reward for turning you into these software police. The disgruntled employee you just fired is a surefire tattler. Don't take a chance! It is not worth it. Make sure all of your software is properly licensed.

Back Up!

There are few worse feelings in business than finding out that your hard drive has crashed and all of your important files are gone. In some cases you can pay thousands of dollars to a company that specializes in retrieving your lost data, but in many cases you are out of luck. Use a service like Carbonite (see carbonite.com) to back up your computer and all of your employees' computers every night via the Internet. It is around $50 a year and worth every dime. A service like Carbonite also makes more sense than a physical backup because should your office burn down, all of your valuable data is stored offsite.

You may think this goes without saying, but if you are running a network, make sure your IT professional is backing up the network nightly. If you know this is being done, do yourself a favor and have them double-check to make sure it is still working. You might be surprised that what you thought was set up and running had actually broken a few months ago and no one knew.

You Don't Always Save Money By Being Cheap

I know someone who once ran a business that required his people to be on the phone and the computer at all times. Their computers were being used to place orders and look up information for customers on the phone. In order to save money, he went out and bought someone else's used computers. In his mind, this was a brilliant move. In reality, it was a disaster.

His used computers came with hidden viruses that caused issues. Because they were older versions with older processors, they were *slow*. These slow and virus-ridden computers only frustrated his staff and customers, leaving the customers with a poor experience and his employees wishing they worked somewhere else. The moral of the story is to make sure your computers properly meet your needs!

Free Internet for All!

I dream of a time when I will have a hyper-fast and free Internet connection everywhere I go. While that may not be as important as solving world hunger, it is just one of my little dreams. The Internet has changed our lives, making everything easier and at our fingertips. It has globalized small businesses and given us access to more information than we will ever need. It, too, often makes us less productive.

Internet access is important in every office. Unrestricted Internet access is a productivity killer. Think about restricting or at least monitoring the sites that your employees go to during the workday. Talk to your IT professional about products that will allow you to block sites that are inappropriate in the workplace, as well as sites that are simply productivity killers such as MySpace and Facebook. (Yes, I still think Facebook is a good marketing tool. Just make sure it is accessible to just the person who updates and monitors it.) Shopping sites and job board sites such as Monster.com may be on your list as well.

If you don't want to block the sites completely, make sure you have a system where you can track the sites each employee uses. You may be surprised to see that the employee who you thought was a little slow is really a shopaholic with a passion for online poker.

Random Thoughts on Technology

Fax = efax

Faxes are still a part of our daily business lives and efax makes it easier to capture and save every fax you get. With this service, you no longer will have to deal with lost faxes. Efax will send every fax to your email address and save them until you can print them out—if and when you really need them.

Simulscribe

I hate checking my voicemail. I don't even have a particularly good reason why I hate checking my voicemail, but I do. A year ago I signed up for a service called Simulscribe. It takes my voicemails, turns them into text, and then emails them to me. Now instead of having to check my voicemails, I can easily read them on my email. I find this to be a huge time-saver, especially when I may be in a meeting where I can't easily check my voicemail, but I can sneak my iPhone or Blackberry under the table and check my email.

Wireless Internet Cards

If you or your employees are out of the office on a regular basis, think about investing in wireless Internet cards. The speed is much better than it was even a few years ago and it will pay for itself many times over in productivity gains. It will pay for itself after a single hotel stay. There is sweet satisfaction one can gain through the revenge on the hotels that nail you for $40/night Internet fees.

Video Surveillance

Video surveillance of your place of business is a must. It is not just banks that get robbed; almost every business can be a target. We have video surveillance in all the hallways of our office as well as over the outside parking area. If something goes missing (and that has happened to us), we can go to the tapes.

Summary

Technology has always been and always will be a game changer. Do not underestimate the importance of having the proper technology in your workplace. Having the proper gadgets will make the customer and employee experience much more enjoyable and, therefore, may be one of the best investments you can make.

Chapter 11

Business Intelligence

There have been many books written on business intelligence. For the purposes of this book, I will boil it down to the process of collecting information about the marketplace in which you operate.

In order to survive and thrive in today's business climate, you must truly understand the lay of the land, including all of your competitors, big and small.

The Marketplace

In order to understand the market you're operating in, you should ask these questions about your marketplace:

- In what geographic area does your business operate?
- Within that area, where are the "prime" areas in which you are, or should be, getting the majority of your business or customers?
- Why is this your prime area?
- How many potential customers are in this area?
- What is the average household income in your area?
- What are the general economic conditions in your area? Is it just average, unaffected by the economy, or are you working in, for example, Detroit and are at ground zero for the economy?
- What are people in your area willing to spend money on right now?

Your Competition

Understanding your competition can be a key part of your success. The more you know about your competitors, the better chance you have of making the proper decisions when a competitive situation arises. Try the following exercise as you consider one of your competitors. After you are finished, go back and try it again, until you have evaluated all of all of your competitors. Your mission is to finish this exercise within the next 30 days. If you don't know the answer to a particular question, leave it blank and move on. However, before the end of the 30-day period, find the answers to each and every question.

WHO IS YOUR COMPETITION?

List each of your competitors and answer the following questions for each.

Name?

_____

How long have they been in business?

_____

In what do they specialize?

_____

How much business do they do in an average year?

_____

What is their reputation in the marketplace?

_____

Are they priced higher or lower than you? Why?

_____

What does their website look like?

_____

What suppliers do they use and why?

_____

Are they getting the same or better prices for product as you?

_____

Are they trying to grow, maintain, or shrink?

_____

Who are their key employees?

_____

Are their key people happy?

_____

Do they have any recurring clients?

_____

Who are their best clients?

_____

What is their reputation on the Internet?

_____

What else do you know?

_____

Now What?

Create a file for each of your local competitors and update it regularly. This information can help you in many ways.

Each of your competitors is better than you at something. Your goal is to figure out what that something is and find a way to make your business more successful.

Knowing how your competition generally bids against you can be very helpful in a competitive situation.

Understanding that they book jobs because they are pushing a new type of material or product that you had not thought about carrying could help you grow your business.

Knowing that a key employee has just left because he or she was unhappy could be a great way to pick up a talented person.

What if you found out that your competition's owner was getting ready to retire and you could pick up his or her clients for a nominal percentage of the business those clients produce each year for a few years?

How To Gather Information About Competitors

Ask questions and listen carefully. The more questions you ask of customers, suppliers, and your own employees, the more information you will obtain.

Your own employees probably know almost everything you need to know about all of your competitors.

GATHERING INFORMATION ON COMPETITORS: THE NO-NO'S

Don't:

- Spy on them
- Rifle through their trash
- Create false reviews on the Internet about them
- Copy their materials
- Ask them to bid your mother's house
- Break any laws at all!

You can gather all the information you need just by asking questions. Points to remember about your competition:

- Bigger does not mean better.
- Years of experience do not always equal quality.
- Most employees are unhappy and thinking about leaving once or twice a year.
- They are just like you and will have problems with customers from time to time.
- We are all better in our niches.

Business Intelligence Outside Your Market

If you want to be the biggest and the best, you need to study the biggest and the best.

The biggest and best may not be in your area, but you still want to know who they are.

Who are the premier players in your business? Who has built the biggest, the highest quality, and the most profitable business in your industry?

Create a file of the top five players in your industry. Answer the same list of questions for each of these large players. After creating the file on each one, keep filling it up.

Bookmark their websites and review them. Ask suppliers to fill you in on what they know.

Use trade shows to gather information. In many cases, these large companies will be happy to share ideas, especially if you are not direct competitors. Your goal is to find out what makes them so successful.

Friendly Competition Is Always Better

It is a small world and it is generally better to be on friendly terms with your competition.

That is not to say you need to go grab a beer on Fridays with them.

You never know when you will come across a job that is outside your scope of work and you may be able to hand it off to someone better suited to handle it. Do this and they will return the favor.

Remember…knocking or generally speaking ill of your competition to a customer will almost always lose you the business.

Business Intelligence: Strategic Relationships

Business intelligence is not just about your market and your direct competition.

It is also about understanding which other businesses in your local area market to your same customer pool.

Think about the local businesses in your area. Which ones are already marketing to your same customers? Take a look at the following examples.

SERVICE COMPANIES

Homeowners	*Business to Business*
Pool cleaners	AC repair
Landscapers	Computer repair
House cleaners	Office cleaning
Window washers	Office security/alarms
Plumbers	

This is just a short list of service companies that exist in your area that are all marketing to your same customers. In most cases, you will have an actual client list that is separate and distinct from theirs.

Create a file for each service you offer and make it your mission to meet with the top competitors from each category.

Why should you do this? Well, they are all in the service business. They are all marketing to the same clients. They all provide unique goods or services that are better than others.

If you are able to share and put into practice each other's ideas, you will only make each other's businesses stronger.

Having an alliance with other businesses will create more business for the two of you. When you come across a lead for another trade and share it with your new business partner, you will have resolved a dilemma for your customer as well as ensuring that this partner will do the same for you.

If you were to create alliances with at least one company in 10 different trades, it would be like having 10 more connected people looking for business for you.

Thinking Outside the Box

This business alliance model works for almost any type of business. If you're thinking that is not the case for you, you just need to think outside the box.

What About...?

...an alliance of four restaurants that cross promote each other. Picture this group of four restaurants: one fish house, one Italian restaurant, one steak house, and one Chinese restaurant. Nobody wants to eat the same food every day. What if each of these restaurants promoted each other with a simple flyer saying, "In the mood for something different? Try a meal from one of our sister restaurants. We know you will enjoy the food and service!" You may be surprised at the results.

...pool cleaners, landscapers, and so on. Do you have a relationship with the local pool supply store and nurseries? Will they send you business?

...a "strip mall." Do you know all the other store owners in your mall? Do you promote each other's businesses? Do you offer the occasional flyer promoting 10% off if they go next door?

...a carwash. Do you have an alliance with the local fast food locations and cross-market? How about a promotion that states, "While we are washing your car, go next door and get a free bag of chips on us with any sandwich order?" The restaurant could reciprocate with a flyer of their own: "While you are eating your sandwich, go next door and get $2 off of a car wash."

...a local hardware store. Do you have an area set up for contractors to advertise their services? Does each of these contractors in turn promote your business?

YOUR ALLIANCE LIST

Who are the local businesses in your area that you should have an alliance with?

Contact: _____

Phone: _____

Email: _____

Website: _____

Contact: _____

Phone: _____

Email:_____

Website: _____

Contact: _____

Phone: _____

Email:_____

Website: _____

Just remember that these alliances need to be created at the owner-to-owner level. If you try to create these relationships without the owners signing off on them, your cross-marketing efforts will not achieve the same results.

Here's the great thing—just like many ideas in this book, as simple an idea as it sounds, almost none of your competition is doing this!

Chapter 12

Back to School

In writing a chapter about going back to school, I'm not suggesting that you turn around and enroll in college, major in psychology, and start a new profession.

I am simply suggesting that you make learning a priority in your life.

Become an expert in everything important in your field. There are always new products, new systems, and new ways to do just about everything.

The Enemy of Learning Is Knowing

One of the biggest obstacles to growing a business is thinking that because you have been in your profession for 15 to 20 years that you are absolutely convinced that your way is the best and only way to do things.

This leads to dangerous behavior.

The Boss Attitude

This mindset can be deadly. If the owner of any business has it, creativity in the organization is stifled and employees feel like their opinions are not as important as the boss's. Over time, this kind of thinking will kill your business. No single person has the "keys to the city " or the answers to all questions.

The Salty Dog

The salty dog is defined as the employee who has been in the business for years and years and has typically forgotten more about the business than you will ever know—and he or she is not afraid to tell you so.

The salty dogs are a huge value to the business because of all the knowledge that they bring, but can also be extremely dangerous because they may believe there is nothing left for them to learn.

It is because of the salty dogs that the phrase, "The enemy of learning is knowing," was coined. No matter what you say, they will look you straight in the eye and say, "I know the best way to do this."

Or worse, they will nod their head, smile, and completely ignore your direction.

Taking the Salt Out of Your Dogs

- They need to feel respected. Take the time to make sure they understand that you appreciate their opinions and respect their experience.
- It is important that they feel like they're being heard. This takes time and lots and lots of actual conversations. You are competing with years and years of history and experience in that noggin' of theirs.
- Ask, don't tell. The best way to get them to try new things is to ask them to "test" a new method of yours and determine which way would work best.

  Telling salty dogs to do anything will only get you barked at and possibly bitten!

Not Invented Here

The organizational equivalent of the salty dog is the "not invented here" attitude.

This mindset generally takes over an entire company when its employees have been working together for an extended length of time. Every company has some degree of this within its organization.

The trick is to not let it infest too deeply into your company. The "not invented here" disease is one that tends to make all new employees feel like outsiders and is a reason why companies have a hard time attracting and retaining new talent.

Learning Is Not Just for You

Learning should be a part of your culture. Encourage your employees to improve themselves and therefore your company. Make learning a team event.

Trade/Industry Associations: Get Involved

Every industry has its own trade association and every trade association has local chapters.

Local Meetings

Local meetings are a great way to meet people in your industry who are doing things differently than you.

These meetings are almost always very friendly gatherings where business managers get together once every month or so to listen to a guest speaker and have dinner.

These meetings give you a chance to share war stories with colleagues who may have already experienced your dilemma and may have answers for you.

Conventions

Conventions are a great way to take a few days away from working in the business and spend some time working "on" your business.

Most associations will have regional and national conventions that you can attend. These conventions will have multiple guest speakers who will address topics that are relevant to your industry. Most conventions also include a large exhibit hall filled with suppliers and other vendors that are relevant to your business.

Suppliers

Your suppliers are a rich source of what is new and exciting in your industry. Go to lunch with them and ask questions. They not only know what is new from a product side, but they will sometimes let you know about innovative things that your competitors are doing. The added benefit of setting up such a meeting is that your supplier will generally pay for lunch!

Build Your Advisory Team

Very few, if any, entrepreneurs have built a significant business single-handedly.

Similar characteristics are shared by all of the most successful companies.

One of the most important pieces of the puzzle is an "advisory team" piece. No one is an expert at everything in a particular field. You don't know what you don't know!

Having the right team to turn to when important decisions need to be made is critical to the long-term health of any company.

The following are the critical advisors who you will need on your "team" in order to grow your company.

Legal

A strong attorney will help you see the legal pitfalls of your pending decisions.

CPA

A solid CPA will help you make smart financial decisions.

One of the biggest reasons companies fail is that they run out of cash! A good CPA can see that dead end coming and may help you avert it.

Banker

A good banker is someone who is a partner in your business. He or she is someone who takes the time to understand what you and your business need in order to grow and stay healthy.

A good banker is someone who you should feel comfortable talking to and who offers suggestions about how your company can become even stronger.

Bankers have a unique perspective in that they don't specialize in one particular industry. They have the benefit of telling you what other companies are doing to succeed.

IT Professional

Your IT professional is a key team member. As your company grows, you will be more and more reliant on technology.

Your IT person should be someone who is "sized right" for your business. In other words, someone who is used to dealing with the challenges of $50 million companies is not the right person to make sure your small business has a website and email.

The most important quality when picking IT people (other than they know what they are doing) is how quickly they respond to clients. Your IT people need to be available when you need them.

You also want to make sure that this potential team member will put the sometimes complicated technological terms in a language that you and your team understand and will be there to help you grow when you are ready for expansion.

Industry Experts and, Yes, Competitors

Utilize your trade associations to build relationships with competitors outside your area.

Many of your fellow business associates have spent years banging their heads against the wall as they learned to overcome problems that you are just now starting to experience in your business.

With rare exception, there is not a business problem out there that has not already been seen and solved multiple times. The solution to your current issue will come by simply talking to the right people.

Alliances with competitors who are in different geographic areas are great ways to share ideas and grow your business.

"Serial Entrepreneur"

A valuable team member is someone who has been successful at more than one start up. The reason you want this person on your team is simple.

These people have a proven track record of accomplishing something more than once.

There are those out there who are running successful new businesses because they just got get lucky. The stars aligned properly, they had the right industry connections, or they hired the right people. That's not saying that someone who has been successful in business was just lucky, but if you find someone who has been successful multiple times, you really have something to learn. Nobody gets lucky over and over again. They will have something to offer because of their vast experience in starting up businesses.

Chances are they have also failed at ventures, so they understand the warning signs better than anyone.

If you can find someone like this, regardless of the industry they come from, they will offer you a very fresh perspective as you begin your path to success.

Mentor and Coach

Everyone needs a coach. From Tiger Woods to the President of the United States, successful people surround themselves with top-notch advisors. One of the most critical people in that mix of advisors is a personal coach or mentor.

This person should be more experienced in business than you are and should be willing to hold you accountable for the things that you say you will do.

A coach is someone you meet with either over the phone or in person for an hour or so once a week or twice a month (depending on your needs).

Your coach will help you do what none of your employees can do—hold your feet to the fire to get your goals accomplished.

Your coach will make sure that what you say you are going to do, you actually do.

This is your confidant, your mentor, and someone who, if you choose wisely, will be an instrumental part of your future success.

Your coach ideally is someone who has "been there and done that" and has the battle scars to prove it.

He or she should be someone who you look up to and are willing to listen to. You must be able to trust the coach completely and be comfortable sharing everything about your business with him or her.

If you hide things or keep secrets, your coach will not be able to truly help you in your quest for success.

CEO Groups

For those of you who have reached critical mass, you should apply for membership in CEO organizations. Here are a few that I have had personal success with.

Entrepreneurs' Organization: EO

The Entrepreneurs' Organization (EO)—for entrepreneurs only—is a global network of more than 7,500 business owners in 38 countries. Founded in 1987 by a group of young entrepreneurs, EO enables entrepreneurs to learn and grow from each other, leading to greater business success.

EO's vision is to build the world's most influential community of entrepreneurs.

EO's mission is to engage leading entrepreneurs to learn and grow.

EO's core values are as follows:

- Boldly Go!—Bet on your own abilities
- Thirst for Learning—Be a student of opportunity
- Make a Mark—Leave a legacy
- Trust and Respect—Build a safe haven for learning and growth
- Cool—Create, seek out, and celebrate once-in-a-lifetime experiences

EO's facts-at-a-glance:

- Total sales of all members worldwide: More than $124 billion
- Total members worldwide: More than 7,500
- Total number of workers that members employ worldwide: More than 1.3 million
- Total number of chapters worldwide: 118
- Total number of countries represented: 38
- Average member age: 40
- Average member sales: $18.4 million per year
- Average member employees: 191

Young Presidents Organization: YPO

YPO's mission is to develop "Better Leaders Through Education and Idea Exchange."

YPO screens its applicants extremely closely because true peer-based learning is the foundation of the YPO mission and experience. YPOers learn from their peers, they exchange ideas, ask for advice, and share best practices in an open and trusting way. CEOs have access to a lot of information, to smart subordinates, and perhaps a few too many "yes men." YPO's strength is a membership of qualified peers eager to learn and interact and grow as leaders.

Vistage

With more than 14,500 members, Vistage International is the world's foremost chief executive leadership organization, providing access to new ideas and fresh thinking through monthly peer workshops, one-on-one business coaching, speaker presentations from hundreds of top industry experts, social networking, and an extensive online content library of articles, best practices, podcasts, and webinars.

This top executive network started from very humble beginnings over five decades ago. One October morning in 1957, a Wisconsin businessman named Robert Nourse met with four fellow chief executives in the office of the Milwaukee Valve Company to test a simple, yet revolutionary idea—sharing knowledge and experiences to help each other generate better results for their businesses.

Soon this group of businessmen was probing, asking questions, and making suggestions. They challenged each other and worked together to solve issues and grow.

My Experience

I have been a member of EO, YPO, and Vistage at different points in my career.

I have never been a good student. In fact I am a college dropout with a GPA that my more educated business partners continually laugh about.

What I did realize, however, when I started my business was that I needed education very specific to running an organization.

I have spent more than 14 years in a combination of EO, Vistage, and YPO and am eternally grateful to the organizations, as well as to the friends I have in each. They all share in the success that I have achieved.

As I look back on critical moments in my career, the people in these organizations were always there to help me navigate the choppy waters.

Other Organizations

Although I have no personal experience with these organizations, let me share other options with you.

Business Roundtable

Business Roundtable is an association of chief executive officers of leading US companies that has more than $6 trillion in annual revenues and nearly 12 million employees. Member companies comprise nearly a third of the total value of the US stock markets and pay nearly half of all corporate income taxes paid to the federal government. Annually, they return $133 billion in dividends to shareholders and the economy.

Business Roundtable companies give more than $7 billion a year in combined charitable contributions, representing nearly 60 percent of total corporate giving. They are technology innovation leaders, with $70 billion in annual research and development spending—more than a third of the total private R&D spending in the United States.

Business Roundtable unites these top CEOs, amplifying their diverse business perspectives and voices on solutions to some of the world's most difficult challenges. Combining those insights with policy know-how, Business Roundtable innovates and advocates to help expand economic opportunity for all Americans.

Business Roundtable believes the basic interests of business closely parallel the interests of American workers, who are directly linked to companies as consumers, employees, shareholders, and suppliers. In their roles as CEOs, Business Roundtable members are responsible for the jobs, products, services, and benefits that affect the economic well-being of all Americans.

Robust participation by member CEOs is a key strength of Business Roundtable. The organization is selective in the issues it addresses, a principal criterion being their potential impact on the economic well being of the nation.

BNI: Business Networking

BNI is the largest business networking organization in the world. It offers members the opportunity to share ideas, contacts, and most importantly, business referrals.

Using its "Find a Chapter" feature, potential members can contact a local BNI director to see why BNI has brought businesses together all across the globe for over 24 years.

Personal Growth: A Commitment to Reading

Some of you love reading and some of you are like me...

Those of you who are prolific readers, well, good for you! You can officially skip this section (read on anyway).

Business Books

Reading fiction or the sports pages does not count. Growth comes from reading business books—books that will cause you to rethink the way you are running your company.

Make it one of your written goals to read one business book a month. If you are truly committed to your team learning as well, you can create the business version of a book club.

Step One: Pick a Book, Any Book

Pick out an easy business book to start reading. Pick one from which you believe your team could benefit. Pick one book for the whole team and then alternate between different departments on a rotating monthly basis. Perhaps you could choose a sales book for the sales team one month, a customer service book for the customer service team the next month, and so on. Four books a year is plenty to require your team to read. If you find your employees are truly enjoying the process, go ahead and increase the number of books to rotate.

Step Two: Time Is of the Essence

Set a timeframe to read the book. Try to choose books that are easily read in less than a month.

Step Three: The Halfway Point

Have a meeting halfway through the month to talk about the first half of the book. This will give you a good idea as to who is really reading and who needs to be encouraged a little. Generally speaking, the employees lagging behind will more likely catch up as they see their colleagues getting animated about the book and receiving your praise.

Step Four: The Review

At the end of the book, divide your people into pairs. Have each pair review specific chapters for which they will eventually give verbal reports back to the entire team. This makes sure the book has relevance to your business and forces people to work together in teams. (Try pairing people who have challenges with each other.) An additional benefit to this process is that it helps to improve everyone's public speaking skills as they present to the group.

Magazines

Subscribe to all of your industry magazines. In fact, have multiple subscriptions so that there are always copies available for your team to read. Read business magazines and websites every month. Find the best articles and forward them to people who may find them interesting in your company.

Websites

The web has tons of sites that are industry specific. There are articles, forums, and blogs, and the writers come from around the country. This is a great way to stay informed about your business.

Chapter 13

Expense Management: Running a Lean Business

K eeping an eye (or both eyes for that matter) on the bottom line has never been more important.

In order to survive in business, regardless of the state of the economy, we all need to pay attention to every penny being spent. No amount is too small.

Far too many business owners do not pay close enough attention to their expenses. Consider how difficult it is to bring in $100,000, or even $10,000, in business. Most of us struggle putting together a marketing and sales program in order to be able to increase our revenue numbers on a consistent basis. Despite this concentrated struggle on revenue, we pay little attention to small expenses that slowly add up to $1,000, $2,000, and even $10,000 a month.

This runaway collection of small expenses happens to all of us. Stop for a minute and consider what those expenses are truly costing you. If your business runs at a 10% net profit margin, $1,000 in basically negates the $10,000 in revenue that you worked so hard to bring in. $10,000 in these expenses negates $100,000 in revenue!

You must be as passionate about cutting expenses as you are about driving revenue.

Here are some tips that, while specific to three industries, will start the wheels turning in your own mind about what you can and should be doing to control costs in your business. (Don't be tempted to skip this section just because your business is not in one of these industries. You'll find that most of these tips apply to all types of companies—including yours!)

Contractors and Service Companies

Materials Estimating

This is a simple, but often overlooked, area of cost savings.

Knowing exactly how much material is required for each job is critical to being profitable.

Are your estimating standards tight? Do you track the difference between the quantity of materials on which you bid and the actual materials used?

Are there areas where you consistently underbid materials from job to job?

Material Suppliers

Have you explored all options with your suppliers?

Are you aware of all the products on the market today and how they may be different from the ones you are using?

Are there products that could be saving you time and money if you used them instead of what you are currently using?

Can one supplier offer you better pricing, terms, or rebates if you buy exclusively from them?

Are you taking advantage of sales and bulk purchases on items that you know you are going to be using on a regular basis?

Inventorying Materials

Stuff walks off of job sites almost daily. In many cases excellent people who would never be caught stealing even a candy bar from the corner market will somehow justify taking home extra or unused materials from your job site.

In many cases, workers feel like carting off with your materials is just something that "everybody does" and, therefore, they don't think of it as theft. Bottom line? If they take what isn't theirs without your permission, they're stealing from you and are hurting your profitability.

What are you doing to control material consumption?

Controlling Inventory

What gets put on the plate gets eaten or taken. Develop a "just-in-time" method for supplying materials to your job sites.

Everyone has seen how if a job has four or five days worth of material stacked up, waste is always higher than when crews are consistently worried about having enough materials to complete that day's tasks.

Take sand paper, for example. (Even if you may not use sand paper in your trade, your trade has a consumable like sandpaper.)

If you give a crew an entire ream of sandpaper at the beginning of a job, they'll only use somewhere between 10% and 50% of that sheet's potential. Check your trash each night and see what you find.

If you limit the sandpaper to a couple of sheets per worker (depending on the job), you will find that each person will use 50% to 80% of each sheet.

It is simple human nature to waste things if you think you have an unlimited supply.

Checking on the Work

Most employees have no concept of "your money."

You are the "rich boss" and what does it hurt you if there is a little waste?

Visit your jobs and go through the trash.

Is every roll of tape being completely used? Are they using too much?

Are they getting every last bit of fertilizer out of the bag or getting lazy and leaving a cup or two at the bottom?

Are they measuring twice and cutting once?

Are they planning out a job to eliminate as much board waste as possible?

Do they get the last drop of paint or glue from a can?

Are they using five times as many nails as they need because they really like the sound of the nail gun?

You must instill in every worker's mind that you are watching everything on a job, right down to the rags and nails.

Focusing on Waste Does Not Mean Lowering Quality Standards

Paying attention to wasteful habits does not mean using lower-grade materials.

Definitely don't substitute inferior products for what was bid.

Don't water down your paint or use two nails or screws where you should be using five, and so on.

Just pay very close attention to waste on your job sites.

Labor Waste: The Big One

How long should a task take?

This is the most important question a business owner should be asking.

You need to know exactly how long every task on a job should take and, more importantly, you need to be holding your employees to these standards.

Your survival depends upon it.

With a proper estimating process you should be able to tell everyone on the job exactly how long each task will take to complete.

Holding workers accountable is the next step.

How Do You Eat an Elephant?

One bite at a time.

Each job must be broken down daily into bite-size pieces.

How many feet of trench should be dug per hour?

How many windows need to be painted in an hour?

How many square feet of tile should be laid in an hour?

Set Clear Expectations

Every worker on the job should know exactly what is expected of him by lunch and, then again, by the end of each day.

This job falls on the foreman, superintendent, and/or yourself.

It is absolutely critical to a job being done on schedule that the entire crew knows what is expected of them throughout the entire day—from the foreman right down to the person pushing a broom.

The job will expand to fill the time available.

If there is no clear-cut expectation of time set by you, the tasks will always take longer than they should and the job will cost you more money!

Bonus for Jobs for Coming in on Time

The only way to bring jobs in on budget is to bonus the people involved for accomplishing this goal.

Put together a simple incentive system that pays your superintendent and foremen a small bonus for each job that comes in under your estimate.

In other words, if you bid your job with a 40% gross profit and they are able to bring it in without sacrificing quality at 44%, give them 2% of the overall job as a bonus.

Everyone needs something to shoot for.

Everything can always be done faster and more efficiently. This must become one of your core beliefs.

There is room in every project to shave a point or two off of labor and a point or two off of materials just by being hyper-diligent and paying attention to every detail.

Your Equipment

How long should your equipment last?

How long does it last?

Do your crews treat it as if it belonged to their old shop teacher? Do they even know where it is half of the time?

Do you have an inventory system and maintenance schedule?

If you answered "not sure" to any of these questions, you have some work to do.

Restaurants

Suppliers

Obviously food costs are a huge expense in the running of a restaurant. When was the last time you reviewed your pricing from all of your suppliers? When was the last time you spoke to different suppliers just to see how much prices may have changed? Loyalty is important and most suppliers will reward it; however, remember you are not married to your supplier. If someone has better prices for the same quality of food, you need to make a change.

Hours

Even though I argued earlier that Subway finally woke up to offering breakfast after all these years, does it make sense for your business? Examine your breakfast, lunch, dinner, and catering business. Take each of these sections of your business and divide the restaurant overhead for each. Do they make profitable sense when you look at each as a separate business unit? Is breakfast profitable for you? Do you happen to be in a location where offering breakfast just does not make any sense? Maybe dinner is where you lose money and you really should just be a breakfast and lunch place. If you are losing money in one area, can it be fixed? New menu? Better quality food? Take a hard look at your model. You may be surprised what you discover.

Food Costs

There is nothing better than a restaurant with an amazing chef. There is nothing more unprofitable than a restaurant whose chef uses unique and expensive ingredients that cost you more than what your market will bear. Truffles are amazing (at least to some people), but if your restaurant is not able to price that kind of item at a point that makes sense, take them off the menu.

Understand your food cost on each and every meal. Determine a food cost percentage that is acceptable for each meal. Don't use lower quality ingredients or provide substandard food (doing that will put you out of business quicker than out of control food costs). However, you do need to decide what percentage your food expense should be relative to your overall cost of producing that particular meal in order to be profitable. Determine that percentage and build a high-quality menu around it. Push your chef; he or she will have the ability to create a profitable high quality menu. If he or she can't (or won't), find a new chef.

Think smaller portions. Far too many restaurants focus on large portions rather than smaller, high-quality portions.

Restaurant Staff

Review your staffing for the entire day. Is everyone being as efficient in the kitchen as they can be? Is everyone pulling their weight or do you have a few too many assistants to the assistant in the kitchen? Are there times when things are slow enough that the waiters and waitresses could be busing tables? (They will love me for that idea.)

Inventory Control

What is your system for managing your food inventory? How do you know that filets and T-bones are not walking out the back door? Are you monitoring even the little things, like garbage bags and paper towels? It all adds up over time.

The Bar

What is your system for managing those friendly drinks that get poured in and around your establishment? How closely are you watching your bar staff and their generosity to friendly cute customers? (I managed a bar in my early 20s. I know this one well!)

Employee Theft

One of the top reasons why restaurants fail is because of employee theft. Too many employees steal not just the food, but cash out of the register. Just because you are an honest person does not mean that everyone else is.

Any veteran of the restaurant business will tell you that this unaddressed problem will become an epidemic in your business. Set clear expectations. Balance the cash register at the end of every shift, if possible, and at the end of the day as a minimum. Watch for the signs from employees who are stealing from you: new clothes, expensive toys that are uncharacteristic of your employees, and so on.

Above all, set expectations from day one. Make it crystal clear that if an employee is caught stealing, he or she will be prosecuted.

Live Entertainment

Live entertainment can make the night feel more fun. It may even bring in more customers who stay longer and order more. These customers may indeed become more loyal and come back more often. Take the time to do a cost-benefit analysis on live entertainment. Is it really adding to your bottom line or is the additional money you are making just going to pay for the entertainment?

Restaurant Summary

Restaurants have a high failure rate for a variety of reasons, not the least of which is that owners are notorious about not watching expenses. I personally know of one restaurant in the Caribbean that went from losing thousands of dollars a month to making tens of thousands a month in profit once the owner finally got serious about watching expenses and fired those who were stealing from him.

Retail

Inventory, Inventory, Inventory

Are you too busy to do inventory? No time to set up inventory controls? No idea of the quantity of any particular product you have on hand at any given time? If so, say goodbye to a chunk of your inventory as it walks out the back door. Without an inventory control system you have the potential of losing as much as you sell.

Dollars Tied Up in Expensive Inventory

How fast does your inventory turn? Are you paying attention to what is selling and what is not selling? Are those really cool high-end items really selling or do you just think they are cool to have? What is the cost of carrying that excess inventory that does not turn as fast as other products in your location? Do the math. You may be surprised at how much it is costing you.

Staffing

Are you staffed appropriately at all times? Are there times of the day when you have too many people on the floor? Can one person staff the store adequately most of the time?

Don't make knee-jerk decisions, but do spend some time watching and tracking the number of people who come into your location at different times of the day and week. Have your staff create a tally sheet for a few weeks of the number of people who walk in each hour of the day. Have them also make notes on how many sales are made from those people. This exercise will give you two very important pieces of information. You will discover what your staffing needs truly are and what quality of salespeople you have. You will see definite patterns where some of your salespeople make sales in seven out of every ten customers, whereas others scare customers from the store. (You need to read this book carefully; hidden sales advice may pop up in any chapter.)

Caution

Remember the story of Circuit City? Just before it closed its doors, Circuit City changed its sales program. It replaced all of its motivated commissioned salespeople with hourly-wage employees with no financial motivation to learn the product line. Circuit City quickly lost its competitive advantage when it lost its highly-motivated and knowledgeable sales force. Many believe this was the final deathblow to the company.

Expense Management Advice for All Industries

Leases

If you have not already done it, talk to your landlord about changing your lease. Regardless of whether you signed a two-, five-, or ten-year deal and the contract states it is nonnegotiable, times have changed. Landlords would rather negotiate with you now than have to find a new tenant. Don't be greedy. A 10-15% cut in your monthly rent will definitely help out your bottom line. Give it a try. You may not be successful, but these renegotiated contracts are much more common than they used to be.

Vehicles

Most employees don't treat company vehicles as if they owned them.

They drive them too hard and don't keep up on the proper maintenance.

Put it in your schedule to spot-check your vehicles regularly. Expect your employees to treat the company truck like they would treat their borrowed father's car.

Expect the vehicle to be clean and free of trash.

If you don't permit your employees to drive the vehicles on personal time, have you ever thought of tracking your vehicles with a GPS so that you know where the vehicle is being driven off the job? A GPS comes in handy, as well, to check if your employees are out driving around town at 80 miles an hour or parked at a coffee shop for two hours.

Purchasing Power

Who is authorized to make purchases in your organization?

What kinds of purchases must you alone okay?

Is there a price limit on certain types of equipment and supplies that can be bought without your approval?

How do you track purchases to each job?

How closely do you review invoices for errors or extra items not needed?

Job Costing

Every job that you do needs to be compared to the original estimate.

It is imperative that the total amount of labor and materials for which the job was bid are compared to the actual labor and material cost on the job.

Every job that you do needs to be reviewed this way so that you can find areas for improvement.

In some cases, you may find that you are consistently underbidding a certain type of project or that your people are always taking longer in a particular area.

Whatever it is, you'll find something that will save you money.

The Office

This is always a tough one. In some cases you need an office out of which to operate.

Others find a way to operate without the leased space. Even in our own businesses, I am constantly amazed by divisions that operate at the same revenue level despite some utilizing office space and the others not.

The ones that operate in a virtual environment are generally much more profitable.

The longer you are in a space, the more people tend to spread out.

You move in and over the years people grab the cube next to them, the bigger office, and so on.

ANALYZING YOUR OFFICE SPACE

Look at the space you have and ask yourself how much of it is really necessary.

- Is the space reasonable for the kind of work your company and employees are doing?
- Could you function just as well with a smaller space?
- How often is the boardroom actually used?
- Could you operate with a storage unit and people working out of their homes?
- Do clients actually visit your space?
- When is your lease up?
- Will your landlord give you a rent reduction to stay in the space?

Outsourcing

Outsourcing as discussed here, is not about sending jobs to countries that most of us have never been to, but is about finding a more efficient way to do the tasks that exist in your organization.

OUTSOURCING IDEAS

Some simple outsourcing examples are:

- Payroll—Payroll is a simple one to outsource, whether it is to QuickBooks payroll or ADP. There is no reason for you to be cutting your own payroll checks and dealing with all the complications of tax withholding and the like.
- Bookkeeping—The simplest way to run your business is by using QuickBooks. I have heard all the arguments on other software, but, candidly, QuickBooks is what we use in our $47 million business and it works great right out of the box.
  Do you actually need a full time bookkeeper or can you outsource to someone who can do it part time?
- Phones—Do you have the need to have your people answer the phone or can you find a professional service that will answer the phones for

---

> you and then text or email you the messages directly, giving you 24-hour coverage and saving staff costs?
> - Others—What other roles exist that do not necessarily need to be fulfilled by full-time employees? What roles could you share with other companies?
>
>   For example, we have had a Safety Consultant for years. For a monthly fee, he helps us negotiate all insurance coverage and makes sure that our safety programs are up to speed.

Office Efficiency

Things can always be done faster. It does not matter what anyone tells you, take the time to watch a task and you will naturally see ways to accomplish it in less time. Owners are natural efficiency gurus. There is something about the fact that it is your money being spent that gives you an added sense of how to make things go faster...even when you have never done the task.

The Little Stuff

The little stuff adds up quickly. Just take a look at your monthly financials and add up all the line items in this section. It is amazing how many costs are not attached to individual jobs. Here are a few of those costs and some suggestions on how to bring them in line.

Cell Phones

Analyze your plans regularly. Are you getting the best price out there? Pay attention to the little stuff that adds up, like text messaging, roaming, ring tones, and so on. Those "extras" can take the bill from $100 month to $300.

Offer employees $50 a month toward their bill instead of giving them a phone. They will take better care of the phone because it is theirs and they will be responsible for their own ring tones.

Postage

Postage meters are expensive! In some cases they cost $100+ per month. For years, postage meters were thought of as a necessary cost of running a business. Not anymore. Check out Stamps.com and get rid of your postage meter forever.

Miscellaneous Office Supplies

Are you paying full price at the local office supply store? Online stores offer a variety of solutions at amazing prices.

Phone Lines

What are you paying every month for your phone lines? How many lines do you have and how many do you need?

Do you need a landline system or could you change to an IP-based phone system? Imagine getting rid of all your landlines and using phones that are tied to the Internet instead. These IP-based phones have functions that most people never even thought were possible, all at a fraction of the cost of a landline.

Internet Service

Compare all of your options. Most of us are paying much more than we need to for our Internet service.

You will be amazed at how much faster your Internet speed can be and how little you will pay for it.

Don't Buy Anything New

Never, never, never buy anything new (except computers; see next section). There are plenty of used office furniture stores in every city in the country. I have never owned a new desk and I never will.

Craigslist and other sources are full of all the used equipment that you need for pennies on the dollar. However, be careful about spending too much time searching. Saving five more bucks after searching an additional hour just doesn't add up.

Computers and Equipment

Where do you buy your computers and equipment? Are you getting the best deal on equipment? Will it be fixed when you need it to be fixed, or are you just buying the cheapest stuff, hoping it will work?

Price scrimping will hurt you here. Buying used computer equipment is not a good option.

I am generally not an extended warranty guy unless it is on expensive laptops and TVs. I have always gotten the better end of the deal buying the extended warranties on these items.

Photocopiers

Check your leases on all your copiers.

Ink Cartridges

Where are you buying your ink cartridges? There are multiple options online to save you a bundle of money.

Cleaning Service

Do you have a cleaning service in your office or retail location?

Shop around and you'll find significant differences in pricing for the same level of service.

STUFF YOU DON'T THINK ABOUT

Consider checking these simple areas for cost savings:
- Cancel magazines you don't read.
- Use a simple water filter instead of a bottled water service.
- Save on electricity:
  Use CFL lights wherever you can.
  Turn off computers and printers when not in use.
  Use a power strip to avoid "phantom power" drain.
  Set your AC at 72 and make sure it is off when the business is closed.
  Place the lights on motion switches and make sure they are off when the business is closed.

The Big Stuff

Legal

Lawyers are said to be a necessary evil.

It seems the longer you are in business and the larger you grow, the more interaction you have with this unique portion of the community.

Here are some tips for the next time you cross paths with this "necessary evil."

If You Are Being Sued...

Check to see if you have insurance coverage for whatever the issue may be. You may be shocked at how many things that you are actually covered for.

You also may be shocked to see what you are not covered for.

Ignore the Dollar Amount

Most lawsuits have a huge dollar amount attached. This is done to get your attention and make you panic.

Very rarely does anyone get anywhere close to what they are asking for (nor do they expect to).

Don't Panic

One of the purposes of a lawsuit it is to make you, your partners, and family panic.

Plaintiffs hope that you lose sleep at night so that you will be more motivated to write them a check quickly.

Yes, Some or All of Their Claim Is Untrue

Many lawyers will throw anything they can into the initial lawsuit.

Claiming not only that you have done their client wrong (which may be true), they'll tack on how you have caused them to lose sleep and perhaps other baseless claims.

Focus on what you know to be true and what you can prove. Don't worry about what they have made up.

Get to the Heart of the Problem Right Away

The first thing you need to do is to find out exactly why you are being sued. Get a clear understanding of what the plaintiff is claiming you did and what you actually did wrong, if anything.

Be objective. Very few lawsuits are filed on the whim of a client or attorney. You did something wrong. What is it?

Take the time to write everything out that you know about the incident in question.

Write down every detail, including dates and times and anyone who can corroborate your side of the story.

Have everyone involved write down all the details as well as they can remember them.

Gather any documents, pictures, emails, and so on, and get ready to tell your story.

Don't Hire the First Lawyer You Talk To

They say that it is a crime that you don't have to pass a test to become a parent (which I agree with).

It is also a crime that all you have to do is pass a test to become a lawyer.

Just because someone has passed the bar in your state and has a nice suit does not mean he or she is a good lawyer.

Get Referrals

Get at least three referrals from business people you respect, not referrals from friends. Everyone knows a lawyer, and just because this recommended lawyer was great in a divorce case or DUI, doesn't mean he or she is a good fit for you.

Make sure the referral is from someone who has actually used the attorney in the past and is speaking from experience, not just, "I heard she was a great lawyer."

What Do They Specialize In?

There are many types of law and they are all very different.

Do not assume that just because a person may be a great real estate attorney that he or she knows how to defend you in a criminal trial (let's hope that never happens, but it is a polarizing comparison).

Check Out the Lawyer's Bar Record

Go online and check out the recommended attorney's record with your state's bar.

Find out exactly what the attorney's history is and make sure he or she has a spotless record.

While you are at it, check out the lawyer who is suing you. It is always beneficial to know your enemy.

Interview Three Lawyers

Lawyers worth their salt will give you an hour to see if there is a good match.

Send the attorney a one- or two-page summary as well as the entire lawsuit.

There is never one simple way to defend yourself in a lawsuit. There are multiple approaches just like there are multiple lawyers. Find out how each one would approach the case.

How will they charge you? How long do they think the process will take?

Have they ever had a case like this before, and if they have, what was the outcome?

Do they know the opposing lawyer?

You need to be 100% comfortable with the lawyer you choose.

Managing Your Lawyer

Speak up, you are in charge! You are the one paying the bills and if you are not happy with the direction that the case is going, you have the right to say so.

Lawyers know the law. It is amazing how many lack simple business sense.

Trust your gut; chances are you may be right!

Settle the Case as Fast as You Can

The most important point to remember about getting sued is to not focus on whether you are right or wrong.

It is much more important for you to get the lawsuit to end as quickly and as cheaply as you can.

This needs to be your attorney's focus. Good attorneys recognize that if they get you out of your pain as soon as possible for as little as possible that you will use them again.

You are in business. You will probably get sued more than once.

Getting your attorney to focus on closing the case quickly is the challenge. Both your attorney and the other side's attorney make their money by billing their time. Be very careful not to get caught up in long drawn-out letters, motions, discovery, and so on. The world is littered with lawsuits where the legal bills were 10 times the actual settlement.

Review All Bills

You are the client and you have a right to review and question all bills.

Lawyers bill for their time. Was it really worth it to spend three hours chatting about other issues or how your weekend was? They will charge you for that, as well.

Being Right Is Not Enough

Right and wrong has little to do with a lawsuit (even though we all wish it would).

You don't have to search for very long to find the story of someone who was sued, was absolutely right, but still lost tons of money.

Once again—if you are getting sued, your number one goal is to figure out a way to settle quickly for as little as possible.

Suing Someone Else

So you are mad. You have been wronged.

You are totally convinced that it is absolutely clear that the other person is dead wrong and deserves to pay.

You have suffered a tremendous amount of pain and suffering because of this wrongdoing.

You are convinced that once a lawyer hears your claim he or she will absolutely side with you and will work toward making everything right.

You *are* right about one thing—you'll be able to find a lawyer who will take your money and agree that you are right. Heck, some attorneys will fan the flames for you, get you all excited about how you have been wronged and how you deserve your day in court (all charged at their hourly rate).

Hold the presses.

If you want to see how they really feel about your case, ask them if they will take it on contingency.

In other words, when they win this case for you, their only compensation is 30% of whatever is awarded to you.

They just sat there and told you that this was a slam-dunk and that you were right, correct?

Well then, they should be willing to do this for 30% of the victory right?

Suddenly your new friend does not seem so excited.

Instead, they tell you that taking cases on contingency is not their business model. They just don't take cases like that.

And why not? Because attorneys know what you and I do not.

Lawsuits take a very long time to argue and even if you are 100% in the right, you can still lose.

They know that at the end of a lawsuit, the two lawyers are generally the only two people leaving with their pockets full.

If two lawyers are willing to take your case on contingency, pick the best and then see about just paying them hourly with a small success bonus.

The only time a lawyer will take a case on contingency is when they truly believe that they will win no matter what and that they can make more money off of the 30% than off of an hourly fee.

After all, they are in business to make a profit, too.

Contracts

Having a good contract is imperative to your business.

But, what is a good contract?

A good contract is one that is suggested by your industry/trade organization as being "normal" for your business.

If you want to understand the potential issues with your contracts and agreements in general, have a contract written by one attorney and to another for review.

I have never once seen an attorney say "this is real quality work." They always say, "well, this is okay, but I would change, this, this, and this."

Contract Disputes

Contracts, whether with a customer, vendor, or business partner, will occasionally end up in a dispute.

A well-written and clear agreement is extremely helpful in all of these cases.

At the end of the day, though, these conflicts will generally end up in a negotiation that in many cases has little to do with how the contract was written and more to do with what was supposed to be the "spirit of the agreement."

In Summary, Your Honor, Now What?

Years ago, I used to fight battles based on what I believed to be my sense of right and wrong.

I took on all comers!

No fight was too big or too small.

If I believed that I was right and the other side was wrong, I would take the fight all the way to the mat.

After many years of spending tens of thousands of dollars on legal fees and despite winning many cases, I forgot the most important part of the victory.

There were many cases where I had won, but there was no way to collect any money or the amount I won was nowhere near the amount I spent in legal fees or in collections.

At the end of the day, I would have been better off just settling quickly or not suing and moving on with my business.

CPA Firms

A good certified public accountant will be an important part of your team.

They will be there to help you with overall business strategy.

Think of the CPA as a partner who you consult before going off in any crazy directions or spending large amounts of money.

All entrepreneurs need someone to help reel them in from time to time.

We get excited, and many of us, especially me, have never met an idea that we did not like.

Running financial decisions by someone who is not as close to the day-to-day business operation and who has seen others do similar things, can really give you a different opinion that may save you tens of thousands of dollars.

Equipment Purchases

Many contractors get caught up in the idea of having the best and newest gadgets.

Contracting is a very male-dominated sport and most of us men have never met a "tool" we did not like.

I still have this problem. As recently as last year, I thought, "wow, with all the money we spend on boom lifts, we should just buy five and shuttle them around."

Now, good thing I have smart partners, advisors, a great CFO and CPA firm or I would have one of those things parked in my driveway most of the time (I would eventually get bored with checking out the peak on my roof) and still needing to rent different types of boom lifts anyway.

I am crazy enough that 14 years ago I actually thought of manufacturing our own paint. Fortunately, I once again had good advisors to steer me away from that one.

Ironically, it came up again just a couple of years ago when a new partner said, "What about this idea?" I was able to help steer us away on my own that time.

Expansion

Expansion is a very expensive proposition. The costs of expansion are generally underestimated.

A solid CPA will be able to help you put together the true cost of expanding your business and be able to look at your plan with a critical eye.

Acquisition

Before you even think that buying out your competitor is a great way to expand your business, have your CPA do a complete review of the other company's financials. Have your CPA tell you exactly what the downsides are.

All you will see when you first consider the acquisition is all the good parts of the deal and none of the downsides. Your CPA will show you the pitfalls.

Budgeting

Many home improvement contractors do not have a budget for the year.

This basic, but important, part of business is something that your CPA can help develop for you.

Based on your past history and your future expectations, your CPA can help put together a basic budget that you can review on a monthly basis in order to make sure you are making the right decisions to make a profit.

Job Costing

Good CPA firms will help you put together and/or review your job costing in order to make sure you understand what is working and what is not working on every job.

Interviewing Key Hires

Use your CPA firm to help hire bookkeepers, accounts payable clerks, accounting managers, controllers, and, if you are large enough, CFOs.

They will ask all the questions that you don't know to ask and will help you get the right person for the job.

Financial Controls

The amount of small businesses that have employee theft is staggering.

In many cases, the culprit is a long-term and trusted employee who has been slowly and methodically skimming money for years.

Your CPA firm can help make sure that you have the systems in place to safeguard your cash!

Remember this phrase: "Trust and verify."

CPAs Are Not Just for Taxes

You're getting the point. Many contractors only talk to their CPA firms when they are ready to file their taxes.

If you bring your CPA in throughout the year to help check your progress and work on the overall business, he or she will save you much more money than you will spend on CPA fees.

No, you are not supposed to always like them. Having a CPA that thinks just like you and really likes your ideas is a dangerous relationship.

The last thing you want or need in your business is a CPA who is just excited that you are paying them and agrees with everything you say.

You need someone who will challenge your ideas. You want someone who will stand up to you and tell you that you are crazy from time to time.

Run, Don't Walk

Just like attorneys, the quality of CPAs is all over the map.

There are many different business strategies in the world and there are many different CPA firms using those different strategies.

If you come across a CPA who is telling you about the newest "scheme" to not pay taxes or some special strategy that only a few of the smartest people are using, I suggest you RUN, DON'T WALK down the street and interview another firm.

If it sounds too good to be true, it generally is.

Remember Arthur Andersen and Choose Wisely

Even big firms have bad ideas. Choose a conservative CPA and you will be protected and kept out of jail.

About 10 years ago, I felt it was necessary to change CPA firms.

We had grown to a size that it made sense to move from a sole proprietor to a larger firm that had a staff to be able to better handle our business. We were expanding into a good-sized, multi-state operation and needed the resources of a larger firm.

Being the kind of guy who just wants to get things knocked off my list, I decide to move quickly. I found a firm recommended by a colleague. Since the firm was large and specialized in contracting, I went ahead and had a meeting, (which, of course, went well) and I signed them up on the spot.

I was able to put a check mark next to "CPA firm" on my to do list, pat myself on the back, and move on to the next executive challenge on my list.

Later that week, I had my monthly meeting with my Coach/Vistage chair.

I sat down to lunch, went over the usual catching up on family and friends, and then got down to business.

The first question was one I was very prepared for and excited to answer. "Where are you at on finding a new CPA firm?"

I smiled and looked my coach right in the eye and said, "Done. Signed up …last week," and, of course, in a my normal cocky way, gave him the, "You are not going to catch me this month" look.

Now, my coach is a very intelligent man who has been around the block many times. I was not the first or only eager entrepreneur who he had dealt with.

He leaned back in his chair, smiled and said, "Great. How many did you interview?"

"How many did I interview? What do you mean? I got the job done, is that not what counts? If I found the right one the first time, why does it matter? Aren't all CPA firms the same? After all, accounting is an exact science. It's math. There is only one way to do it, right?"

I think I will remember that meeting for the rest of my business career as one that really took the air out of my sails and reminded me why I believe every business person needs a coach.

It was not about getting the job done. It was about the process of learning from the meetings. Every CPA, lawyer, or other professional will approach problems from different ways. Those different approaches don't always match your needs. Take your time to find the one who does.

Chapter 14

Estimating and Pricing

Estimating and pricing are two completely different pieces of your business.

Estimating is the "art" of figuring out exactly how long a particular task will take to complete.

Pricing is understanding your business model, your market, and your overhead well enough to be able to set a price for your services and turn a profit.

Many business people think of estimating as something that is only for contractors. However, almost every business has estimating as a component of its daily activities.

For contractors, properly estimating the hours and materials on a given job is critical to their success or failure. But they're not alone. Even though it is more obvious in the contractor world, every successful business needs to understand how long various tasks will take and the cost of materials used. In order to accurately price your goods or services, you must know what they are costing you.

Examples

Mechanics

The majority of auto mechanics have software that tells them how long a given task should take an average mechanic. Using this information, they are able to come up with the price they charge their customers who come into their shop. How many mechanics, though, actually compare their actual labor times to the estimated times? What if you realized that by training your people to be more efficient, you could beat the "generic" standards set up in the software? With that information in hand, you could price your jobs more competitively and become the low-cost automotive repair leader in your market.

Caterers

Estimating food cost is critical to your success. What do you do to track and compare estimates to actual costs?

Carpet Cleaners

How long should it take to clean one room? How much do the products cost to clean that single room? Does it take all of your employees the same amount of time and materials? Do you compare crew to crew?

Manufacturing

Custom manufacturing can be a nightmare for cost control. These companies will hire manufacturers to build prototypes or to outright manufacture different products. I have personally seen companies lose an entire year's profit on poorly estimated projects.

Restaurants

How long does it take to create your chef's newest creation? What are the food costs involved and can you charge enough for it when you account for the extra staff time and food cost?

Estimating System

Having a system for estimating is a key component to your business. The "gut call" estimating system that many business owners use is just not going to carry you though the larger and more challenging jobs.

An estimating system can be a simple spreadsheet. On that spreadsheet is a breakdown of each task by employee hours and by cost of materials. The system can also be a robust piece of software that will do it all for you.

Estimating Software and Books

There are some great estimating software programs, as well as books, on the market today. Most industry and trade groups can direct you to these resources. Keep in mind that these estimating standards are only guidelines. Your mission should be to create your own set of standards that reflect the efficiency that you are building into you business. If you are able to get the work done 20 percent faster than the numbers in the manual or software you bought, your opportunities will grow exponentially. By paying close attention to these numbers, you have the opportunity to be the low-cost leader, still maintain your margins, and grab more market share.

The Horrors of Underestimating

Everyone has seen it and everyone has done it.

You quickly take a job that was supposed to be a simple project. You put some quick numbers together without paying much attention to the details.

Later you find out that it really took you or your guys twice as long as you thought because you took a guess at the scope of the job and didn't properly measure the project.

> **AVOIDING UNDERESTIMATING**
>
> Here are a few reminders to help you avoid the horrors of underestimating:
>
> - Pay close attention to the details. Closely review each section of the job to make sure you fully understand the scope of work that will be required.
> - Measure twice just to make sure. Many a blown estimate is due to an improper measurement of the time required to do the job.
> - Understand your labor costs and materials costs. What is the total average wage of the staff, including taxes and burden? What are the exact costs of all materials? Don't forget the little stuff, making sure to include all the regular consumables that you will use on the project.
> - Count the extras for specific projects, including storage, equipment that you don't own and need to rent, and travel.
> - Triple-check your numbers. Math errors are a terrible way to blow an estimate.

Pricing

Once you have a clear understanding of your job or product costs, you need to mark up the price to account for your business overhead and, of course, for your profit.

Your overhead should take into account all costs that are not directly related to the job. Include in this overhead costs associated with marketing, office, trucks, rent, utilities, your salary, and so on. These are all part of your overall overhead.

Mark Up

Mark up varies wildly by industry. It can be anywhere from 10% to 50%, depending on everything from overhead to market conditions.

It is critical that you understand what you need to charge your customers in order to cover your expenses and turn the profit you desire.

Most of your competitors have the same basket of direct costs that you do. For the most part, you are all pulling from the same labor pool and are paying roughly the same wages for your staff. Your materials cost should be very close to one another. The only difference between your price to your competitor's price is how much you each mark up the job.

Prices Are All Over the Map

I am constantly amazed at how prices are so different when I go to buy just about anything or especially when I have a project done around my home. There are really only a few reasons why these prices can be lower or higher.

- The company over- or underbid the job. This is generally due to a lack of an estimating system and/or not paying attention to the basic steps listed earlier in this chapter.
- Business overhead is either very high or very low and therefore the service or product is priced accordingly.
- The company is using a cheaper or more expensive grade of materials.
- The company is willing to take the job just to keep their guys working.
- The company really has no clue what they are doing and they're just guessing.
- A salesperson, in addition to selling, is also pricing and estimating. He or she just wants the job since the salesperson is paid on revenue not gross profit.

Just To Keep My Guys Working

This is a phrase uttered by too many service companies and contractors too many times.

They are way too willing to take a job that barely covers their costs just so they can keep their guys busy.

This all-too-common practice only helps to lead to the contractor death spiral.

The concept of taking jobs just to keep your guys busy only leads to you having to spend hour after hour babysitting a job that is not making you a dime.

The job never turns out the way you expected. The customer is never as cool as you thought he or she would be (considering the amazing discount they are getting and that you are working for free).

Do yourself a huge favor and give your guys the time off to chase some side work so that you have the time to focus on what should be your number one priorities—marketing and sales.

It is impossible to focus on finding profitable work if you are spending all day on jobs that don't make you any money.

You Will Never Make It Up with Volume

Far too many people think that it is just fine to take work at little to no margins because they ultimately will make it up in volume.

You are not a major grocery store or a huge gas station.

Small business is not a volume business.

If you were to book so much work that you increased your volume tremendously, your overhead would also increase proportionately.

More work means more equipment, more trucks, more supervision, more office staff, and so on. More volume always translates into more overhead. More overhead generally means less profit, not more.

Job Watch!

Understand the size and scope of jobs that you are comfortable taking.

The death trap for many business owners is taking the job that is much larger than the jobs that are in their "sweet spot."

The Allure of Easy Money

For any business owner, a large job can seem like a path to riches.

What's not to like? One job for a zillion dollars, all in one location, regular work for your staff, only one customer to look after, and *all that profit!*

It's time to start looking at buying a new boat!

If it were only that easy.

Large jobs generally mean larger headaches.

Not to say you should never go after larger jobs, but here are the things you need to think about first.

Experience

Do you have the experience within your business to take on a project of this scope and size?

Do you have the knowledge to be able to properly estimate the project?

Resources

Large projects are significant cash and resource drains on any business. Larger companies pay slowly and have a tendency to cause major cash flow challenges to small businesses.

Chapter 15

Big Opportunities

The appeal is sometimes just too tempting. The opportunity presents itself whereby your business can explode by making a deal with a potential client that will exponentially increase your revenue. Is this a gift from heaven, or a deal with the devil?

Big Box Retailer

The call comes in and all of a sudden your world is turned upside down. You are bouncing off the walls. Buyers from your industry's "big box retailer" just called and they are interested in carrying your product.

You start to do the math. Each unit they want wholesales for $20. Your cost is only $14. They have 1,000 locations, and each location should be able to sell 100 units a month. You begin dreaming. Their stores have thousands of people a day rolling through them and these customers all want your product. The numbers are staggering. Those 100 sales per 1,000 locations multiplied by a $20 retail price is $2 million in revenue per month and, wow, $600,000 in gross profit per month! Your bottom line is now 10 times what it was.

How does this sound to you? If you're drooling (so did I at one point in my career), read this chapter carefully.

Big Box Buddies

When you start your relationship with your new "partner," you will more than likely be working with a single merchant who is in charge of a product or line. This will be your new "big box buddy."

Big box retailers do not have partners.

You are a vendor. You are not a partner. Do not fall for the sales pitch. Big box retailers only care about their bottom lines and what drives revenue. If you have something they want, they will be excited to have it, at least in the beginning. They will tell you that you are partners and you need each other equally. They need your unique product for their customers and you need their distribution.

A marriage made in heaven.

Don't buy it.

Pricing Pressure

Once your product or service has been tested and they start a roll out, the relationship begins to change. Expect that you will be called to headquarters once a year, at a minimum, to talk about price. Your "partner" will want you to lower what you are charging them. Whatever margin you had going into the deal will be eroded over time. They will actively source other suppliers of your product or service and pit their pricing against yours. If you want to keep their business, you will need to lower your price point.

In many cases, your big box buddy will have his or her personal bonus tied to how much he or she can bring down your prices each year. Big box retailers tell their customers that they are low cost leaders. These low costs come on the backs of people like you.

Even if you have a great relationship with your big box buddy, you can count on one thing. They will leave you. They will quit, get fired, or get promoted every 18 to 24 months. When your new buddy arrives, all the rules will change.

Advertising Dollars

Another little trick is the big box retailer's "co-op advertising" dollars program. This little program was undoubtedly not brought to your attention when the relationship started. After all, you didn't really expect your new partner to advertise the product for you did you? Remember, though…you're partners. Expect your big box buddy to hit you up for small amounts of money to cover a "few promotions" at first that are guaranteed to improve sales (or so they say). As time passes, these "promotions" will become the norm until eventually you are required to write a sizable check every year just for the privilege of doing business with them.

Slotting Fees

Don't like your shelf space? Your big box buddy can take care of that, too. Just write a check—sometimes a BIG check—and your buddy will give you premier eye level shelf space.

Payments

Big box retailers are notorious for paying their vendors slowly and then hitting them with extra charges when they do. Expect to be paid in 90-120 days and to be shorted on your invoice, no matter what promises your buddy makes.

The Extra Surprises

Prepare yourself for extra travel expenses, dedicated staff, and a whole host of expenses that you did not initially count on when you were drooling over potential profits.

Sales will be slower than you planned and slower than what your big box buddy promised you.

The End

Your relationship can end faster than it began. Many of these relationships are ended quickly, sometimes with as little as a month's notice. If you move forward and do accept the big box retailer's offer, you really need to have a plan for what happens if that portion of your business is suddenly shut off. This can be very scary if, in catering to your big box retailer, you start to ignore your past customers who now represent a small portion of your business.

Sour Grapes

If all of this big box retailer advice sounds like sour grapes, I have done my job. I know too many small business people (including myself) who were mesmerized by the lure of easy big box retailer money, only to be one of the many small business corpses they've tossed aside.

The mistake I made almost cost me my company. I was excited to see what I could learn from people running an $80 billion company. What I learned is that entrepreneurs are still some of the smartest folks I have ever met and that large companies, with some notable exceptions, do not generally have as talented people as those you may have in your business.

If you decide to move ahead with a big box buddy, proceed at your own risk. You have been warned! My conscience is clear.

Other Businesses

Similar types of large-scale and low-margin opportunities exist in most businesses.

Restaurant Catering

The catering business can be a great way for a restaurant to improve profitability. The issue here, though, is very similar to the big box retailer relationship.

Let's say you find a large hotel or conference center that wants you to handle all of its breakfasts, lunches, and dinners. This can be a huge boom to your business, but may become the same challenge that retailers have with big box retailers. If you are looking into one of these types of relationships, go back and reread the last few paragraphs. The situation you are getting into is almost identical.

Auto Mechanics

Fleet maintenance opportunities can grow your business overnight. Be careful.

Dry Cleaners

Uniform cleaning can bring in daily business at high volumes. The margins, though, tend to be minimal. Bid these with great caution.

Cleaning Services

Large office building or factory cleaning can turn your mobile housecleaning business into a major undertaking. Do your homework and make sure you have the staff and expertise to handle this large endeavor.

Your Business

Whatever type of business you own, there are similar large-scale opportunities. Proceed with caution and know your risks. They can be a godsend, but only if approached properly.

Staff Crossing Over: Like a Fish Out of Water

Staff members typically become very good at one specific type of work.

Those who are excellent dealing with residential customers will have a high degree of customer awareness and understanding of customer expectations. They will be accustomed to dealing with all the ins and outs that come with this type of work.

Putting your crack residential crew into a new construction project, for example, is like putting fish out of water. Everything from the terminology to the flow of work is different.

The same is true if you take employees who are used to dealing in a commercial environment and put them in a residential environment. All of a sudden expectations are different. They are now expected to deal with the customer directly and, of course, all the customer's silly requests!

Another good example of erroneously reassigning your employees is in the restaurant business. Taking kitchen staff members who are used to dealing with banquets and reassigning them to your high-end gourmet restaurant could be a recipe for disaster. They might be miserable and ineffective.

It is enough to drive your people to quit.

I am not trying to say that you should never try anything new. If you do decide to embark on such an adventure, make sure that you understand the differences and be prepared to train your employees accordingly.

Opportunities Outside Your Area of Expertise

Cash Flow

Large contracts also require a large commitment of cash.

Payroll will still need to be paid regardless of when you get paid for these large jobs.

Materials will need to be paid or set up on job accounts with joint checks so that you get the terms you need.

In many cases, large jobs don't pay for 60 to 90 or even 120 days.

If you are not set up to be able to fund the cost of not getting paid for 120 days, you should not be taking these contracts.

Your business will not survive.

Bonding and Insurance

Large companies may require specific types of insurance and bonding that you may not have.

Read the contract very carefully and make sure you are capable of providing the level of insurance and support that are required in the contract.

There can be a huge price difference in carrying $1 million of insurance versus carrying $5 million.

Bonding on jobs is another requirement you cannot overlook.

Estimating

If you are not 100% confident in your estimating, run away from the large project.

Small errors on $10K jobs are challenging, but they become huge nightmares on $100K jobs.

There is nothing like spending $125K to produce a job that nets you $98K. This happens all of the time.

Being Low Bid

If you find yourself being the low bid on a job, try to find out where everyone else is.

If you find everyone else submitted bids within 5% of each other and you are 25% less, you are about to lose your shorts!

Final Thoughts on Going Outside the Box

For the record, I don't recommend that you stay solely in your box and never try anything new.

What I am trying to say is that before you venture out into the world that is new to you, make sure you do your homework!

KEYS TO BEING SUCCESSFUL WHILE EXPANDING INTO LARGER OPPORTUNITIES

- Keep your eyes and ears open—listen, listen, listen.
- What happened to the company you are potentially replacing? Did they go out of business? Try to find this company and have a conversation.
- Interview other vendors that deal with the same large company.
- Read your contract thoroughly.
- Watch your cash.
- Don't let one customer become more than 35% of your business.
- Have an escape plan ready for when they pull the plug on you.
- Don't be greedy—know when to say no to more markets.
- Watch your overhead. It will grow, grow, grow!
- Fight to maintain your margins.
- Because the best lists always go to 11...Don't drink the Kool-Aid.

Chapter 16

Management

There are so many schools of thought on managing people that when you search for management books on Amazon you get 95,965 results.

You could spend the rest of your career just reading management books and never actually manage a single person!

Since none of us have the time, unlimited wealth, or interest to spend that much time learning the nuances of every management philosophy, I thought I would distill my years of experience into a few simple paragraphs that have not yet failed me.

There are five basic aspects to managing people in any organization. These five components are the same regardless of the industry or size of company you run.

The five management components are:

1. Job mapping
2. Understanding/communication
3. Expectations management
4. Incentive management
5. Culture

Job Mapping

The Right Seat on the Bus

The first part of managing is to find people who fit the type of work you need to have done.

You need to make sure the person you have in a particular spot has the skill set and attitude to get the work done.

You can't take a person who is a salesperson by nature and try to make this person an accountant.

You can't take someone who is a computer programmer and put this person up on a ladder and ask them to just hammer away.

You can't take someone who really does not like dealing with the public and put this person in charge of customer service.

One mistake we all make is taking those who are star performers with great attitudes and assuming that they will be good at anything we give them to do. That practice just does not work.

Attitude Is Everything, Right?

A person's attitude is the key to having the right person in the right seat.

But, the question is, "What is the right attitude for the job at hand?"

It is easy to pick the excited person who has great customer service skills and who is always positive to be a salesperson or to deal directly with customers. But, do you really want that person as your bookkeeper or controller? You want the person who is much more cautious, controlled, and perhaps a little pessimistic to be in charge of your finances. You want someone who does not believe everything he or she hears from employees out in the field about when an invoice is going to be paid. You want someone who, in general, has a healthy distrust of those sales types. You want someone who feels the need to squirrel away nuts for a rainy day. In general, you want a bookkeeper or controller who will watch your back.

Skills Required for Each Job

Take a look at each job in your organization. What are the basic attitudes and skills required for each of the roles in your company?

ROLES IN YOUR COMPANY

Make a list of the roles in your company:

Sales _____

Office Work _____

Customer Service_____

Superintendent _____

Server _____

Bartender _____

Bus Boy_____

Foreman _____

Laborer _____

Other _____

What skills and attitudes are associated with each role?

1. _____
2. _____
3. _____
4. _____
5. _____
6. _____
7. _____
8. _____

Your Employees

Now make a list of your employees and gauge them on the same list of skills and attitudes.

Do they match up with their current role in the company?

Is there a better seat on the bus for them?

Different Skills and Attitudes

If you do this simple survey on the roles and the individuals in your organization, you will see that you have some people improperly placed in jobs.

In many cases, such employees are in a role that they thought you wanted them to have. They are not happy in it, but feel they would disappoint you if they told you that they wanted to change roles.

This process of "job mapping" is the first step to building a functional and manageable company.

Understanding/Communication

Many companies can be a place of stress and frustration for the owners as well as for the employees.

Many people believe stress and frustration are just part of doing business in any industry. They think working with customers and dealing with their expectations, battling deadlines, and so on, make for the high stress level.

If you are experiencing stress and frustration in your company, it's not coming from the customers.

The stress and frustration you are experiencing is coming almost entirely from the poor communication that is within your organization.

Communication—No, Not Text Messaging

This poor communication is not about phones, emails, or text messages.

It's the way in which we deliver the message and the way in which everyone hears the message we are delivering.

We all communicate differently.

For example, how many times do you think hard-driving entrepreneurs have frustrated their accountants for no other reason than the tone of voice they're using?

The key to proper communication is to understand everyone's personality profiles. You'll know the best way to communicate your message to others if you know what makes them tick. They'll not only understand what you're trying to tell them, but will be excited to go out and do what you're asking them to do.

The key to proper communication is much more than slowing down and making sure that your employees actually hear what you are saying. When many business owners think about communication their immediate response is, "I am a great communicator. No one ever misunderstands my directions. I am crystal clear." Communication is a two-way street. The fact that you are "crystal clear" in your communication does not mean that your employees feel like you are a good listener. They may not feel like their concerns are being heard.

Your employees are on the front lines of your organization. They hear your customers' questions and concerns on a daily basis. They hear each others' questions and concerns. They may be willing to share with you what they know, but only if you are willing to listen.

Take the time to open the lines of communication between you and your team. Don't say you have an open-door policy and then be grumpy with everyone who wants to talk to you. Truly have an open-door policy and make it a point to listen to your team daily.

Walk around your workplace. "Management by walking around" is an old term, but a great one. You will learn amazing tidbits about your team if you just take the time to visit with them while they are doing their daily jobs.

Personality Profiles

Through a simple series of questions, personality profiles can give each person a 10-plus page description of who they are and, more importantly, how they deal with stressful situations.

Wikipedia does a much better job of describing DISC than I can.

DISC

DISC is the four quadrant behavioral model based on the work of William Moulton Marston PhD (1893–1947) to examine the behavior of individuals in their environment or within a specific situation (otherwise known as environment). It therefore focuses on the styles and preferences of such behavior.

Marston graduated from doctoral studies at Harvard in the newly developing field of psychology and was also a consulting psychologist, researcher, and author or co-author of five books. His works were showcased in *Emotions of Normal People* in 1928 among others.

In 1948, Walter V. Clarke established his new business, Walter V. Clarke Associates, to utilize the years of development and research he had undertaken after listening to a lecture at Harvard by Prescott Leckey that postulated that it was possible with a high degree of accuracy to determine and predict the long-term behavior of an individual based upon a set of questions. Working with Marston, he was able to name four vectors of behavior, namely Assertiveness, Sociability, Tranquility, and Dependence, and the means to identify the relative propensity of individuals to behave according to these predictive scales.

This system of dimensions of observable behavior has become known as the universal language of behavior. Research has found that characteristics of behavior can be grouped into these four major "personality styles" and they tend to exhibit specific characteristics common to that particular style. All individuals possess all four, but what differs from one to another is the extent of each.

For most, these types are seen in shades of grey rather than black or white, and within that, there is an interplay of behaviors, otherwise known as blends. The denotation of such blends starts with the primary (or stronger) type, followed by the secondary (or lesser) type, although all contribute more than just purely the strength of that "signal".

Having understood the differences between these blends makes it possible to integrate individual team members with less troubleshooting. In a typical team, there are varying degrees of compatibility, not just toward tasks but interpersonal relationships as well. However, when they are identified, energy can be spent on refining the results.

Each of these types has its own unique value to the team, ideal environment, general characteristics, what the individual is motivated by, and value to team.

Although the original company to create behavioral assessments, Walter V. Clarke Associates, is still operating, many other systems based upon this original work have been developed, especially by people who originally worked with Clarke, and these have mostly used the DISC notation. There are probably several thousand derivatives of this work. Only a few of these give credit to Clarke, including Bill Bonstetter from TTI and Success Insights in America, and Nathan Richards from Personality Insights Australia.

DISC is also used in an assortment of areas, including by many companies, HR professionals, organizations, consultants, coaches, and trainers.

Method

The assessments classify four aspects of behavior by testing a person's preferences in word associations (compare with Myers-Briggs Type Indicator). DISC is an acronym for:

- Dominance—Relating to control, power, and assertiveness
- Influence—Relating to social situations and communication
- Steadiness (submission in Marston's time)—Relating to patience, persistence, and thoughtfulness
- Conscientiousness (or caution, compliance in Marston's time)—Relating to structure and organization

These four dimensions can be grouped in a grid with "D" and "I" sharing the top row and representing extroverted aspects of the personality, and "C" and "S" below representing introverted aspects. "D" and "C" then share the left column and represent task-focused aspects, and "I" and "S" share the right column and represent social aspects. In this matrix, the vertical dimension represents a factor of "Assertive" or "Passive", whereas the horizontal represents "Open" vs. "Guarded".

Dominance: People who score high in the intensity of the "D" styles factor are very active in dealing with problems and challenges, while low "D" scores are people who want to do more research before committing to a decision. High "D" people are described as demanding, forceful, egocentric, strong willed, driving, determined, ambitious, aggressive, and pioneering. Low D scores describe those who are conservative, low-keyed, cooperative, calculating, undemanding, cautious, mild, agreeable, modest, and peaceful.

Influence: People with high "I" scores influence others through talking and activity and tend to be emotional. They are described as convincing, magnetic, political, enthusiastic, persuasive, warm, demonstrative, trusting, and optimistic. Those with low "I" scores influence more by data and facts, and not with feelings. They are described as reflective, factual, calculating, skeptical, logical, suspicious, matter of fact, pessimistic, and critical.

Steadiness: People with high "S" styles scores want a steady pace, security, and do not like sudden change. High "S" individuals are calm, relaxed, patient, possessive, predictable, deliberate, stable, consistent, and tend to be unemotional and poker faced. Low "S" intensity scores are those who like change and variety. People with low "S" scores are described as restless, demonstrative, impatient, eager, or even impulsive.

Conscientious: People with high "C" styles adhere to rules, regulations, and structure. They like to do quality work and do it right the first time. High "C" people are careful, cautious, exacting, neat, systematic, diplomatic, accurate, and tactful. Those with low "C" scores challenge the rules and want independence and are described as self-willed, stubborn, opinionated, unsystematic, arbitrary, and unconcerned with details.

In summary, DISC allows you to better understand your employees. I have found them to be so dead-on accurate that each time I start working with a new person I send them a copy of mine. Armed with my personality profile, they know exactly what they are getting themselves into.

The web is also full of many tests that are skill based. You can have cashiers tested for math aptitude, mechanics tested for technical skills, and so on. The list goes on and on. You truly don't need to just trust your gut.

Expectations Management

There have been countless studies that perform "deep dives" into why people fail at their jobs.

The studies all come to the same conclusion.

People fail at their jobs because they do not know what is expected of them.

Most people don't go to work each day with the intention of doing a really bad job that will possibly get them fired (you are right; there are exceptions to every rule and everybody has had one of these employees, but hold it for now).

Most people go to work hoping to please their supervisors.

The challenge, time and time again, though, comes when what you expect and what they *think* you expect are not aligned.

The Basics

Do your employees truly understand your expectations in the office and on the jobsite?

If they were asked these basic questions, would their answers surprise you?

For fun, ask your employees this list of 10 questions and see what you get. You may be surprised at what you discover.

EXPECTATIONS QUESTIONNAIRE

1. What are the expectations for the following:
   a. Starting time?
   b. Breaks?
   c. Ending time?
   d. Personal and sick days?
   e. Vacations?
2. What do deadlines mean in this organization?
   a. Fast and hard
   b. Soft and squishy
   c. Do they matter at all?
3. Work product questions

   Example—contractor:
   a. What are the quality expectations on your jobs?
   b. What should a work site look like from a cleanliness standpoint?
   c. Punch lists
      • What is an acceptable punch list?
      • How many items should be on a customer punch list?
      • What does "done" mean?

   Example—restaurant:
   a. How long should a customer have to wait for a beverage, appetizer, meal, or dessert?
   b. What does "clean" mean in the kitchen?
   c. How many times does a meal need to be ordered to remain on the menu?

---

4. Communication
    a. How long should it take to return a phone call?
    b. How long should it take to return an email?
    c. How long should it take to return a text?
    d. What is an acceptable message on voicemail?
    e. What should a signature line on an employee's email look like?
    f. What does it mean to be on time?

5. Marketing
    a. Do you have business cards?
    b. Do you know how to take down information from a customer about another potential client?
    c. Have you "role played" and practiced how to talk to a customer about the company?
    d. Is there a bonus for new leads and does everyone know how much it is?

6. Appearance
    a. What is the dress code?
    b. What is the policy on hair grooming, jewelry, tattoos, and so on?
    c. How is one expected to maintain the company vehicles?

7. Pay structure
    a. Do you understand how and when you get paid?
    b. Do you understand how you earn a bonus and when it gets paid?
    c. Do you understand how you can earn a raise?

8. Advancement
    a. Do you understand where you fit in the company and why you are important?
    b. Do you understand what your next step would be if you perform above expectations?

9. Your company
    a. Do you know your company's "commercial"?
    b. Do you know the top reasons why customers choose this company?
    c. Do you know and carry with you any company references?
    d. Does the boss practice these items with you regularly?

10. Consequences
    a. Do you understand the consequences for not knowing the answers to these questions?

Expectations Management: The Next Steps

Almost everything within a business should be broken into a series of tasks. Every role within a company has a list of daily tasks that different people will perform.

Your big challenge is in determining how long each task should take your employees to complete. Almost every task the average employee completes can be done 25% faster and still stay safe. (Okay, driving a car should not be done 25% faster—remember, I said *almost*.)

Start by making a list of the top five tasks that your people are responsible for accomplishing everyday. The ideal situation is to find a task that more than one person does repetitively. Find out how long it takes to actually accomplish the task. This task could be something as simple as entering data into a computer or cleaning a certain area of your shop. If there is more than one person performing a task, you are almost guaranteed that there will be two different amounts of time associated with the task.

Start by Asking Questions

How long does this take? Why do you do it that way? You will be surprised at the answers. Generally, they will be something like, "I don't know how long it takes, I have never checked" and "I was taught to do it this way so I have always just done it this way." The majority of people don't really know how long individual tasks should take and therefore the time allotted for the task expands to meet the time available.

Look for New Ways

If you take the time to watch how even the most mundane of tasks are done in your business, you will innately find new ways to speed up the process. As a business owner, you already have the "efficiency" gene. It is right next to the "I'm the one paying for all this" gene. Most business owners are substantially more efficient at the majority of tasks in their organization.

Encourage Employees to Speed Up

Have contests to see who can get things done quicker while maintaining the quality and safety standards that you require. Offer bonuses for efficiency improvements and publicly recognize those who are making a difference.

If you make these steps a part of your everyday routine, you will easily see an improvement of 20-25% in your efficiency, which, of course directly translates into less expense and higher profit.

Incentive Management: Share in the Profits

Many of you believe you are paying people a great hourly wage and/or a great salary and that should be enough to get the job done correctly.

You're right. You are paying to get the job done correctly. But is that all you really want? You are better served if your people go above and beyond just getting the job done "correctly" every day.

What you really want is for every customer not just to thank you, but also to rave about you.

If you really want higher profit margins and want customers to be thrilled about you, you need to encourage your people to do so with bonuses.

Step One

Set up a program in which supervisors share in the wins when profit and quality exceed expectations. Bonuses and profit sharing are earned through extraordinary performance. Salaries and hourly wages are for maintaining the status quo.

You'll achieve amazing results after your supervisors understand that they share in the profits by focusing on profitability and quality.

Your material waste will drop significantly as your employees begin to view the cost of the materials coming out of their own pockets. They will quickly realize that any waste is counted against their bonus and they will find new ways to make sure that everything is used properly.

Miraculously, they will find new ways to get their job done efficiently. Ineffective workers will suddenly disappear from jobsites, offices, restaurants, and shops, as supervisors suddenly have no interest in keeping the slower people on their team.

At least one of your supervisors will suddenly want to fire the same guy who you have been wanting to get rid of for years because your supervisor all of a sudden discovered how slow he works.

The difference now is that the supervisor realizes keeping his slow brother on the payroll is costing him money!

It is amazing the efficiencies that you will find in your business when you tie your key people into the profit.

Step Two

Now that you have successfully implemented Step One, you need to roll the program out to the rest of your workforce. Again, this does not have to require massive expenditures.

In the service and construction industries, you should incentivize enough so that everyone understands that when a job comes in under "X" hours and "X" material cost, that they, too, will share by receiving "Y" dollars.

If you are in a retail environment, incentivize people based on shrinkage, increased sales, and repeat customers.

Every business is a little different, but if you look hard enough you will find great ways to incentivize your employees and thereby increase your profits.

After implementing this step, you will have everyone in your organization focused on driving more business and higher profit margins.

Step Three

Office costs have a tendency to creep up over time.

Make sure that whoever runs your office is bonused to keep costs down and not incentivized to add people to your overhead.

Work on a plan that gives office managers a percentage of the money saved when the overall office costs come in under an agreed-upon amount.

Overall

When you put in the time and effort and get all of your key people to watch your bottom line (because they will share in the win), your life will suddenly change.

No longer will you be the "Lone Ranger" who is the only one out there caring about the bottom line. You will have a group of partners who will care as much as you do about the company!

Culture—The Glue That Holds It All Together

You, the CEO and owner, decide your company's culture.

Every company has a culture. Every culture is as unique as the business itself. Employees wear the company's culture on their sleeves.

It only takes a few minutes of talking to people within an organization to get a feel for the culture.

Define Your Company's Culture

Take a moment to answer these questions. A picture of your culture, or lack of culture, will appear.

- Does it revolve around you and only you?
- Are people afraid of what you will say or do?
- Are your employees free to speak their minds?
- Do you encourage the sharing of ideas?
- Does everyone want the company to make money and succeed?
- Do your employees socialize at work?
- Do your employees socialize outside of work?
- How does everyone define hard work?
- How does everyone define play or having a good time as a group?
- What do you want your company culture to be?

It is up to you not only to define your company's culture, but also to make sure one exists.

If people are excited to come to work every day, genuinely care about the well being of the company and their fellow employees, and feel like they are trusted and respected, amazing things will happen.

Chapter 17

Meetings: Communication Is Key!

Meetings are necessary evils in every business. The challenge is making sure that your meetings are as productive as possible and that your employees actually look at the time they spend in meetings as productive and not a drain. I have put together a list of different types of meetings that you should be having with your employees. Each type of meeting serves a specific purpose, so read carefully.

Weekly/Bi-Weekly Team Meeting

The weekly or bi-weekly team meeting is the workhorse meeting. The following sections list nine tips that apply to this type of meeting (as well as most meetings).

Tip One

Overall team/management meetings should be limited to no more than once a week (ideally once every two weeks).

Tip Two

Start with a positive focus. In meetings with fewer than 10 people, go around the room and give everyone 60 seconds to say one positive thing about the business and one positive thing about his or her personal life. This sets a positive tone for the rest of the meeting.

Tip Three

Everyone wants a company update from you! Most business owners don't understand the degree to which their employees are yearning to understand your thoughts on the business and how outside economic forces may impact the business.

Tip Four

Celebrate successes! Company meetings are a great time to recognize your team's contributions.

Tip Five

Don't fall in love with the sound of your voice. Limit your speaking time. Make sure everyone has a chance to say his or her piece.

Tip Six

Listen, listen, and listen some more. You have hired smart people; make sure you listen to their input.

Tip Seven

Agendas and clocks are a must. Every meeting needs a written agenda that is distributed in advance. Each topic needs to have a set amount of time allocated for discussion.

Tip Eight

Be a participant; get over the need to chair every meeting. Let your staff take turns chairing the meeting, keeping the schedule, gathering the topics from others, and creating the agenda. You will be amazed at how much more seriously they take meetings once they have had a chance to run one!

Tip Nine

Meetings must start and end on time—no excuses! Have your team agree to a start time and set agreed-upon penalties for being late. In my company, those arriving late do 25 push-ups. Some people have a $20 fine that goes into the company "party" fund. Either way, make sure everyone agrees on the penalty.

Project Meeting

The project meeting is a meeting in which a team working on a specific project gets together. The team may meet once or twice a week in order to review the project's progress. Here are some tips for running productive project meetings.

Tip One

Make sure that everyone who is attending these meetings has the schedule well in advance. Everyone is busy and schedules change. If you do not stick to the meeting schedule, the project will never get done.

Tip Two

Participants should be limited to those who are directly involved with the project. Those who are just curious or feel the need to have their fingers in everything are a distraction and hindrance to getting the project finished. The core participants should be chosen and required to attend each meeting.

There may be a need to pull in people from other parts of your organization for input. These invitees should be brought in only when the group has specific questions. Remember, everyone would rather be part of a new and different project than the regular job at hand, but if we were all involved with new projects, the core business likely would not get done.

Tip Three

The project group needs to have one leader who is responsible for keeping everything on track. This person does not need to be you! How will your people ever grow to the next level if you don't let them take leadership roles?

The leader is responsible for the meeting agenda, keeping track of each member's tasks, the overall completion of the project, and, of course, reporting back to you on the progress.

Tip Four

Being part of a new project team is a privilege (depending on the project, of course). Each member of the team needs to understand the importance of the project and the importance of getting their assigned part of the project completed before each and every meeting. They need to know that failure to do so will mean removal from the project team or worse.

Tip Five

The meeting requires someone to take notes and document the progress. The scribe should rotate to a different team member (other than the leader) at each meeting.

Tip Six

People who are on a project team are on it for a reason. Everyone should understand that their voices are equally important. Ultimately the leader will decide the project's direction (with your input, of course). Some of the best ideas come from the most unlikely places. Encourage everyone to speak up!

Tip Seven

Resist the temptation to be in every meeting. Furthermore, resist the temptation to personally control every aspect of your business. Your input is important, of course, but remember you are much more impactful when you show up from time to time to give praise and a gentle (or not-so-gentle) nudge, than if you are constantly in your team's face. Your people will never grow into better leaders without giving them a chance to steer the boat from time to time.

Company Lunches or Breakfast Meetings

Company lunches or breakfasts are a great informal way to spend some time with your employees. They serve a couple of purposes. They allow you to show your appreciation for everyone's hard work and allow you to give a brief company update.

Tip One

These meetings do not have to be in a formal environment. Ours are done in the company parking lot or in the warehouse. When the company was much smaller, we just brought take-out into the break room. It truly is the thought that counts. A company favorite of ours is having the management cook breakfast for everyone.

Tip Two

Prepare a brief company update. Let everyone know how you are doing (keep it positive, always). Use this time to single out people who have performed above and beyond. Make a big deal out of those who are making a difference. Introduce new employees and tell everyone else why you hired them!

Remember this is meant to be a *short* announcement. Keep this part of the "meeting" to 10 or 15 minutes. Everyone will tire of your voice long before you do.

Tip Three

One of the key elements of this meeting is to allow everyone to socialize. Make it a point to sit with people with whom you don't normally have a chance to sit and talk. They will appreciate getting your time and you will learn things about them and your business that you never would otherwise.

Tip Four

Once a quarter bring in a lunch speaker. There are plenty of people out there who would love to come and talk to your group for an hour. How about a speaker who is focused on healthy living? How about a speaker who can show everyone the power of properly investing in IRAs? A supplier coming in to talk about the industry may work for your business. If you put your mind to it, the list is endless.

Morning "Pump Up!" Meetings

This meeting can be as simple as five minutes before you open the doors in the morning or the first 30 minutes of a salesperson's day via a conference call. The point of this brief get together is to focus everyone on the day ahead. Make sure everyone's attitudes are in the right place and that people are clear on what is important for the day. This meeting is especially important for any outside or inside sales force. During Home Depot's early years, this meeting was a part of every day and the morning "cheer" was a key part of meeting.

Tip One

Keep it brief! This is not meant to be a big long dissertation about the state of the economy. Its purpose is to focus employees on what's important that day.

Tip Two

Everyone should get 30 seconds to say what is their biggest priority for the day. This allows everyone to get focused and realize they will be held accountable to that statement later in the day.

Tip Three

These meetings should be no larger than five to eight people. The meetings will drag on far too long if the groups are larger. In larger organizations, managers or team leaders can lead the meetings and you can drop in on them to say hello.

Tip Four

Look for ways to keep these morning pump ups interesting and fun. Tell a (clean) joke. Share a new idea. Keep the meeting lively.

Daily "Wrap Up" Meetings

The daily wrap up meeting is all about holding people accountable and celebrating success. This short 10- to 20-minute meeting is designed to allow everyone who was part of the morning meeting a chance to share with the group what they accomplished during the day.

Tip One

Praise in public; reprimand in private. From time to time people will not accomplish what they said they would in the morning. Praise loudly those who did what they said they would do. Everyone will get the point when you are silent when someone says, "I did not get to my biggest priority today." It may take a couple of weeks, but everyone will get the message.

Pull the constantly poor performers aside privately and have a long chat about their performance and your expectations.

Tip Two

Use peer pressure to your advantage. The wonderful thing about these meetings is that your people will start to manage each other. No one wants to be the person who constantly shows up not accomplishing what they said they would. Eventually their peers will start calling them out in the meeting. In my mind this is much better than the boss constantly being the one pointing out mistakes.

Tip Three

Encourage the group to give each other tips and ideas to improve their days. This works especially well with salespeople who may be having a tough time getting a meeting with a particular client.

Tip Four

Look for new ideas to toss out at everyone. Get them excited for the next day regardless of how good or bad the day was. Find a funny story and share it. These wrap ups can get old if you don't work on keeping them fun and interesting.

The One-to-One Meeting

The one-to-one meeting is a manager's best tool. It is a one-hour meeting once every week or two with those who directly report to you. This meeting is designed to give your "direct reports" the essential quality time that they all crave.

It is very easy to get caught up in the process of growing a business and to forget how important it is to spend time with the people who are a critical part of the operation.

Your people need your time, no matter how independent they seem, no matter how self-motivated they are. It is imperative that you take time for them as individuals.

Tip One

One-to-ones need to be scheduled in advance and must be a regular part of your month. The topics and issues that are brought up tend to build on each other. If you miss even one of these meetings, you will lose the momentum you were building.

Tip Two

One-to-ones are not a time to harp on issues that are not getting done the way you want them to be done. There is plenty of time for that the rest of the week. One-to-ones are employee development time. This is an hour for you to build a better relationship, trust, and understanding with your "direct reports". It is an opportunity for you to understand the business and or personal roadblocks that may be in the way of their success and offer up suggestions when appropriate.

Tip Three

This is not your time; this is their time. It's not about you. This is not a time for you to spend telling stories about the business or your personal life. This is a time for you to listen to your people. They should drive the topics and tell the stories. Everyone needs an opportunity to be heard.

Tip Four

Like all meetings, one-to-ones need agendas in advance. The agenda is not yours, but theirs. You will probably need to help outline a solid agenda for the first couple of meetings in order to set the tone.

SAMPLE ONE-TO-ONE MEETING AGENDA
8:00 am Meeting starts
Topics:
- Roadblocks where I need some help on Project X (15 minutes)
- Update on my personal growth plan/advice needed (15 minutes)
- Suggestions I have for increasing profitability (15 minutes)
- Some personal stuff I want to share (15 minutes)

The agenda does not have to be formal, but it does need to be well thought out. If necessary, increase the one-to-one by 30 minutes when your people hit their grooves.

Additional Reading

If you want even more information about running effective meetings, try reading Patrick Lencioni's *Death by Meeting*. This book is a staple for anyone who is regularly running or taking part in meetings.

Chapter 18

Dream Management or Whole Life Management

This topic, although not a lengthy one, is important enough to warrant its own special chapter.

Our employees spend the majority of their waking days at our places of business. It is very easy to get wrapped up in the idea that all we care about is getting the job done and the resulting bottom line.

Far too many business owners and managers take an approach that is best described as "If it is not about this business, then I don't want to hear about it during business hours." This style of management is not only outdated, but also detrimental to the healthy growth of any organization.

The days of the corporate drones are long gone. Years ago people went to work, went home, watched TV, had dinner, watched TV, and dreamed of the day when they would retire. They were "happy" because they did not know any better.

Today's workforce is a much more diverse group. They have dreams and ambitions that transcend the work place. They have very full lives outside of work. They have hobbies, special interests, charity work, and some even have side businesses. They have goals and dreams that are much bigger than your business. They may not be dreaming of retirement, but they may be dreaming of leaving your company unless you decide to embrace and support their dreams and ambitions.

You're probably thinking, "Their personal lives are their personal lives. I don't need or want to be a part of any of it."

This is absolutely your prerogative. Just like everything in this book, you can pick and choose whether or not to follow my advice. Do so at your own risk.

So what exactly do I mean by dream management?

Let me start by saying that I am not recommending that you start managing your employee's personal lives the same way you manage tasks at work. I am recommending that you are aware of what is important to them and do your best to support them in their dreams and ambitions outside of work. I am suggesting that you encourage them to have hobbies and interests outside of work and family. I am suggesting that you walk them through the goal chapter of this book and encourage them to create their own written goals—both personal and professional goals. I am suggesting that you find out what is truly important to them and support them as best you can in order to help them achieve their goals.

Starting a Business

What if their dream is to start a business? Why would you want to encourage that? Fight it all you want. Most employees do dream of starting their own businesses. I am not suggesting that you go ahead and start creating your competitors. Fortunately, the majority of people who dream of starting their own businesses never do. However, a large portion of the few who do end up leaving their jobs to start something new have not thought through things as well as they could have. They are not prepared and lack sufficient knowledge and capital to be successful. In most cases, they have not flushed out their model and end up leaving their jobs only to find out that entrepreneurship was not meant for them.

The question then is, how do you support someone who wants to have his or her own business?

Step One

Educate them on just what it means to have your own business. Tell them your war stories over lunch. Tell them about the times that you were the last to get paid and the challenges that you have been through. Give them the "behind the scene tour" of the business. All of your employees (except for your bookkeeper) think you make a lot more money than you actually do. (The bookkeeper, on the other hand, is wondering why you bother to do what you do!)

Step Two

Flush out the model. Encourage them to share their idea with you. Sign an NDA (non-disclosure agreement) if they are worried about sharing. Take some time and look at their business plan or encourage them to create one if they do not have one already. Ask questions (there will be many to ask). Have they researched the market? Do they understand the competition? Does the business make logical sense? Do they have enough cash saved to do it the right way? Remember, they will be planning and dreaming about this regardless of what you say. You might as well be a part of the process.

Step Three

Offer to mentor them through the process. Carve out a half hour every other week to have a coffee and help them with their plans. Don't you wish someone offered to help you when you were getting started? Who knows, maybe you will end up with a small piece of someone's great idea.

Step Four

Encourage them to test the model out in the evenings and weekends to make sure it actually works. It makes no sense to quit their job until they are absolutely sure that they can pay their bills with their new business. When they complain about working two jobs at the same time, remind them that the greatest thing about being an entrepreneur is the ability to choose when you want to work your 80-plus hours a week!

Step Five

When the time is right, let them go. In the small percentage of cases where someone actually pulls it all together, has the cash, the plan, has fully flushed out the model, and is ready to leave…let them go. Be proud of your small part in starting up the new business and wish them luck. The good thing is that you will have seen this day coming for some time and you will have had plenty of notice to find a solid replacement.

Managing Happy Employees

For most people, the process of dream management is much simpler.

It is about understanding how important softball tournaments are in your employees' lives and supporting them in their goals to run a marathon or maybe compete in a triathlon. Or maybe offer to pay for the first three months of their gym membership because they want to lose weight.

It is realizing that what they really want and need is extra personal time and providing a fast track so that they can ride in the toll lanes. It's taking the time to look at the photographs and oil paintings of those who are artists. It's about going to listen to them perform live with their band.

It's about allowing them to take the time off to see their kid's soccer game. It's about reading their novels. It's about helping them find courses that they want to take in completely unrelated subjects to your business. It's about rearranging their work schedules so that they can go back to school.

It's really about going out of your way to encourage interests outside of your place of business. The list goes on and on.

At this point I am suspecting that some of you are wondering what the possible business benefit could be from doing all of this. Your employees will be happy people, will work harder, and will spend less time looking for a new job.

If you are anything like me, you will find that you get tremendous personal satisfaction from helping people have a well balanced life and being more to them than the guy who signs their paychecks.

If you want to learn more about this concept, I recommend *The Dream Manager* by Matthew Kelly.

Chapter 19

Goals

The most successful people I know are all goal-oriented people.

The fact that you are in business for yourself means that you must share this characteristic as well. When I ask a group of entrepreneurs if they would describe themselves as goal-oriented, close to 90% of the room will put up their hands. This is pretty much what any of us would expect.

However, when I rephrase the question and ask how many people take the time to write down their business goals and make a plan to achieve them, the room's hands drop down to only about half of the room.

When I change the question yet again and ask how many people take the time each year to write out their personal goals and make a plan to achieve them, only about 10% of the hands are still up.

Even though business owners are some of the most goal-driven people that you will meet, many do not take this important step in the goal process. A goal not written is only a wish. Effective business owners write their goals down and have a systematic method of reviewing them.

Write It Down

Let's face it; you are busy! Small business owners are some of the busiest people on the planet. You spend most of your days and evenings multitasking between customers, suppliers, accounting, and employees. Your mind is spinning at a hundred miles an hour and ideas are popping above your head like tiny bubbles. Some are good ideas and some are best lost forever. You might tell yourself to make that mental list. After all, how long can it be? Well…it should be very long, indeed.

Your list of ideas is lengthy because it includes not just ideas you have for yourself, but also for everyone who works with you. It is a list of topics you need to discuss with your suppliers, accountants, customers, lawyers, employees, and family. Your list can easily be made up of a hundred different "to do" items in a single week, all of which are important and need to be addressed in a timely manner.

With all this going on, how do you expect to remember the goals that dance around in your head from time to time? How are you expected to have an action plan to accomplish the items on this mental list? The reality is that "mental lists," especially for your goals, are not an effective way of accomplishing much. Despite the obvious, many people who hear this say to themselves, "I can remember all my goals, no problem." My answer to them is, "Then you don't have enough goals!"

I believe in written goals and in written plans to go with each one of the goals. I also believe in tracking and grading goals on a monthly and quarterly basis. I know, I know; this sounds like something that those who organize their spice rack alphabetically would do. Although I'm not the spice rack organizing type, I am detailed and methodical when it comes to my goals.

So why is it so vitally important to write everything down in such detail and make sure that results are graded? The answer is simple. We only get one chance on this planet and that time goes by quickly. The older we get the quicker time seems to fly. In the blink of an eye a week can go by and, if you're not careful, very little can get accomplished. In two blinks, it is next month and before you know it you're a year older and you'll never get that year back. I know this sounds a bit like an "I'm going to miss you when you are gone" speech, but it's true…time flies!

How many friends do you know who keep talking about what they are going to do *someday*? Maybe you have family members who are always saying how they are going to start losing weight or eventually start back at the gym again. Any of you know someone who says that they are going go back to school and get those skills they need to get a new job? Do you know anyone who swears they are going to learn a new language? The list goes on and on.

The first mistake that these people likely make is not writing down their goals. Writing down your goals is the first step in committing to the process of actually accomplishing them. Written goals get accomplished 90% more than unwritten goals.

The Writing Process

I am going to share with you my process for writing my yearly goals. This is something I have been doing for decades and is a big reason why I am able to lead as full a life as I do.

Step 1

Take it seriously. Your written goals are your GPS to the future. Without them you don't know where you are heading and may get lost, distracted, or end up in a completely different place than where you wanted to be or should be.

Create goals at the same time every year. The last two weeks of December is goal-setting time. This is not to say that you should wait until the last two weeks of December. You can start right now. The trick is to do a major overhaul of your goals once a year, preferably at the same time of the year.

The process really does take two weeks. During that time you should be constantly thinking about the year ahead and contemplating the year that is just wrapping up. What went well? What did you accomplish? What do you want to accomplish in each part of the year ahead?

Take lots of notes and dream big! Be honest with yourself about past years and about the nagging things that never seemed to get done.

You should generally edit the list five or six times before you are happy with the finished product.

Step 2

Separate your business life from your personal life.

You should have two sets of goals: your business goals and your personal goals. I believe in a balanced life and in order for that to happen I need to achieve as much in my personal life as I do my business life. Both sets of goals are equally important, but if I were to pick one over the other it would always be the personal goals.

Step 3

Think of your goals in different time horizons. Some are things that you can and will get accomplished in the next month. Others are 90-day projects. Some may be six-month goals, one-year goals, or even five-year goals. Just make sure you are realistic about how long each will take and the time frame you are giving yourself.

Step 4

Make sure your goals are SMARTER:

- S-Specific
- M-Measurable
- A-Attainable
- R-Relevant
- T-Time Bound
- E-Evaluate
- R-Reward

Specific

Be specific about what it is that you want to accomplish.

An example of a non-specific goal: "I want to be able to run a good distance."

An example of a specific goal: "I want to run a 10K."

Measurable

Your goal needs to be something that you can easily measure.

An example of poorly measured goal: "I want to lose some weight."

An example of a measurable goal: "I want to lose 10 pounds in the next six months."

Attainable

An attainable goal is one that is one that is within your reach. It cannot be a goal that is so outlandish that you have no chance of accomplishing it.

An example of a poorly attainable goal: "I want to lose 20 pounds in two weeks."

It's hard to give the example of an attainable goal. This depends completely on you and what is realistic in your situation. Following the weight-loss scenario, an example of an attainable, healthy goal: "I will begin walking for 30 minutes every evening after dinner."

Relevant

Your goal should make sense considering your current situation and what is important at this time of your life.

An example of non-relevant goal: "I want to learn Japanese this year."

While it may sound like a fun thing to do, if you do not have a specific reason to learn Japanese such as for an upcoming trip, for a new Japanese business venture, or to be able to communicate with Japanese-speaking friends, you are not likely to actually accomplish the goal.

Every goal needs to be relevant to your personal or business situation at the time you set it.

Time Bound

Every goal needs to have a time frame attached. Without a time frame, the goal is floating out in space and won't likely ever get accomplished.

An example of a non-time bound goal: "I am going to grow my company to $20 million in sales."

An example of a time bound goal: "I am going to grow my company from $500,000 in sales this year to $1.2 million in sales next year. Three years from now I will be at $5 million in sales and by the end of my 10th year in business I will be at $20 million in annual revenue."

Evaluate

Every goal needs to be evaluated on a weekly, monthly, quarterly, or yearly basis. This frequency of evaluation depends on the time frame of the goal. Attach such an evaluation frequency to each goal.

Reward

Every set of goals needs a reward. The rewards you set for yourself are important. They will help to keep you focused and keep "your eyes on the prize" when motivation drops.

A great personal example of this is the writing of this book. I agreed to write it under a very tight deadline. I have a full-time job, as you know, and a wife and four kids. During the same short eight-week period I had to deliver the book to my publisher, I traveled an average of three days a week for business, had a family vacation, and trained for *Ironman Brazil*. My reward? I am a closet techie and my eyes are on the iPad that was just released. Once I deliver this book on schedule to my publisher, my reward will be the new iPad. I kept my eyes on the prize, especially during the times where the simple goal was not enough to keep me writing long into the night.

Step 5

Dream big—BHAG!

> B-Big
>
> H-Hairy
>
> A-Audacious
>
> G-Goal

Think about the big things that you want to accomplish in your life. Think about the crazy things that you want to accomplish in your life. Write them down.

Step 6

How do you eat an elephant?

There is only one way to eat an elephant, of course, and that is one bite at a time. You accomplish a BHAG the same way. One step at a time. Make sure all of your BHAGs are broken into small bite-size pieces. Measure those "pieces" by writing them down and checking them off as you accomplish them. Each bite-size piece of the goal that is achieved gets you one step closer to completing the big goal!

Step 7

Think small. Sometimes the little things in life are some of the most important and are often overlooked.

A great example of a small, but important, thing in life is flossing. Flossing is a small daily task that many people overlook. Lack of flossing leads to gum disease and ultimately the bacteria from gum disease causes heart disease. Not flossing can cut years off your life. Think small and don't overlook the little things.

Step 8

It's not just about you. Your goals involve others. You can and will have goals that touch other lives. Write them down and keep track of them.

Examples could range from spending a week in May on vacation in Hawaii with your wife to teaching your 6-year-old how to ride a bike with no training wheels by June. A company goal that involves others might be to launch by February a program to make all of your senior managers better public speakers.

Step 9

Your goals are not etched in stone. As a year progresses, priorities change and your goals may need to change. What was important three months ago may not be important now. It is important to remember that your written goals are a fluid, ever-changing map and as plans change, so do your goals. Feel free to strike some off, change others, and add new ones as the year goes on.

Step 10

Evaluate and reevaluate your goals! Check your progress weekly, monthly, and yearly.

Grade yourself on your progress: A—B—C—D—F.

You decide what each letter grade means to you! The trick here is to be brutally honest with yourself and work to fix the areas in which you are failing.

Step 11

Don't take yourself too seriously. Life is short; enjoy it and enjoy your goals. Don't be a slave to them. If you have written goals and don't accomplish everything every year, don't fret. Even hitting 60% of your yearly written goals means you are accomplishing twice as much as you would if you had no written goals. Give it a try and you will be amazed at what you are able to accomplish.

Step 12

Find an "accountability partner" who you can share and review your goals with quarterly. It is important to find someone who views the process the same way that you do. If you have 10 categories with three goals in each category and the person you are considering as an accountability partner only has three goals in total, you are not a good match.

As partners, you need to review each other's progress and give brutally honest feedback where it makes sense.

Example Goals

Now for the fun stuff. Each section of my business and each part of my life has room for improvement and, therefore, should have goals associated with each.

As it is sometimes easier to learn by seeing an example, I'm going to show you the categories that I divide my goals into each year with a few sample goals I have had in those categories over the years. I'll also include some that I have made up as examples.

Keep in mind that each of these examples is just a heading and that there is usually a list of activities and action dates that are linked to that specific goal. This is especially true in the case of business goals.

BUSINESS GOALS

Sales:
- Grow sales from $500K in Q1 to $600K in Q2, $750K in Q3, and $800K in Q4
- Hire two new salespeople by the end of Q1
- Find one new "major" client relationship each quarter
- Run one full day sales training each month

Marketing:
- Redo the marketing program with new marketing message by the end of Q3
- Review all marketing sources for cost per lead and job; cut the fat by Jan 31
- Find online marketing options by April 14

Expenses/Profit:
- Set up new expense-management system by the end of Q1
- Renegotiate pricing with all suppliers by March 15

- Maintain 37% gross profit numbers throughout the year
- Obtain 12% net profit after my salary for the year

Office:

- Find one full day training classes each six months for customer service people
- Evaluate need for office space and examine outsourcing options with decision about lease renewal by June 12
- Review system for buying office supplies by end of Q2
- Hire an accounts receivables person by end of Q3

Other:

- Organize my desk and files by January 15 and keep them organized for the year
- Send five handwritten notes to clients or employees each week
- Allocate one day a month for myself to spend quality time thinking and planning (time to work on the business while not in the business)
- Find a personal coach by Feb 30

So there is a good example of a set of written goals for a business. This is a solid list of high-priority items that need to be accomplished this year. For most business people, this business list is the easy part. The harder part is what is yet to come—the personal goals. Here is an example of a set of personal goals.

PERSONAL GOALS

Health:

- Run 45 minutes three times a week
- Run a 10K in September
- Cut fast food down to once every two weeks; bring lunch
- Physical, dentist, and optometrist by March 1
- Regular vitamins

Family—Marriage:

- Plan once-a-week date nights with my wife and stick to it!
- One weekend a quarter with no kids (with Grandma's help)
- Force myself to watch *Dancing With the Stars* with my wife

Family—Kids:

- No training wheels by end of June for the little one
- Bonding time: lunch or dinner with each one individually once per month
- One weekend camping trip with each kid individually this year

Family—All:
- Plan a one-week summer family vacation
- Friday night family movie nights
- Family dinner at least four nights a week
- Family board games and hanging out time Sunday nights

Extended Family:
- Golf with Dad once a month
- Mom and Dad to the house for dinner at least once a month

House:
- Re-paint the house by September
- Change out the sprinklers to drip irrigation by March 15
- Vegetable garden planted by May 12

Finance:
- Refinance mortgage by June 15
- Pay down the $14,000 in credit card debt that is left
- Put away $10,000 for kids' colleges
- Review trust and retirement IRA by June 30

Personal:
- Read one pleasure book and one business book per month
- Play piano for two hours a week; learn one new song a month
- Floss
- Cut TV to one hour a day

Other categories:
- Spiritual
- Hobbies
- Charity
- School
- Kids' schools

(The list is can be as long as you want it to be.)

Your Turn: Writing Your Goals

There is no time like the present to get started on your goals. You don't need to wait until the end of December to get started. Go ahead and get started now.

Written goals are a significant part of every successful person's life. If you follow this system faithfully for one year, you will accomplish much more than the previous year of unwritten and unmeasured goals.

SETTING GOALS
Business Goals
Sales goals:

1. _____
2. _____
3. _____
4. _____
5. _____

Marketing goals:

1. _____
2. _____
3. _____
4. _____
5. _____

Expenses/profit goals:

1. _____
2. _____
3. _____
4. _____
5. _____

Office goals:

1. _____
2. _____
3. _____
4. _____
5. _____

Other:

1. _____
2. _____
3. _____
4. _____
5. _____

Personal Goals

Health:

1. _____
2. _____
3. _____
4. _____
5. _____

Family—Marriage/Significant Other:

1. _____
2. _____
3. _____
4. _____
5. _____

Family—Kids:

1. _____
2. _____
3. _____
4. _____
5. _____

Family—All:

1. _____
2. _____
3. _____
4. _____
5. _____

Extended Family:

1. _____
2. _____
3. _____
4. _____
5. _____

House:

1. _____
2. _____
3. _____
4. _____
5. _____

Finance:

1. _____
2. _____
3. _____
4. _____
5. _____

Personal:

1. _____
2. _____
3. _____
4. _____
5. _____

Spiritual:

1. _____
2. _____
3. _____
4. _____
5. _____

Charity:

1. _____
2. _____
3. _____
4. _____
5. _____

Other: _____

  1. _____

  2. _____

  3. _____

  4. _____

  5. _____

Other: _____

  1. _____

  2. _____

  3. _____

  4. _____

  5. _____

Other: _____

  1. _____

  2. _____

  3. _____

  4. _____

  5. _____

Chapter 20

Protect Yourself, Your Company, and Your Employees

The majority of this book has been about how to "build " your business. This book cannot be complete, though, without having a chapter about how to protect yourself and your employees, not from "evil doers," per se, but from people that you will run across every day in business.

Advertising/Marketing/Branding

Beware of the advertising people who want you to commit to large marketing spends without the ability to do a small test. Every week, it seems, you hear about another business owner who "invested" thousands of dollars into a marketing campaign where the return was negligible. If it can't be tested and tracked (reread the marketing section if you don't understand) for less than $1,000, there is no need to try it. Remember, you are not Coca-Cola; you are not building brand awareness. You just need customers!

Consultants—Business Coaches

There are some consultants and business coaches who are worth every dime you pay them. There are others, though, who are trying to make a living off of some formula or implementing what they have learned from the books they have read. Here are some tips in choosing a consultant or business coach.

The Specialist

If you are choosing a "specialist," make sure this person truly is a specialist. There will be many times in your business career where you may need to hire a consultant for a specific project. For example, you have an accounting systems change and need help implementing a new software package. Or you're looking for a risk management expert or a sales training consultant. If you are going to take this step, make sure the person you are hiring specializes in your specific need. The last thing you want is to hire someone who says they are "confident they can figure it out" while charging you X dollars per hour to do so.

The Generalist

Business coaches are a valuable addition to your team. However, unless this person has been a successful entrepreneur in her own right, she will have limited value to the entrepreneurial business owner. If you are in the middle of a startup trying to figure out how to find customers and make payroll, you want advice from someone who has already been in your shoes and was successful in them. Someone who had an amazing career at a Fortune 500 company may not have a clue how to start a business effectively. Although these "experts" may have vast amounts of experience in many categories, if small business ownership is not one of them, this person is not a good fit. Don't be fooled. Running a $500 million or even $50 million company is very different from running a $1 million company. You want your consultant to have "been there and done that" and have been successful at it as well!

Degrees

Don't be fooled by an MBA or PhD degrees or any other group of letters behind someone's name. Business schools today are minting MBAs to thousands who have limited or no work experience. Many of these are hired by large consulting firms and sent to work on small projects (like yours or mine). Remember, in many cases it's easier to stay in school than to face the real world!

Don't Be Wowed!

Don't hire the first one to walk in your door. Remember, the consultant who comes to your first meeting is the *sales* guy! If he works for a medium to large firm, his only job is to sell you on a consulting package. Then he sends in the newly-minted MBAs to regurgitate the last business case that they read. If this is a one-person show, this person is there to sell you on his services. His personal income depends on making the sale to you today! Interview multiple people for the same project.

Be Wowed!

If you are not excited about what this person or firm has to say when they are sitting across the table during the first meeting, you should run, don't walk, away. Remember their job is to *sell* you on their services; if they can't knock your socks off in the first meeting, they never will.

Check References

Just like with a job interview, if a consultant can't easily turn over 10 or 20 references, find someone who can. I am sure you have a list of a 100 or so satisfied customers (you better) and so should your potential consultant.

Don't Commit

This goes without saying, but every consultant will want you to sign a long-term engagement. Under no circumstances should you sign anything other than an hourly-rate agreement. Their job is to get you to commit to a long-term deal. Your job is to keep them on their toes with the fear that at any time you might cancel the project.

Banks

After having lived through the 2008-2009 home loan disaster, we are much more suspicious of banks. Stay that way. Banks are a business. Their job is to turn a profit by moving money. Make no doubt about it; banks are not a charity. Here are a few tips for dealing with banks.

Banks Specialize

Don't assume that because you were turned down at one bank, you will be turned down at another. Banks tend to specialize in different types of businesses. They tend be more comfortable loaning to businesses with whom they have an existing relationship. Some banks don't like restaurants, some don't like contractors, and others stay away from retail. Before you sit down with a bank representative, make sure you know how the bank feels about your industry and how many customers the bank has that are like you!

Banks Need To Understand Your Business

Many business owners make the mistake that banks only want to see your financials and make 100% of their decision based on the numbers. That could not be further from the truth. Good banks take the time to understand the business you are in. They want to know you and understand where you have been and where you are going. Don't make things up or exaggerate your prospects. Banks see this everyday and are not easily fooled.

Interview 5 or Even 10 Banks

There have been a couple of times in my career where I needed to find a new bank. I was amazed that even though we presented the exact same package to every bank, they all looked at it differently. Some banks turned us down completely while the range of offers from the others was absolutely amazing. Our offers from these banks varied up to three times on the line of credit size and the fees they charged.

Banks Are Not Venture Capitalists

Banks do not lend to startups that have no assets and security. Save yourself and them the time and hassle. If you are a startup and need cash for your next idea, call on friends, family, or angels/devils (I will cover angels/devils next), but not banks.

Everything Is Negotiable

You make your bank money. You are its customer. Assuming you are a good customer and not a "dead beat" (who is fortunate just to have a bank account), it is not out of the question to negotiate your rates and fees with your bank. They know how competitive it is to obtain good clients and they don't want to lose you!

Read the Fine Print

Before you get overly-excited by the large line of credit that has just been offered to you, make sure you read the details. Go through all of the "bank covenants" with your CPA. Bank covenants are the terms of your agreement. They are written by the bank to protect itself. They may cover multiple topics from your reporting requirements (monthly, quarterly, or yearly financials, for example). They may include how far out your receivables can get and how much money you, the owner, can take out of the business. Before you sign and close the deal, make sure you understand all of the terms. The last thing you need is for your bank to deny purchase of new equipment you need to grow your business because you are outside your "covenants." This happens all of the time.

Relationships Matter

At the end of the day, your banking relationship is only as good as your personal relationship with your banker. If you take the time to make sure the bank always knows where you are, you will have a better chance of building a long-term bank relationship. When you have the right bank relationship, the bank is your partner through good times and tough times. From my own experience, because of the strong relationship between my company and my bank, our line of credit was renewed with a 25% increase in fall of 2008 when the stock market was crashing, banks were not lending, people were talking about a pending depression, and our industry was "obviously" heading into the tank. Was this due to our financial strength or the strength of the relationships? I tend to think it was because of our relationship.

Angel/Devil Investors and Venture Capitalists

I will be completely honest with you. I have never taken any money from an angel investor or venture capitalist. I have borrowed money from family and friends and paid a much higher than normal rate of return for their generosity. Many have had a tidy additional stream of interest income for years from us.

The main reason that I have never taken any money from people who wanted equity is simple. The loss of control. When you take money from angel investors or venture capitalists, you are bringing on a new partner.

This partner is not someone that you have known for years and came up with the business idea together, vetted it, tested it, and mortgaged your homes to run it. This partner is more than likely a professional investor who has much more experience doing what they do than you do.

Professional investors are generally looking for one thing and one thing only; a return on their money in a certain amount of time. They generally don't share your passion for the business. Their time horizon may not match yours.

You've been warned. However, if you do choose to go down this path, here are a few tips.

Interview as Many as Possible

Just like a bank, you don't want to take the first or only deal that falls in your lap. Take the time to interview as many investors as you can.

Check References

Before agreeing to any deal, you will want to talk to people who they have invested with in the past. You will want to make sure you get references of successful deals. More importantly, you want to talk to those who they had deals with that failed. Keep in mind that those with the successful deals will love them. You want to find out how the investor reacts when things go badly. What happens when their backs are up against a wall and they are in danger of losing their investment? Do they role up their sleeves and pitch in, fire the entrepreneur, or abandon the project? If they try to tell you that they have never had a failed deal, run very fast in the opposite direction. Even if it is true (which it probably is not), they have not experienced failure and you don't want to risk being their first.

Partner?

It's not just about the money. This person will be your business partner for years to come. Do you like them personally? (You better.) Do you feel like you can be completely honest with them? (You better.) What does your gut say? Do you trust them? (You better.)

Nothing sucks the life out of an entrepreneur more than waking up everyday and going to work to deal with a partner who he or she doesn't enjoy working with, especially one who put in all the money! Remember, one of the reasons you started your own business was because you did not want to have a boss anymore!

Time Horizon

Expectations around time horizons are one of the most critical conversations you can have with your new "partner." Investors are generally looking to make their investment and then get out in a three- to five-year time frame. If you are looking to build a business that you can pass on to your kids, your interests are not aligned. Think about what happens when their time frame is up. Do you stay? Is the company sold and you now have a new boss? Is this really what you wanted when you said that you wanted your own company?

The Lure of Easy Money

Don't let yourself get caught up in the "projections" game. You will feel the pressure to put together a plan that is enticing to investors. The question is whether or not it is realistic. A big part of obtaining an investor is showing this person the growth in revenue and profit that your business will have over a five-year period. The challenge is making it look enticing enough to invest in, while keeping the numbers realistic.

This is generally difficult for most entrepreneurs to do, because we are an optimistic group who is passionate enough about our product and service to believe that everyone in the world will want to buy from us. On one hand, this is our greatest strength. It is our passion that drives our businesses. On the other hand, it is that same passionate optimism that gets us into bad situations.

Whatever you commit to with an investor is what they will hold you accountable to, no matter how naïve you were or how much the market conditions have changed. Imagine the pressure that will be on you if you don't hit your numbers. If you think having a boss was bad…

Equity

How much equity are you giving up? In many cases you may be giving up 51% of the equity and essentially all of the control. You'll hear the standard argument. "Would you rather have 100% of a very small pie or 10% of a very large pie?" It is not that simple.

What if you end up with no pie because someone has the power to take it away from you? What if you could end up with 60% of a medium-sized pie with fewer headaches? What if, instead, you give up pieces of the pie to key employees and build your business with a committed team? (That's what we did). What if it was going to take you 10 years to get where you are going instead of five, but the 10 would be much more enjoyable than the five? Remember, equity = control.

The Devil Is in the Details (Literally)

Before you sign any deal and take any money, make sure that you have had the agreement reviewed by an attorney and CPA who are both familiar with these types of deals. What are the terms of the deal? How much money do you really get? Does it come in all at once or at different milestones? Do you have control over how it is spent? What happens in the case of a disagreement? These are only a few of many questions that a professional team will help you with.

Sometimes the Best Deal Is No Deal

Having spent 20 years in the entrepreneurial arena, I can say that the most stressed entrepreneurs I have met are the ones who took outside venture money. They are generally the ones who always talk about "when they sell" or "how stressful things are" or "their lack of a good night's sleep" or " been preparing for my board meeting for a week now." Many of them remind me of the autoworker who is counting down the days until his or her retirement. They can't wait to get out.

On the flip side, the entrepreneurs like myself and my partners have conversations about how "we can do this for 20 more years" and "what would we do if we sold? We would have to start something up new, which does not sound like fun." Maybe we have not grown as fast as we could have (who knows?) but I can guarantee you one thing, none of us has to worry about being kicked out of the company we started because we had a challenging quarter or two.

Insurance

Insurance is one of those issues that many business owners don't pay enough attention to. It is hard to keep writing checks for something that you have never used and may *never* use. Invariably, the minute you cancel it or decide to cut back your coverage, you'll need it.

Here are a few points to keep in mind about insurance.

Your Broker Should Not Be Your Best Friend

If your broker is one of your best buddies, think about changing brokers. An insurance broker is someone who you need to keep at arm's length. Your negotiations with them will always be tenuous and this person needs to be pushed in order to get you the best deal possible. Your best buddy may not feel the need to call in "favors" from his contacts to keep your business. He's confident you're not going to leave him.

Don't Use Just One Broker

Even though a broker will tell you she needs an exclusive deal, it is not the law; it is only her wish. Of course, she doesn't want to have any competition. In the event that you are having trouble finding brokers to play by these rules (sometimes it is tougher depending on your size), separate your different types of insurance needs and dish them out among different brokers.

Give your liability insurance to one, your auto to another, and your workers' comp to yet another. The only way you will learn about the insurance racket (which you need to understand) is by dealing with multiple brokers and asking lots of questions. Having multiple brokers is also the only way to keep them all honest.

Over time, you will find the right brokers. I have found the right ones, but I still keep one for liability insurance and one for workers' comp. They both work hard to take over the other's side of the business.

The Renewal Trick

For the first 10 years or so of being in business I used to believe what my brokers told me. I would always get my renewal offer on my insurance 24 hours before my policy was about to expire. When I complained, they would always say the same thing, "Jay, you don't understand how busy it is this time of year. I don't get any of my renewal offers back until a few days before they are due. I can't get quotes from anyone *now*."

For years I bought this line until I finally put my foot down and said, "I want all renewal offers on the table 45 days prior to the expiration of my insurance or you are fired." Amazingly enough, I now get insurance quotes 60 days prior to expiration.

It is in your broker's best interest to wait until the last minute so you don't have time to shop anywhere else. This is why many small business owners end up with sub-standard insurance policies that do not cover them when they need them and at costs that are radically higher than they need to be paying.

Specialists

All brokers are not created equally. Brokers specialize by industry. Insurance companies specialize by industry as well. If you are an auto mechanic and your broker is used to dealing with restaurants, chances are they will not have the right relationships to get you the best price or best coverage.

Apples to Apples

Policies are not created equally, either. There are subtle differences in almost every policy and quote that you will get. These differences can be everything from the policy limits, to deductibles, to what is actually covered. Insurance language is tricky and there are many shady companies that will offer you what looks like a great price for insurance that is essentially worthless when you need it. A broker should give you a side-by-side comparison of the policy. In the insurance game, the cheapest deal may also be a worthless deal.

Claims: Be Careful

Don't try to get your premiums back every year by making claims every time someone steals that new piece of equipment. The more claims you make, the more your insurance will go up in the next renewal. Liability insurance is for catastrophic claims only. (Workers' comp is different. You, of course, are required by law to report all work-related injuries.)

Understand Your Risks

There are many types of insurance; liability, auto, earthquake, workers' comp, environmental, and so on. The list goes on and on. Do not assume that your policy covers all of your risks. It more than likely does not. Be honest with your broker about how your business operates so that he can make sure you have all the proper coverage.

Workers' Comp: Yes, You Need It

No one is truly exempt from workers' comp. It is dangerous to dodge having workers' comp on your employees. Many small businesses will try to set their employees up as independent businesses that they believe are workers' comp exempt. Others will just decide to pay cash and hope that nothing happens.

FACT: If someone is injured at your place of work, you are responsible.

You are responsible even if you hired a separate business or sub-contractor to do work for you. If this sub-contractor is injured at your place of business and does not have his or her own workers' comp policy, you can and will be held responsible.

It's not fair, but there are plenty of workers' comp attorneys suing business owners every day for this reason alone. And why shouldn't they? The lawyers will always win this one. The law is on their side, not yours.

Being in business is tough enough. Losing your business and going personally bankrupt because of an injury is something that happens more often than you would want to believe.

Your Employees' Safety

The best way for me to sum up this point is by giving you my philosophy on safety.

Someone will get injured at your place of business. Statistically, it is a fact—eventually it will happen. When it does happen, I hope it is not serious. No matter how serious it is, you will need to look yourself in the mirror and ask yourself one simple question.

"Did I do everything I could have done to stop the injury from happening?"

You will need to live with the answer to that question for the rest of your life. And if it is that you did not and the injury is tragic, I guarantee you that it will haunt you in the middle of the night for the rest of your life.

If you don't have a properly written safety program and, more importantly, a culture of safe work practices led by you, the owner, find a qualified safety consultant to put one together for you immediately. This is not something that can wait until next month.

Safety requirements are very different in every industry. Responsibility for safety, regardless of the exposure, always rests with the business owner.

Summary

I do not want you to believe that all consultants, bankers, marketing folks, and insurance brokers are "evil doers." The vast majority of them are great business people just like you.

Unfortunately, just like most businesses, a small percentage of bad ones give the good ones a bad name. I am confident that the "good" ones who would read this chapter will agree with everything in it.

Chapter 21

Business Planning

You need a business plan and every plan should be written down. Here is an outline for writing a business plan from the SBA's website at SBA.gov.

Writing the Plan

What goes in a business plan? The body can be divided into four distinct sections:

- Description of the business
- Marketing efforts
- Finances
- Management

Agendas should include an executive summary, supporting documents, and financial projections. Although there is no single formula for developing a business plan, some elements are common to all business plans. They are summarized in the following sections.

Elements of a Business Plan

- Cover sheet
- Statement of purpose
- Table of contents

The Business

A. Description of business
B. Marketing
C. Competition
D. Operating procedures
E. Personnel
F. Business insurance

Financial Data

A. Loan applications
B. Capital equipment and supply list
C. Balance sheet

D. Break-even analysis

E. Pro-forma income projections (profit and loss statements)

F. Three-year summary

G. Detail by month, first year

H. Detail by quarters, second and third years

I. Assumptions upon which projections were based

J. Pro-forma cash flow

Supporting Documents

A. Tax returns of principals for last three years

B. For franchised businesses, a copy of franchise contract and all supporting documents provided by the franchisor

C. Copy of proposed lease or purchase agreement for building space

D. Copy of licenses and other legal documents

E. Copy of resumes of all principals

F. Copies of letters of intent from suppliers

Understanding Your Market

You should have a solid written business plan that will force you to understand the market you are in and outline how you will grow your business.

The Challenge with Business Plans

The challenge with creating long business plans is that, while they are helpful in the beginning to get the ball rolling, they tend not to get updated as much as they should and sit on a shelf until the business is highly successful or fails.

Many of you (including me) may not be big on writing a 35-page business plan, so here's an outline of a nice and simple five-to-eight page plan. This small plan tends to be used more frequently and is easier to update as things change.

Either way, both the large and small versions make great reading after the fact.

The Basic Plan You Need

The following sidebar contains a basic framework for your plan. This is not the type of business plan you'd use to raise capital, but is a plan in the practical sense. It includes points you need to understand your business in order to be successful.

BASIC BUSINESS PLAN

Describe the type of business:

- What is your business/trade?
- What types of work do you specialize in?
- What is your experience in each of these areas?
- Why did you choose to operate in these areas?

Describe the location of operations:

- Which geographic locations do you operate in?
- What geographic boundaries have you set, if any? Why?
- Describe the demographics for this area.

(All of this information can be plugged in from the business intelligence section of this book.)

Describe the competition:

- This section should contain the complete business intelligence information you have built.

Describe the marketing efforts:

- This section should contain everything you learned from the Branding/Marketing/Lead Generation section of this book.

Describe the financials:

- Your profit/loss projections for this year.
- Your profit/loss projections for the next two years.

Describe the personal information:

- An organizational chart of the people you now employ.
- A projected organizational chart for 12, 24, and 36 months from now. This chart should match with your financial projections.

Summary

I do understand that creating these plans is not something that many of you want to spend your time doing. There are some people who are really good at writing fancy plans and others who are really good at just working and getting the job done.

Take the time, regardless of which of these types of people you are, and write down your plan. Use the resources you have in your company—your partners, employees, and board of advisors—to help put this plan together.

The financial plan and budget are probably the most important parts of the business plan and they are something you'll want your CPA to help you with.

Review your plan (especially the budget) every month and make sure you are on track and that all points still make sense. Make adjustments as the business changes.

You will get much further with a simple eight-page plan in which every item on it means something to you than you will get with no plan or a 50-page plan you never read again.

Chapter 22

Conclusion

I have spent 20-plus years building my business. Without exception, at the conclusion of each year, I admit to myself that I learned more this year than I did in any other year in business.

Even though I dropped out of college, I have dedicated a huge part of my adult life to learning and surrounding myself with people much smarter than I am. I realized early on that I did not have enough knowledge alone to be successful in business and that I needed to commit myself to my own education. I still feel the same way today as I did 20 years ago.

If you were to remember only one or two points from each chapter of this book, these are my suggestions:

- **Branding:** Once you have decided who you are and what you stand for (based on your customer feedback, of course), you and your employees need to walk the talk! Your brand is not just a catchy phrase; it is a way of life!

- **Marketing:** Marketing is a fickle beast. What works for one trade does not always work for another. Every market is different and potential customers in those markets respond differently to advertising. In order to successfully create a sustainable lead program you need to test each new marketing program and continually track the results.

- **When Things Go Very Bad:** It is a new age of customer service and even the customers who are wrong are now right.

- **Leads:** A lead is just that, a lead. It is not a promise of a sale. It is up to you to turn every lead into a customer for life.

- **Sales, Sales, Sales:** Customers buy from people who they like and trust. Don't give them a reason to not like you.

- **Sales Management:** There is no such thing as an independent salesperson. Every salesperson, no matter how amazing he or she is, needs support, training, and encouragement. If you are not committed to this process, do not hire salespeople.

- **Employees:** Hire slow and fire fast. Understand that there is a big difference between recruiting and hiring. You want to be a recruiter.

- **It's Your Time:** The tools that got you to where you are today are not the same tools that will get you where you want to be. Focus on your priorities as a business owner.

- **Customers:** The basics have not changed. You need to treat your customers the way that you expect to be treated.

- **Technology:** We will never go back to the way it used to be. You need to have mobile access to your email and you need to learn how to text.

- **Business Intelligence:** A CEO understands the market to which he is selling and the competitors that are in it.

- **Back to School:** You are never too old to learn. The way we historically have run businesses will never be successful again. It's time to learn new tricks.

- **Expenses:** Every dollar you spend is a dollar less in your pocket for your family. Focus on the little stuff when it comes to expenses. If you don't, your existing profit will disappear.

- **Estimating and Pricing:** Without utilizing a systemized estimating and pricing model, you cannot grow your business.

- **Big Opportunities:** Sometimes the best decision you make is to walk away from a big opportunity.

- **Management:** Hold people accountable. Be fair, and don't forget to be fun.

- **Meetings:** Having people take control of your meetings is an amazing way to help your people grow in their roles. Remember, no matter how busy you think you are, one-to-ones are how you connect with, grow, and keep your best employees!

- **Dream Management:** You will spend more time with your employees than you will with your family. Take the time to find out what they want out of life and help them achieve it. And do it not because you want anything in return, but just because it is the right thing to do.

- **Goals:** The most successful people who I know are all extremely goal-oriented. Written goals enable you to maximize your weeks, months, and years by reminding you what is important and what needs to be accomplished. Try it! You will not be disappointed.

- **Protect Yourself:** Just like in any business, the unsavory characters can give good people a bad name. Do all of your research and carefully interview all the relationships you have in business.

- **Business Planning:** The plan you drew up 90 days ago is no longer relevant or accurate. Review and revise your plan every three months.

This book is filled with a ton of information I have learned over the years. My mode of learning came mostly the hard way.

If I did not go into as much depth as you would have liked on any particular topic, then I encourage you to build your advisory board, find a mentor, talk to your competitors, and get involved with your local trade associations.

Conclusion

If reading is your thing, I hope you enjoyed this "primer."

You are the CEO of your company. You are responsible for everything that happens in your organization. The most important thing you can do for your business is carve out time to work on it.

Remember, if a simple guy like me from a mining town in northern Ontario, Canada, who dropped out of college in order to paint houses can build a business that spans multiple states and employs a couple thousand people, being successful should be easy for you!

Index

H

I